"Over the years, Dave Ulrich and Norm Smallwood have produced a number of seminal pieces that change the way we think about HR and leadership. They have done so once again with *Leadership Brand*. As the leadership challenge reaches a near-crisis stage in many organizations, this book offers both the insight and practical tools to make a difference."

> —Bob Gandossy, Global Business Leader, Hewitt Associates, and author of *Leading the Way*

"I am recommending *Leadership Brand* to every leader I coach! It is essential that you know and communicate 'who you are' as a leader—*Leadership Brand* shows you how."

> —Marshall Goldsmith, executive coach and author of the *Wall Street Journal* number-one business bestseller *What Got You Here Won't Get You There*

"With complete clarity and rigor, Ulrich and Smallwood focus on one of the most pressing challenges in business today—how to create and support leaders who uniquely express the values and brand of the company. Using a wide variety of tools and diagnostics, *Leadership Brand* brings insights and inspiration to this fascinating topic. A compelling read for any executive interested in leadership and a must-have for those tasked with nurturing and developing leaders."

> —Lynda Gratton, Professor of Management Practice, London Business School, and author of *Hot Spots*

"Organizations live and therefore change over time. The principles behind *Leadership Brand* describe intentional methods by which an organization's value proposition to multiple stakeholders can be made sustainable over time and across leadership changes. Not just an organizational journey, one's leadership brand aligns both an organizational and personal brand promise with both actions and deeds."

> —Doug Hawthorne, President and CEO, Texas Health Resources

"*Leadership Brand* has a durable and lasting quality that will impact our understanding of leadership. It shifts from reporting isolated but qualitative case studies to a dynamic and sustainable theory of why leadership matters and what it requires. Moving from leaders to leadership then to leadership brand generates a fresh conceptual vision of where the field is headed."

—Omar Kader, Chairman, Pal-Tech, Inc.

"Clearly, Ulrich and Smallwood have developed a different and valuable way of thinking about 'leadership brand,' a rationale that validates it, and actions that can lead to a distinctive leadership approach for many organizations."

—Jon Katzenbach, Founder and Senior Partner, Katzenbach Partners, and coauthor of *The Wisdom of Teams*

"For GrupoNueva it is of paramount importance that our entire workforce develops into protagonists of our vision, values, and triple-bottom-line strategy. This is especially true for the senior leadership of the company, who embody this purpose. This leadership behavior, when recognized by all of our stakeholders as an attribute of our company, becomes both the culture of the organization and the leadership brand of our people. Understanding the processes for developing a leadership brand and corporate culture is a valuable insight that Ulrich and Smallwood masterfully illustrate in their new book. A must-read for all concerned with building strong leadership cultures and seeking to capture the value derived from them."

—Julio Moura, Chairman and CEO, GrupoNueva

"As usual, Ulrich and Smallwood are on the cutting edge of leadership theory and practice. *Leadership Brand* is a creative and useful reframing of the critical activity we call leadership. Any professor, consultant, administrator, or manager should take to heart the importance of building their leadership brand."

—J. B. Ritchie, Professor of Organizational Behavior, Emeritus, Brigham Young University

"*Leadership Brand* explores the realities of what it really takes to build that rare leadership brand that sets an organization apart from the competition and connects leaders with customers, shareholders, and employees in a unique and differentiated way. Ulrich and Smallwood create a framework that any organization can use to create a leadership brand and deliver on its brand promise to employees and customers."

—Libby Sartain, Chief People Officer, Yahoo! Inc. and author of *Brand from the Inside: Eight Essentials to Emotionally Connect Your Employees to Your Business*

"A must-read for twenty-first-century leaders! Finally, a book that peels back the layers to root causes of leadership challenges; followed by useable templates for achieving superior results."

—R. Dixon Thayer, CEO, I-trax, Inc.

"Dave Ulrich and Norm Smallwood make an insightful contribution to the literature on leadership, showing a practical pathway that can lead to authentic, enduring, flourishing leadership for any organization. The authors deeply understand the profound difference between finding leaders to run an organization and building leadership that will sustain that organization."

—Mike Volkema, Chairman, Herman Miller

Leadership
Brand

Leadership Brand

*Developing Customer-Focused
Leaders to Drive Performance and
Build Lasting Value*

Dave Ulrich
Norm Smallwood

HARVARD BUSINESS SCHOOL PRESS
BOSTON, MASSACHUSETTS

Library of Congress Cataloging-in-Publication Data

Ulrich, David, 1953–
    Leadership brand : developing customer-focused leaders to drive performance and build lasting value / Dave Ulrich, Norm Smallwood.
        p.   cm.
    Includes bibliographical references and index.
    ISBN-13: 978-1-4221-1030-0 (hardcover : alk. paper)
    ISBN-10: 1-4221-1030-3
    1. Leadership. 2. Executive coaching. 3. Organizational learning. I. Smallwood, W. Norman. II. Title.
    HD57.7.U44 2007
    658.4'092—dc22
                                                                                            2007009122

The paper used in this publication meets the requirements of the American National Standard for Permanence of Paper for Publications and Documents in Libraries and Archives Z39.48-1992.

We dedicate this book to our mothers:

Karin Ulrich

Elizabeth Anne Smallwood

Contents

Preface

WE HAVE SPENT OUR CAREERS trying to figure out how to build organizations that help employees, customers, and investors succeed over time. Some of this work has focused on how human resources (practices, departments, and people) can add value. We have worked on how HR practices can build value-creating organization capabilities. We have worked to upgrade the quality of HR departments so that they have a more strategic focus. And we have studied, cajoled, and framed how HR professionals can deliver value through the competencies they demonstrate.

But organizations that deliver value over time ultimately require leadership attention. Our study of leadership began with a simple premise: leaders must deliver results. We argued that the leadership field has become so enamored with competencies and personal characteristics of leaders that the leader's job to also deliver results was almost forgotten. Our book *Results-Based Leadership* encouraged a balance between leadership attributes and business results, and balance across four business results (investor, customer, employee, line manager). As we discussed these ideas with senior executives in publicly traded companies, we realized that many of these executives were particularly interested in the topic of investor results. This led us to a better understanding of intangible value as perceived by the investment community (owners and analysts). In privately held companies and government institutions, these ideas resonated because they provided a logical framework for making intangibles tangible in a manner that increases confidence in the future. *Why the Bottom Line Isn't!* (subsequently retitled in softcover as *How Leaders Build Value*) was written to help leaders determine how to build intangibles that create at least half of sustained market value.

As we continued to explore how leaders make a sustainable difference to investors and customers outside the organization and to employees inside, we recognized two shifts that need to occur to more fully enable leaders to create sustained value. First, we needed to shift from studying *leaders* to studying *leadership*. It is easy to be enamored of a great leader who has charisma, personality, emotional intelligence, and charm and who delivers great results. Celebrity leaders have become de rigueur on the covers of business magazines, and most of us like to identify and admire them. But these leaders do not represent *leadership*. Leadership represents the cadre of leaders within an organization. Good leaders do not just build their personal credibility; they build the organization's leadership capability, or the capacity of the organization to sustain future leaders. Second, as we explored the criteria of effective leadership, we realized that many firms had shifted to building leadership, but those that succeeded focused on how leaders inside the company connected a firm to the customers and investors outside the company. Some firms, even without being completely conscious of it, have shifted from *leadership* to *leadership brand*. In these leading companies, those outside the firm become key monitors of the quality of leadership inside the firm. Investors worry about confidence in future earnings as evidenced by intangibles, many of which come from leadership. Customers often worry about a firm meeting their needs over time, which again comes from quality of leadership.

To more fully understand the relationship of leaders to leadership, we drew on our personal experience to find a helpful analogy: mothers to motherhood. An individual mother is a powerful figure as a member of a family. However, the concept of motherhood is focused on nurturing the next generation of children so that they can grow up to be contributing members of society and make their families proud. It's the same with leaders and leadership. Individual leaders are important members of an organization, but building leadership is even more important to create the next generation of leaders who can deliver results; but then building leadership brand matters most because it ensures the delivery of the right results. That's why we dedicate this book to our mothers.

To better understand leadership as defined by external criteria, we derived and have worked to develop the metaphor of a leadership brand. We can still recall the day when we used this metaphor in a talk in Toronto. It sounded right, but we did not know what it was. We had talked a lot about a firm brand as an extension of product brand and as a metaphor for the culture of the company. We had seen brand used to help employees join a firm (the employee brand) and to help employees build a personal reputation (you as a brand). But when we started to talk about leadership brand, we felt it was something different.

As we applied the metaphor of brand to leadership, our thoughts began to get clearer about what it meant and its impact. Leadership brand is the identity of the firm in the mind of the customers made real to employees because of customercentric leadership behaviors. In other words, leadership brand occurs when leaders' knowledge, skills, and values focus employee behavior on the factors that target the issues that customers care about. Leadership brand is an extension of an organization's brand or identity because it shows up in the behaviors and results of leaders throughout a firm in a manner that bridges employee and customer commitment.

When we wrote this book, we had a fundamental choice: do we want to write a book about the leader's responsibility to *build* a leadership brand, or do we want to write about a leader's responsibility to *be* a leadership brand? Good leaders do both. They build a brand in their organization, and they role model the brand by their personal behaviors. We chose in this book to focus primarily on the role that leaders have to build a leadership brand in their organization. The book lays out specific steps leaders can take to build such a leadership brand. We end by focusing on how the firm's leadership brand must align with an individual's personal brand to be successful.

This book is written for leaders who are primarily responsible and accountable not just to lead but to build leadership. The audience includes senior line managers but also HR professionals who help architect and deliver the quality of leadership. The ultimate success of a leader may be defined by what happens after the leader moves on: are the next generation of leaders prepared for the future uncertainties they will face? We hope in this book to answer this question with both conceptual insight and practice tools.

The concepts related to leadership brand are based on our beliefs about leaders and leadership.

- We believe that leaders matter, but leadership matters more. We have all experienced a gifted leader who engaged all of us—our hearts, minds, and feet. Dynamic leaders enlist us in a cause, and we willingly follow their counsel. But leadership exists when an organization produces more than one or two individual leaders.

Leadership matters more because it is tied not to a person but to the process of building leaders.

- We believe that every leader has a responsibility to create a leadership brand that translates customer expectations into employee behaviors and that outlasts the individual leader. Leaders who focus only internally, either on themselves or within their organization, make a serious mistake. Value is defined by the receiver more than the giver, and leaders who create value understand those outside their organization who define value. These stakeholders include customers who buy products and investors who put in capital. When customer and investor expectations shape what leaders know and do, these leaders are focused on the right things.

- We believe that branded leadership can be developed. While individual leaders may have a host of personal predispositions and styles, the principles that underlie branded leadership can be mastered. In this book, we lay out six steps that any leader can take to create a leadership brand. Each of these steps is based on a simple principle. Leaders who understand the principles and turn them into practices will establish a leadership brand.

- We believe that individual leaders need to role model the brand they advocate to others. We observe what others do more than what they say. If a leader espouses one set of actions and does another, the ensuing hypocrisy undermines the leader's credibility. Leaders who build a brand but act in ways opposed to the brand will not be believable. Aligning personal brand to leadership brand authenticates and embeds the leadership brand.

- We believe and have experienced leadership brand in all types of organizations. Commercial organizations have customers who buy their products or services, and need to develop and then embed their brand to meet future customer expectations. Not-for-profit organizations (ranging from schools to churches, NGOs, etc.) also need a brand to create a mind-set among their constituents. When this external brand identity becomes internalized through what leaders know, do, and deliver, these organizations are much more credible. Government agencies also increase or decrease their political goodwill by the leadership brand they create. Leaders at all levels of these diverse organizations shape and are shaped by the leadership brand of their organization.

- We believe that all organizations have a leadership brand, either explicitly crafted and deployed or implicitly perceived and randomly perpetuated. Our hope is to help leaders craft a leadership that explicitly meets investor, customer, and employee needs.

- We believe that leadership brand can be changed. Firms have worked to change their brand (e.g., from a plump Pillsbury Doughboy to a fit one). Leaders can also change the leadership brand within their firm and can change their personal leadership brand.

The sum of these beliefs is that we have enormous confidence in the future of leadership practices. Much of this confidence comes from personal experience with exceptional leaders who not only fulfill the demands of being a leader but also help establish a leadership brand within their organization.

We are particularly indebted to colleagues who have heard these ideas, read drafts of chapters, and made constructive comments (even if we did not agree with them all). Included in this list are some of the best thinkers in the study of leadership: Dick Beatty, Jim Bolt, Richard Boyatzis, Jay Conger, Mark Effron, Bob Eichigner, Bob Fulmer, Robert Gandossy, Marshall Goldsmith, Gary Hamel, Bill Joyce, Omar Kader, Jon Katzenbach, Steve Kerr, Jim Kouzes, Dale Lake, Ed Lawler, Morgan McCall, Paul McKinnon, Henry Mintzberg, Karl Moore, Mike Panowyk, Jeffrey Pfeffer, Barry Posner, C. K. Prahalad, Bonner Ritchie, Judy Rosenblum, Paul Thompson, Warren Wilhelm, and Jack Zenger. We are also lucky to have caring and insightful colleagues in our firm at The RBL Group (www .rbl.net) who have shaped much of our thinking, including Wayne Brockbank, Erin Burns, David Creelman, Jim Dowling, Starr Eckholdt, Dave Hanna, Dani Johnson, Kurt Sandholtz, Kate Sweetman, Ernesto Uscher, and Jon Younger. We are very grateful for support from Ginger Bitter and Judy Seegmiller, who help us keep our chaotic schedules organized and provided specific support for this book. We are most indebted to our wives, Wendy and Tricia, who put up with our obsessions with these ideas and all of our late nights and weekends to write them. They have been patient and supportive beyond any reasonable expectations.

We are also very grateful to Hilary Powers, who continues to be our "write knight," gifted at turning our musings into comprehensible English. And we are pleased to have an engaged and involved editor in Melinda Merino, who probes with grace and encourages with gentleness.

As we have said, we dedicate this book to our mothers, who were noble exemplars of the process of investing in the next generation. And we are grateful to our children, who we hope will have lives that move beyond our weaknesses and will create their own brand.

Of course, we are ultimately responsible for the ideas in this book, and we hope that they frame some of the future discussions around leadership.

—Dave Ulrich
Norm Smallwood
March 2007

1

Branding Leadership

IN THE PURSUIT OF LEADERSHIP, thousands of books and articles have been published. So why one more? This book focuses on what we call the leadership brand and offers two insights into how to increase the quality of leadership.

First, *leaders* versus *leadership*. They're not the same thing. Both matter. Focusing on the leader emphasizes the qualities of the individual and how he or she leads and engages others. A leader focus works on the knowledge, skills, and values a leader demonstrates and works to help individuals become more proficient in their ability to direct others. Focusing on leadership emphasizes the quality of leaders throughout an organization, not just an individual leader and the systems and processes that create these leaders. Great individual leaders may come and go, but great leadership endures over time. An effective individual leader may not be very good at building leadership—that is, at developing processes that help other leaders grow and develop.

An exceptional individual leader may deliver outstanding results for a while, but the quality of leadership is what sustains results, allows organizations to align with changing strategies, and builds confidence from employees, customers, and investors. Here are some cases in point:

Case 1: The Footsteps of a Giant Make Deep Holes

A large and successful firm grew through the innovation and energy of its founder, who was creative, insightful, and prescient. He gained acclaim as the ultimate entrepreneur—someone who knew what to do and how to do it. He was renowned as a leader, but he insisted on making most of the firm's strategic choices even as the firm grew. Most of the information about the firm flowed to, from, and through him, and most of the authority to act came from him. When others gained influence, he directly or indirectly undermined them, even to the point of having them removed from the company. When he left, the board had to go outside for the next leader—and brought in someone who meandered both personally and strategically, thus beginning the demise of the firm.

Case 2: What We Do Is What We Know How to Do

Another firm succeeded for many years by efficiently producing products. Its leaders were masters of the supply chain, the production process, and the distribution channel. Eventually, however, increasing competition pushed the firm to seek more revenue from services. Realizing that current customers saw it as a source of products and nothing else, its leaders wanted to change the firm's image—but they themselves had grown up and succeeded with a product mentality. They had good instincts for designing, manufacturing, and delivering products but not for providing exceptional customer service, and the firm lost its footing in the new economy.

Case 3: Paring Back to the Bone Leaves No Muscle

For the last five years, a third firm has been working to do more with less. Its leaders have recognized competitive pressures and responded by reengineering, downsizing, delayering, outplacing, and outsourcing. All the numbers look great—except one. In the past the firm could always count on its *leadership bench*—the top fifty leaders and leadership positions each had at least one backup fully qualified to move into the next higher job. With all the consolidation, however, the ratio of backups to key positions is now under 0.5:1—and still sliding. Competent and productive as the leaders in place are, the firm faces a leadership crisis: its current leaders are moving toward retirement, and the potential leaders in the next generation lack the experience that builds a leadership bench.

Case 4: Everything We Know We Want Isn't All We Want

Yet another firm did spot the impending leadership crisis and—well aware that leaders make a difference in sustained business results—set out to find out what leaders know and do that matters most. It built a competence model by identifying both high- and low-performing leaders, then specifying specific behaviors that distinguished the two groups. It used the resulting list of competencies to hire, pay, and train leaders . . . but something was still missing. The survivors pass all the competency tests, but somehow they don't inspire much confidence in their ability to respond to future business challenges.

The message is the same all four times. Real leadership is not just about the person, it's also about the process. People today may be good leaders, but the firm may lack leadership. Leaders today may be fully competent, but the firm may have gaping holes in the next generation of leadership. Firms plan to source future leaders internally but often find it necessary to go outside for the next round of talent. Leaders matter and so does leadership. Both are necessary for leadership to become an organization capability.

Where do firms go wrong? It often comes down to the basic difference between *leaders* and *leadership*. Recent approaches tend to focus on building individuals as leaders rather than building leadership as an organization capability for the firm. While we admire and learn from individuals who are magnificent leaders, the ultimate test of a firm's leadership strength comes from its overall capacity to produce leadership that delivers stakeholder confidence in future results. To better understand leadership as an institutional process rather than an individual set of traits, we draw on a simple concept. Being a leader focuses on the person; building leadership focuses on the organization that creates leaders.

Our second contribution in this book is to shift a focus on leadership from inside to outside the organization. Most efforts to build leaders and leadership concentrate on what happens inside the person and/or inside the organization. Internal studies of leaders emphasize the attributes of effective leaders and show that leaders need to possess strong intellectual, emotional, and social intelligence. Internal studies of leadership emphasize the leadership pipeline and how to invest in the next generation of leadership. But these internally focused studies of both leaders and leadership often miss a simple point, and that is that leadership can and should also focus on the things that go on outside the company as much as or more than what goes on inside the company.

When we first began to talk about the external dimension of leadership, a prominent participant in leadership development told us that his company already had leadership competency models and succession planning systems, and he challenged whether we were suggesting anything new with these ideas. We asked him a simple question: to what extent do the competencies that your firm uses to define effective leadership reflect customer expectations? He confessed that his firm's competency model was based on the behaviors that distinguished high- and low-performing leaders inside the firm, and that neither customers nor investors had been considered in crafting its model. With the external focus in mind, he revisited his firm's competency model and discovered unique knowledge, skills, and values that leaders throughout his organization should demonstrate to meet customer and investor expectations. Customers and investors in this particular market favored firms that were innovative, quick responders, and globally connected. Yet, in his company's leadership competency model, behaviors like creativity, risk taking, and global insight were underrepresented, with a greater focus on setting goals, executing strategy, and having personal credibility. He realized that the competencies identified from focusing only on leaders inside the organization were incomplete without including external expectations. While such an external focus may not completely change expectations of leaders, it can tailor and focus leadership to meet the unique requirements of its customers and investors.

These two dimensions (leader and leadership; inside and outside) form the core of what we call the leadership brand. Figure 1-1 visually captures this idea. Most leadership work starts with cell 1 (competent leaders), which identifies specific individual leader competencies to deliver desired business results. The next step is to align this leader competency model with organization systems such as talent management, performance management, succession planning, and 360-degree feedback tools to build the next generation of leaders (cell 2, leadership capability). Some (including most popular business magazines) report on the importance of leaders' developing a personal reputation that distinguishes them from others (cell 3, celebrity leaders). These studies emphasize how individual leaders become prominent by their personal

FIGURE 1-1

The evolution of leadership

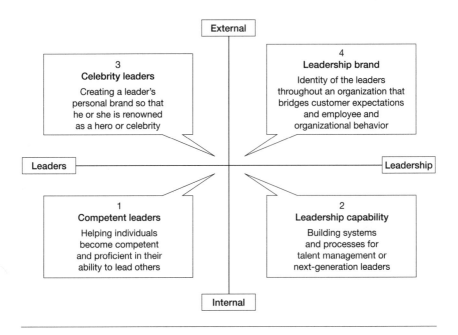

brand and reputation. We want to build on this work but focus on how leaders at every level of an organization can be prepared to turn customer expectations into employee and organizational behavior (cell 4). We call this the leadership brand. Simply stated, *leadership brand is the identity of the leaders throughout an organization that bridges customer expectations and employee and organizational behavior.*

In workshops when we talk about leadership, we ask participants to divide 100 points across the four cells, depending on how much of their leadership attention (rhetoric, training, development plans) has focused on factors in each cell: competent leaders, celebrity leaders, leadership capability, leadership brand. Inevitably, the majority of the 100 points go to competent leaders and leadership capability, as participants report that most of their leadership development emphasis is on developing their personal attributes. They are trained to be more emotionally and socially adept, to set direction, and to build relationships of trust. We think that this personal focus on building better leaders is helpful, but it may not lead to the institutional support required to sustain leadership within an organization. Leadership requires thinking about the X factor, or the systems and processes that build the next generation of leaders, especially leaders who will respond to future customer and investor expectations.

Studying leadership as a brand is a timely and important topic in part because leadership matters. Research supports it and experience confirms it. Leadership makes a difference. Jack Zenger and Joe Folkman found that in branches of a mortgage bank where the branch manager scored in the bottom 10 percent of leaders on a leadership effectiveness survey, net losses averaged $1,176,000 annually during their time with the organization. In branches where the manager scored in the top 10 percent on the same survey, net profits averaged $4,500,000 during the same period. They also found, in a different financial services firm, that leaders in the bottom 30 percent on the leadership assessment averaged 19 percent turnover, while those who scored in the top 10 percent had turnover of only 9 percent.[1] Other scholars have found that differences in executive leadership explain as much as 45 percent of an organization's performance.[2] In reviewing the importance of leadership and talent, Bradford Smart found that leaders who are top talent (A players) have 94 percent higher productivity than average leaders; more-talented investment banking associates are twice as productive as average associates; return to shareholders of top-talent firms is 22 percent higher than for those with average talent; the top 3 percent of programmers produce 1,200 percent more lines of code than the average programmers; and the top 3 percent of sales leaders produce 250 percent more than the average.[3]

Clearly, organizations that perform better over time have leaders who seem to know and do something that produces sustained results. But it is not the individual leader who sustains such results; it is the strength of the leadership bench that promotes investor, customer, and employee confidence in the future, which translates into higher market value.

Goods and services that command higher market value than their competitors come from strong brands. Everywhere we go, we buy or see clothes with the Nike swoosh or the Polo logo. We drive cars that have distinctive styles embodied in their brand and emblazoned on their hoods. Our laptops, notebooks, wallets, pens, and watches are all branded to maximize differentiation. We choose products in part because their brand reflects our self-identity. So it's a natural extension to regard the provision of a sustainable leadership advantage as a *leadership brand.* This mental step allows us to clarify the definition of leadership as an intangible value and thus to help both individual leaders and whole leadership cadres become more effective. It gives us a vantage point for a new look at three old questions:

- What makes leadership effective?

- What can be done to build more effective leadership?

- What is the value of building high-quality and recognizable leadership?

Straightforward as they seem, these questions are not easy to answer. They require thinking not only about the person as a leader but about the process of building a leadership brand. They require not just looking at effective leaders and what they know, do, and deliver but looking at the organization processes that engender future leaders. Leadership brand offers unique insights into these three questions.

Leadership brand accepts that effective leadership must include a personal journey, but it is not complete without an organizational exploration. The last twenty years have seen a profusion of models for how to be or build better individual leaders. Leaders need to be transformational and create fundamental change in their organizations; to be visionary and articulate a point of view about the future; to be primal and release emotional intelligence; to demonstrate good principles through their behaviors; to lead through both science and art; to be resonant and renewing for themselves and their organizations; to be courageous in taking and making decisions.[4] Many have focused on what leaders should learn about what successful leaders have done; they adapt lessons from historically high-impact leaders like John Wooden, Attila the Hun, Colin Powell, Jack Welch, Rudolph Giuliani, Gandhi, Abraham Lincoln, and Jesus Christ.[5] Yet even with all these models, the leadership demand continues. From all these studies has emerged an understanding of the basics of what leaders know and do; but although such basics are necessary, they are not sufficient for effective leadership.

By focusing on customer and investor expectations, leadership brand ensures that those who lead deliver value to those who receive the outcomes of their leadership efforts. Brand shifts attention to the way what happens *inside* the firm connects to what happens *outside*. Effective leadership is not just about what leaders know, do, and deliver, but about how that knowledge creates value to customers and investors outside the organization. If you think of what happens inside a firm as one island and what happens outside with customers and investors as another, then the function of the leadership brand is to form the bridge between the two—providing a way for leaders to translate what outside stakeholders know the firm for into what employees accomplish inside the firm.

Leadership brand also helps with building the next generation of leaders. Those who invest in brands are less focused on a single product than on the reputation of the firm as a whole. Developing leaders is not just about the individual who receives the development but also about the development processes themselves. These processes become as much a part of the leadership brand as the leader who is created by them. Just as a product or firm brand is not a random or haphazard event but a series of integrated choices, leadership development as a brand comes from an integrated set of choices about how to develop and prepare the next generation of leaders. This goes beyond the quantity of leaders—the capacity and size of the leadership pipeline.[6] It focuses on the ability of future leaders to respond to changing customer expectations.

Finally, leadership brand shows up in recognizable and distinct leadership. Firms with a leadership brand have an abiding and enduring reputation. When their corporate brand becomes intertwined with their leadership brand, the corporate brand endures and outlasts any single individual leader.

Cases of Leadership Brand

Leadership brands exist in large or small, public or private organizations and are explicitly linked to a firm's brand. A Nordstrom customer knows that the employees and mangers will give her excellent service. A Disney theme park guest assumes that employees will be upbeat, friendly, and gracious. McKinsey clients understand that consultants will bring the latest management knowledge to bear on their problems. 3M, Herman Miller, and Google work hard to earn and keep their reputations as innovators, so they encourage leaders who take risks, seek alternatives, and experiment with new ideas. Marriott, UPS, and UBS focus on delivering outstanding service, so leaders spend their time identifying and connecting with targeted customers, and are assessed according to their ability to deliver exceptional customer service. In cases like these, the desired brand in the minds of those outside the firm translates to a set of employee and organizational behaviors. By focusing on customer and investor expectations, these companies shape what leaders know and do. Table 1-1 shows examples of how firm brands can connect to leadership brands.

The following cases demonstrate how a firm's brand can be translated into a leadership brand.

Canadian Tire

Since its founding in 1922, Canadian Tire has had a unique position in the Canadian market.[7] The firm began in Toronto to service the growing Canadian automobile industry. While it started out in the automotive parts business, it quickly diversified its product offerings to include camping equipment, radio supplies, and a variety of private and other brand household accessories. With the proliferation of automobiles, it also expanded into service stations in the 1950s and continued to enlarge its retail operations. Today, the corporation is a growing network of interrelated businesses, engaged in automotive (PartSource), retail (Canadian Tire Retail and Mark's Work Wearhouse), financial services (Canadian Tire Financial Services), and petroleum (Canadian Tire Petroleum).

These businesses offer a unique mix of products and services that leverage Canadian Tire's core capabilities and exemplify its vision to be Canada's most respected and trusted retailer. This vision also declares

TABLE 1-1

Branded leadership

Firm	Firm identity *This firm is known for . . .*	Leadership identity *Leaders at this firm are known for . . .*
Wal-Mart	Everyday low prices	Managing costs efficiently; getting things done on time
Lexus	Relentless pursuit of perfection	Managing quality processes (lean manufacturing and design, Six Sigma) to improve constantly
P&G	Managing brands	Defining and growing brands in the marketplace
McKinsey	Analytical, smart strategists	Managing talent and organizing people into teams to solve client problems
Apple	Innovation and design	Creating new products and services outside the industry norms
Baxter Healthcare	Entrepreneurial spirit	Fostering innovation and trying new things
PepsiCo	The next generation	Building the next generation of talent

the company's desire to be passionate about retaining each "customer for life" by providing consistently friendly, knowledgeable service; exciting loyalty programs; and fair pricing across all its businesses. Canadian Tire has near-universal brand recognition throughout Canada, with unaided brand awareness of 97 percent. Its stores are located within fifteen minutes of 91 percent of the population, 40 percent of Canadians shop Canadian Tire stores weekly, and nine out of ten adult Canadians shop at Canadian Tire at least twice a year. These statistics demonstrate the strength of the Canadian Tire brand identity.

Canadian Tire wants to build a reputation of being a trusted partner in bringing new products and innovation to the market in each of its various businesses. It wants its customers to see the Canadian Tire brand as one that they trust, where they can count on great service, a brand that is Canadian, and delivers on all its promises. It believes that its mix of businesses offers products and services to customers throughout their life cycle—from buying their first bike or pair of skates, to purchasing products and services for their first car and/or home, and even purchasing a line of comfortable clothing from Mark's Work Wearhouse throughout their life.

Canadian Tire also wants to be recognized for its commitment to the communities it serves. It is usually among the first to respond to disasters in the communities in which it operates, and has a history of community investment that people recognize. For example, in 2005 and 2006 they have helped more than sixty thousand financially disadvantaged kids.

When a customer passes by or has an experience in any of Canadian Tire's businesses, the company wants that customer to think:

- I have trust in the people who run this business.

- It has good products/services and fair pricing.

- It always has something unique and different, which delights me.

- The Canadian Tire loyalty program (Canadian Tire "Money") provides me with additional savings throughout its mix of businesses.

- The staff is happy to see me, help me, and answer my questions.

- It is a *Canadian* operation.

- It does a lot to support my community.

By ensuring that customers validate these images through consistent experiences, Canadian Tire hopes to have customers for life.

To establish and ensure this strong external customer brand, Canadian Tire has implemented a number of initiatives and programs. It has articulated a vision and values that align with customer expectations. Its vision is to create sustainable growth by being Canada's most respected and trusted retailer. It hopes to grow from the strengths of leveraging trust in its brands, its unique mix of products and services, its ability to capitalize on the interrelatedness of its businesses, and its innovative customer loyalty programs. It is committed to treating its people, its customers, its partners, and its shareholders with unwavering honesty, integrity, dignity, and respect.

As it works to create leaders who guide its approximately fifty thousand employees, Canadian Tire works to assure that these leaders will demonstrate behaviors congruent with these customer expectations. These leaders in turn work to make sure that employees understand what the firm wants to be known for by its customers. The company has also created performance management, recruiting, and development systems to ensure that leaders behave in ways consistent with the firm's brand.

But, even more important, executives have worked to evolve Canadian Tire's leadership model to provide a common, simple framework to attract and develop leadership that embodies their firm brand. Canadian Tire's leadership brand model includes four dimensions that executives believe confirm and encourage the company's desired customer expectations:

- *Business leadership:* Focuses on building the strategic context to build each business in ways that enhance interrelatedness in building customers for life

- *People leadership:* Focuses on leading all employees so that they are committed to building customers for life

- *Personal leadership:* Focuses on building individual capabilities and attributes that build customers for life

- *Results leadership:* Focuses on executing business results that build customers for life

The executives have also developed specific leadership behaviors within these four dimensions of leadership that focus and differentiate expectations at different levels of management.

Canadian Tire also encourages leaders at all levels to be sensitive to and focused on customers. It has sophisticated customer engagement channels including an "Idea-tion" process in which customers, business leaders, and product suppliers collaborate to create new products. It tracks customer perceptions on multiple brand attributes and ensures wide understanding of firm performance against these attributes within its leadership teams. Many leaders spend considerable time visiting operations at the front line, whether in stores, at distribution centers, at call centers, or on the road with field employees.

The internal leadership development activities are aligned with the desired external customer brand. Connecting leaders throughout the company to external customers makes the desired customer experience more likely to happen. And, the firm has had remarkable financial and customer success for the past eighty-five years.

Bon Secours Health System, Inc.

In 1824, a group of twelve women responded to the devastation of the French Revolution by forming a Catholic religious community in Paris dedicated to bringing compassion and care to the sick and dying and to help those in need feel a sense of charity and the love of God. As more women joined the original twelve, the group became more formalized and expanded its service whenever and wherever this care was sought.[8] Today, the Sisters of Bon Secours is an international Catholic religious congregation of women who bring the healing presence of Christ to the world by being "good help to those in need."

The identity of the Sisters of Bon Secours is marked by their commitment to witness to the healing mission of Christ through their participation in the struggle to create a more just and humane world, as expressed by their life of prayer and service in various ministries: hospitals, hospices, rehab centers, wellness centers, clinics, parishes, long-term care facilities, home care agencies, community centers, and social service organizations. In these various ministries, they serve as caregivers, spiritual directors, chaplains, mission leaders, administrators, case managers, community organizers, counselors, and board members. Their distinctive gift—their brand—is to bring God's healing, compassion, and liberation to people in need. Special attention is given to those who are poor, sick, or dying by helping to alleviate their suffering and bringing them a message of hope and assurance that there is a God who loves them. They have captured it in the following descriptors of their work:

- We care for the sick.

- We pray with the dying.

- We comfort the lonely.

- We listen and respond to the cries of the poor and aged.

- We cry with those who mourn.

- We help people return to health and wholeness.

- We embrace them in their joys and sorrows.

- We support them in their search for God and in their struggle to experience the redemptive meaning of suffering.[9]

Guided by this identity and branding, the Sisters came to the United States in 1881 to provide home care for the sick and dying. As health-care practices changed, so did the way the Sisters responded; they opened their first hospital in Baltimore in 1919, followed by additional hospitals and care centers throughout the eastern part of the United States. In 1983, they formed the Bon Secours Health System (BSHSI) to provide skilled, unified management and professional resources for all Bon Secours health-care operations while preserving their healing mission and Bon Secours' tradition of providing quality care to all, especially the poor, sick, and dying.

In recent years, Bon Secours Health System leaders have realized that to sustain their external mission, they must have leaders at all levels who demonstrate the espoused patient-centered values in their day-to-day behavior. Successful BSHSI leaders respond to their own personal "call" and embody the values of Bon Secours and the Catholic health-care ministry when addressing operational realities to produce strategic results. The spiritual resources of the Catholic health-care traditions, their own personal faith and spirituality, and the spirituality of their co-workers supply day-to-day meaning and the deep grounding, motivation, and resolve necessary to carry out this health-care ministry. They call this *reflective integration*, and it is at the centerpiece of BSHSI's Continual Development System (CDS) philosophy regarding its leadership and development of people. The CDS philosophy is depicted in the form of a cross combining four "clusters" or areas of leadership competency: action (creating real world results), focus (effective performance guided by operational realities), values (balancing operational performance and the ministry's faith-based values), and vocation (the unique call to serve those in need, especially those who are poor or dying). Reflective integration, as noted above, holds the four clusters in creative dialogue, thus enabling all four sets to be actualized. For each of these four clusters or areas of leadership competency, the organization has identified both foundational competencies (those skills expected of all leaders at BSHSI) and differentiating competencies (those skills expected of outstanding leaders). These results are captured in table 1-2.

Bon Secours believes that as leaders throughout BSHSI develop and demonstrate these competencies that its desired brand for patient and resident care will be realized. The competencies were developed by considering how those who use their services need to feel and what experience they need to have. With this outside-in approach, Bon Secours was able to identify the internal leadership requirements to continue to live up to its mission. As David Jones, senior vice president of human resources, has commented, "The Sisters of Bon Secours have been around for over 180 years, but their numbers are diminishing. They have become very intentional about sharing their ministry with lay leaders who can help sustain the ministry for another 180 years. The competency model was designed to identify and develop ministry leaders who have the capability not only to run a successful health-care

TABLE 1-2

Bon Secours leadership model for reflective integration

Competence	Foundational	Differentiating
Vocation	Integration of Catholic health ministry	Responding to the Bon Secours mission
Focus	• Customer focus • Analytical thinking • Conceptual thinking	• Information seeking • Performance excellence • Being clear and decisive
Action	• Organizational awareness • Teamwork and cooperation • Impact and influence	• Leading change • Shaping the organization
Values	• Integrity • Self-control	• Understanding self and others • Developing self and others

business, but to effectively carry the mission of the Sisters well into the future."

To deliver on this competency model, the organization has crafted detailed performance management and development process whereby leaders anywhere in the system know how they are expected to live up to their external brand and how well they are doing at living up to those values. It has established proficiency levels in behavioral terms for leaders at all levels of the company. By building a bridge between their external mission and these internal leadership practices, Bon Secours ensures the realization of its mission.

Bon Secours invests heavily in ensuring that leaders live the externally focused behaviors. This is done through assessment, education, and development. In assessment, Bon Secours continually assesses its leaders against the standards it has set to ensure that these leaders stay focused on serving customers in the right ways. In education and development, it offers courses and development assignments to help leaders learn and grow.

In this not-for-profit organization, the concept of leadership brand persists. The desired external identity is made real to employees through a disciplined and focused set of leadership behaviors, identified with the customer in mind.

Drugstore.com

Drugstore.com is the leading online provider of health, beauty, vision, and pharmaceutical products.[10] Its number-one position in online sales makes drugstore.com one of the fifteen largest drugstores in the United States. With more than 8 million customers served since its founding in 1998, the company has filled more than 25 million orders and has achieved a 90 percent customer satisfaction rating. Much of its success is due to maintaining a keen focus on the customer, having leaders who are customercentric, and being agile enough to respond to needs and seize market and product opportunities.

From the start, drugstore.com's mission has centered around five elements of value proposition:

1. Breadth and depth of product assortment—more than twenty-five thousand SKUs

2. Convenience and the quality of the shopping experience

3. Excellent value

4. Privacy

5. Trusted source of information

As a result, drugstore.com has pioneered the way customers shop for health and wellness products online. Through innovation and market savvy, drugstore.com has shifted the way customers learn about, shop for, and purchase health, beauty, personal care, and wellness products.

Leaders at this high-tech, growth company have worked diligently to ensure that all company activities are focused on the requirements of external stakeholders, particularly customers and investors. As with many venture capital funded start-ups, drugstore.com's first growth period (1998–2003) was about realizing a vision: to launch a Web site that allowed customers to buy items online. During this period, the leadership brand was to instill confidence in both the external funding and customer world, and among employees. Just as the external world came to trust that the company would deliver on its promises, internal employees were attracted because of their confidence in leadership.

The second period (2004–2006) involved refining the business model and improving execution, and at its core, it was about placing the business on a path to profitability. In this period, the leadership brand shifted from building confidence to ensuring execution. Successful leaders were those who delivered what they promised, which was beyond creating a dream to working in reality. Drugstore.com's brand of leadership took rapid shape with the 2004 hiring of a seasoned executive as CEO: Dawn Lepore, a veteran of more than twenty years at Charles Schwab. Her hiring signaled to the market—and to employees—that what mattered, and what has characterized leadership at the company since, were some prevailing themes: believing and striving to stretch and exceed, a sense of urgency, grounded optimism, a "no" on self-promotion and a "yes" on collaboration, and leaders, at every level, committed to the company's purpose. At drugstore.com, they found that the strength of the leadership brand in an organization rarely exceeds that of the person at the top.

Beginning in late 2006, the focus entered the third phase: accelerating both revenue and profit growth through channel and category expansion (increased competitive differentiation). In this period, drugstore.com's brand will evolve and strengthen. Shifting from "getting to profitability" to "growing profitably" will require that every leader continue to focus on execution and agility while at the same time focusing on making and following through on select "big bets." Like many other midsize companies, the company must do so with little margin for missing goals. And thus, its leadership brand, now more than ever, puts a premium on "balancing"—long term and short term, strategic and tactical, planning and execution, being functionally strong and cross-functionally agile, developing yourself and others, being quick and thorough. By demonstrating these behaviors, today's and tomorrow's leaders at drugstore .com will respond to changing customer and investor expectations. From a leadership standpoint, the company has prepared for this third phase in three significant ways: building a growth-savvy leadership team; dedicating its focus on articulating and driving a future-oriented, values-centered organization culture; and connecting customer, personal, and organizational leadership to major aspects of how the business is run.

In this rapid-growth start-up company, the leadership brand has evolved, as have customer and investor expectations. But gaining the right leadership assures customers and investors that the company is responsive today and stable for the future.

Defining a Leadership Brand

In each of the preceding cases (representing large versus small and public versus private companies), leadership brand builds leadership more than leaders, and focuses on the outside more than the inside. To fully understand how to build a leadership brand, we need to explore what goes into a leadership brand. We propose that any brand consists of two major elements: the fundamentals (what we call the leadership code) and the differentiators (see figure 1-2).

Both fundamentals and differentiators are necessary. If we turn to the automotive business, for example, the chassis, drive chain, suspension system, and other components must be designed and manufactured with excellence despite being out of sight. Then the visible brand differentiators of body style, finishing, and accessories can make the car appeal to one market segment or another—but no matter how good a car looks on the surface, its market share will shrink if its internals turn out to be lousy. In textiles, the quality of fabric and the ability to manufacture clothing that maintains its fit are invisible basics that can be turned into visible fashion design through style, colors, materials, and labels.

FIGURE 1-2

Elements of leadership brand

A leadership brand has both invisible fundamentals and visible differentiators of its own. As stated, leadership brand is the identity of the leaders throughout an organization that bridges customer expectations and employee and organizational behavior. Traditional leadership is from the inside out, and leadership brand is from the outside in. Bridges come in many forms and sizes, but first and foremost they must get the invisible basics right, the structural engineering and support that allow them to withstand everything traffic and weather can throw at them. Likewise, leaders must get the invisible basics right: efficiently organizing and delivering the fundamentals that keep their products and services at levels that meet and exceed customer expectations. And just as once its foundations are solid, a bridge can hang from suspension towers like the western end of the San Francisco Bay Bridge, cantilever from pier to pier like the eastern end, or take any number of other airy or earthbound forms, a solidly grounded leadership brand can move on into the visible brand differentiators: the elements customers perceive as valuable.

The Fundamentals: Leadership Code

As we worked to make sense of the leadership fundamentals, which we call the leadership code, two questions came to mind:

- What proportion of leadership brand may be attributed to the leadership code? For a product brand, the equivalent question is, How much of it stems from the inner, invisible, and efficient processes making up the product?

- What are the key lessons and insights to be found in the leadership code? For a product to work efficiently and differentiate itself as a brand, its inner workings must be understood and efficiently managed. Likewise, the leadership code synthesizes and integrates studies of leadership and shows what all leaders must know and do.

Looking at the proportion of leadership code that is generic, as opposed to differentiated, shifts the focus away from the age-old question of whether leaders are born or bred—which recent research puts at fifty-fifty.[11] (That is, half of leaders' abilities grow from heritage and half are learned from experience.) The leadership code represents the predisposed or learned behaviors that help make leaders effective. What we want to know is how much of leadership brand is generic and part of a leadership code shared by all leaders, and then, of the generic part, what it really entails.

To answer these two questions about leadership code, we turned to experts who have extensively studied leadership. Scholars in the field have both theoretically and empirically made enormous strides on both questions. We picked thought leaders with a long history of leadership theory and research (as opposed to those with a single point of view or study). Among that group, we looked for published theory about leadership (we wanted those who understood not only *what* made leaders effective but *why*) and for evidence of empirical assessment of what makes effective leadership (we wanted those who tested their ideas with evidence, and we found that this group had participated in over 1 million leadership 360s). We asked them both of our questions, and believe that their insights help define the leadership code.[12]

When we asked colleagues how much of a leadership brand represents universal shared elements, we got answers ranging from 50 percent to 85 percent, which implies that no definitive answer has emerged at this point, but the direction is consistent. Although some of our most valued colleagues estimate that the leadership code covers very close to everything known to constitute good leadership, we prefer to go with a lower percentage, which brings us closer to the majority of our field. Our working hypothesis is that the code covers somewhere in the 60–70 percent range. This approximation seems especially useful because it coincides with what thought leaders in the area of product brand maintain; they regard about 66 percent of the qualities of branded and reasonably effective generic products as shared, leaving a similar proportion of the qualities of the branded products as characteristic of their brands. These common elements may be termed *derailers* (things that cause leaders to fail if not avoided), *competencies* (things leaders must know and do if they are to succeed), and *commitments* (focus required of leaders), or attributes, or dimensions; regardless of label, leaders clearly need to acquire and master some core factors. Knowing these will not guarantee being the branded leader, but not knowing them will almost certainly cause a leader to fall short of success.

If 60–70 percent of leadership effectiveness is shared among leaders, then what is it? What have all the different studies of leadership shown? What are the lessons that emerge from all this work? It would take far too long to summarize all the leadership research done to date.[13] However, as we examine exemplary studies of leadership, we can begin to identify some patterns that unravel the leadership code. Our synthesis of this work suggests that the code of leadership comprises five dimensions (see figure 1-3).

- *Strategists.* Leaders need to have a point of view about the future and be able to position the firm for future customers.

- *Executors.* Leaders need to be able to make things happen, to deliver results, to make change happen, to be technically literate, and to build organization systems that work.

- *Talent managers.* Leaders need to work with their current employees, to motivate, communicate, and encourage them.

- *Human capital developers.* Leaders need to work on future employees, to delegate and build future talent.

- *Personal proficiency.* Leaders need to gain personal credibility through their ability to learn, act with integrity, exercise social and emotional intelligence, make bold and courageous decisions, and engender trust.

Leaders who do the code and master the basics have the foundations for leadership. There really is a codebook for leadership: a set of fundamental, must-do things leaders ignore at their peril. The vast body of leadership theory and research has established the essentials. The leadership code is the essential foundation of the leadership brand. Without excellence in these core elements of leadership, leaders will fail. With these basics in place, leaders can move on to begin shaping their organization's leadership brand, and their own.

FIGURE 1-3

The leadership code

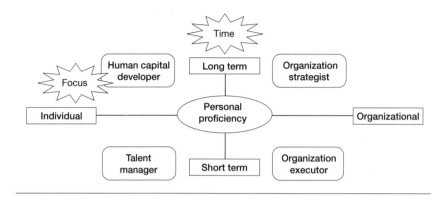

As we work with companies to build leadership, we start with the leadership code. Most companies have developed competency models for leaders. When we map their models against the code, we can begin to test the robustness of their model. In one company, they identified twelve competencies, but nine of them fell into the personal proficiency domain of the code. Another company had ten competencies, but eight of them fell into the execution quadrant. By comparing their leadership competencies to the code, companies can develop a more complete leadership model.

In other work, we explore more deeply the leadership code, but in this book, we examine in some detail the differentiators. Both are important to a sustained leadership brand.

Leadership Brand Beyond the Code

A leadership brand includes the leadership code but goes beyond. The leadership code refers to the 60–70 percent of the core attributes that all leaders must possess. But leadership brand also requires unique and differentiated skills to deliver value to today's and tomorrow's key stakeholders (the next 30–40 percent that differentiates leaders). Leaders must be able to adapt their fundamental skills to the strategies and goals of their own business. Building a leadership brand requires attention to both the basic and essential, and the advanced and differentiated elements of leadership.

The metaphor holds up better today than it would have if proposed even a few decades ago. Product brands still surround us, but the emphasis in the brand business has shifted from product to firm. To a greater and greater degree, it is less a specific product that entices the customer and more the reputation of the firm.[14] When airports went to branded vendors (Starbucks, McDonald's, Chili's), revenue in food-service locations—which hadn't changed—went up about 40 percent. It was not the products but the brands that communicated value. When a no-name hotel turned into a Hyatt, the same room in the same location with many of the same features earned about 20 percent more per night. Product-oriented brands like these ultimately show up in corresponding firm brands—and, even though the idea itself is relatively new, firm brands are sustained and enhanced by the corresponding leadership brand.

To possess a leadership brand, leaders must think and act in ways congruent with the desired product or firm brand. As firm strategy evolves, so must leadership brand. This is why focusing on both the basics and the differentiators is so important. A leadership brand today that reflects a product-driven organization may need to evolve tomorrow to reflect a service orientation instead, to avoid the fate of the company in the second case that opened this chapter. For a company to make this evolution, the core elements of leadership must be in place for the next generation of leaders; then leaders can realize that they have to align their expertise to the unique challenges they face. Leadership brand requires that leaders master the basics and adapt to the distinct requirements of their strategy.

Leadership brand should reflect a firm's brand. When a firm has an identity in the mind of customers, the expectations that flow from that identity need to be made real to employees through the firm's policies and culture. Leaders at all levels of an organization can transfer customer identity into leadership actions.

Reframing leadership as a brand offers a number of insights into leadership effectiveness and creating sustained and consistent leadership that will enhance firm value. In appendix A we review the criteria for product and firm brands and how they apply to leadership brand.

Leadership Brand Matters: A Tour of the Book

A firm with a leadership brand wins on multiple dimensions—with investors, with customers, and with employees.

It wins with investors because investors will grant higher market value for similar earnings supported by a strong leadership brand.[15] That is, quality of management or leadership gives investors confidence in the future and leads to higher share price. Each year *Fortune* has Hay Group prepare its reputation index, which includes a dimension on leadership and repeatedly shows that firms with a higher reputation have higher market value. This same finding is consistent with the recent research on the importance of intangibles. Intangibles represent the market value of a firm beyond its book value, and in recent years the ratio of market to book value has gone up dramatically.[16] Of course, as noted, if the perceived brand value is not rooted in reality, or if the brand does not transfer to the demands of new consumers, the brand image fades. But branded leaders are often in firms with a price-earnings (P/E) ratio higher than typical in their industry because high quality of leadership increases customer and investor confidence in the future.

To test this hypothesis, we averaged the P/E ratios over a ten-year period by industry. It's not possible to declare that companies with a ten-year track record of higher P/E ratios have better leaders. But it's tempting. Obviously, the past ten years doesn't tell us anything about the next ten years, but this P/E comparison within an industry does show the relative importance of intangibles. Let's look at a few industries:

- In beverage manufacturing, Coca-Cola is the intangible champ, with an average P/E over the last ten years of 36.55. This compares with 28.75 for PepsiCo and 19.76 for Cadbury Schweppes. Note that in the last few years, PepsiCo has beaten Coca-Cola's P/E ratio since shedding its restaurant business—Taco Bell, KFC, and so on.

- In aerospace, Boeing wins with a 26.2 and continues to look as if it will stay on top, with Airbus's woes, for the next ten years. Contrast this with General Dynamics at 17.05.

- In wireless equipment, Qualcomm leads with a ten-year average of 44.09. Contrast that with Ericsson's 35.46.

- In general business, General Electric wins the confidence of investors with an average of 27.58, which contrasts with Philips at 21.59 or Siemens at 18.96.

Again, these P/E differences are not solely due to quality of leadership, but leaders make decisions that increase or decrease investor confidence in future earnings. Since it is the job of leaders to build investor confidence in the future, Coca-Cola, Boeing, Qualcomm, and GE have won the quality-of-leadership race in their respective industries. These leaders have created the conditions over the last ten years whereby their quality of earnings is higher than the quality of earnings in competitors. We can also say with confidence that the next ten years may show a different story.

Firms with branded leadership win with customers because the customers have confidence that their needs will be addressed in a consistent and appropriate way. Nordstrom wins in the service game because its leaders are branded with a service mentality. People there don't have to ask for permission to serve customers; they just do it as a reflection of who they are. And customers respond with very high customer share. Nordstrom defines its target audience as customers who spend $1,000 every six months on products the chain sells, and it has established that its service brand is a major factor in driving how much of that $1,000 gets spent at Nordstrom stores rather than at competitors.[17]

Firms with branded leadership win with employees. A consistent and effective leadership brand applies with employees just as with the outside world. It means that employees know what to expect, eliminating productivity- and engagement-draining dissonance between their public and private worlds. One leader told us that he treated his best customers as if they were his best employees and his best employees as if they were his best customers. The relationship between employee engagement and commitment and customer delight is well established. When employees are engaged, customers are more likely to come back and spend more.

If a firm makes a customer brand promise of timely and responsive behavior, the same brand should be reflected in employee relations. Herman Miller wants to be branded as the innovator in the office furniture business, and so it consistently creates innovations in products and services to customers. When a firm extends and consistently applies the leadership brand, that same spirit of innovation permeates how leaders at all levels treat employees, offering creative and flexible approaches to employee terms and conditions of work, work settings for employees, and work processes that put the firm's money where its mouth is and help people bring the brand to life.

How to Build Leadership Brand

If a strong leadership brand is a source of value, then the question is, How can such a brand be built? We propose six steps for building leadership brand consistent with the outline of this book (see figure 1-4).

Steps for Building Branded Leadership

In this book, we'll take a detailed look at the following crucial steps for building leadership brand.

- *Step 1: Build a case for leadership brand*—When asked for their top business priorities, many executives talk about gaining market or customer share, growing in new markets, innovating products, and reducing costs. We believe that most priority to-do lists should include developing leadership. Building individual leaders focuses on the personal attributes of company leaders; a case for leadership brand shows why leadership is a means of accomplishing other organization goals (market share, global growth, innovation, or cost), but also an end in that it creates an intangible value in the eyes of key stakeholders. (This is the topic we develop in chapter 2.)

FIGURE 1-4

Building branded leadership

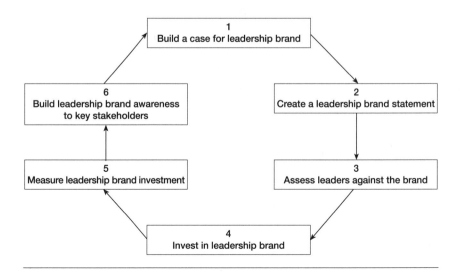

- *Step 2: Create a leadership brand statement*—A statement of leadership brand articulates the leadership reputation in terms of attributes the leader must have and results the leader must deliver. An individual leader statement focuses on personal requirements to effectively lead; the leadership brand statement connects the firm's external reputation with the day-to-day actions of its internal leadership. (This is the topic of chapter 3.)

- *Step 3: Assess leaders against the brand*—Once the leadership brand is delineated, leaders can be assessed by how well they have set up the basics and "behave the brand" as they deliver results, and by how well they grow the requisite skills and perspective as they progress through the leadership pipeline. HR practices must also be assessed and aligned to sustain the brand. At each leadership development stage, the brand assessment may differ. The assessment includes both the core elements of leadership and the brand differentiators. This assessment may be done by one person or through organization practices such as 360-degree feedback. (This is the topic of chapter 4.)

- *Step 4: Invest in leadership brand*—Firm or product brands don't happen by accident, and neither do leadership brands. Leading companies (identified by reputation and leadership mobility) invest in specific practices that instill the leadership brand. These investments include training, development experiences, and life experiences. (This is the topic of chapter 5.)

- *Step 5: Measure leadership brand investment*—Measuring leadership results has two parts. First, it is important to know which leadership investments work best in which organization setting. This means tracking both the leadership investment (such as coaching) and the outcome of the investment (behavior change, financial results, intangible value). Second, the leadership investment should respond to the need presented in step 1. That is, if the case for leadership is to build a growth strategy for emerging markets, then the measurement of leadership success is the extent to which the expected growth strategy is taking hold. (This is the topic of chapter 6.)

- *Step 6: Build leadership brand awareness to key stakeholders*—Leadership brand shows up in the reputation of the firm as seen by multiple stakeholders. The CEO is the brand manager of leadership and should take the initiative to communicate the efficacy of the leadership brand to interested stakeholders. Tying leadership to long-term reputation becomes a basis for why leadership as a brand is more important than individual hero leaders. (This is the topic of chapter 7.)

These six steps can serve as a leadership brand index that will inform you of how well your organization is doing at building leadership brand (see assessment 1-1). This index will give you an overall score and point you to where you should focus to be more effective.

ASSESSMENT 1-1

Leadership brand index

Dimension of leadership brand	Question *To what extent does my organization . . .*	Low				High
Building a case for leadership	1. Have a clear linkage between leadership and the strategy of my business?	1	2	3	4	5
	2. Have leaders who pay attention to leadership?	1	2	3	4	5
Statement of leadership brand	3. Have a unique logic for what leaders stand for and are known for?	1	2	3	4	5
	4. Connect leadership behaviors to customer expectations?	1	2	3	4	5
Assessment of leadership brand	5. Identify gaps in the next generation of leaders?	1	2	3	4	5
Development of leadership brand	6. Invest in training experiences to develop leaders?	1	2	3	4	5
	7. Invest in job and development experiences to develop leaders?	1	2	3	4	5
	8. Invest in life experiences to develop leaders?	1	2	3	4	5
Measurement of leadership brand	9. Gauge the effectiveness and efficiency of leadership efforts?	1	2	3	4	5
Reputation of leadership brand	10. Ensure the awareness of all stakeholders to continue to invest in leadership brand?	1	2	3	4	5
	Total					

Key:

45 and higher: You have a branded leadership within your organization. Buy your stock now. It will have higher intangibles.
35–44: You have many of the key elements in place. Identify those areas where you are lower, and focus on them.
25–34: There are many areas that you need to focus on. Pick the one that you think can have the highest impact, and get started.
Under 25: Get started, do something, anything, and invest in leadership.

Putting It All Together

By following these six steps, a firm can create a leadership brand that differentiates the organization to employees inside and customers and investors outside. Creating this brand requires commitment from individuals throughout an organization. Boards of directors need to encourage and pay attention to leadership brand; senior executives need to sponsor leadership brand initiatives; HR professionals need to design and facilitate the creation of a leadership brand (see chapter 8).

Ultimately, leadership brand should affect individual leaders. It is impossible to sustain an organization's leadership brand unless and until individual leaders align their behaviors with it. As leaders at all levels of the company learn how to master the essence or core of leadership and demonstrate the requisite differentiators of leadership brand, they add value to their organizations (see chapter 9).

The leadership brand metaphor adds value to the understanding of becoming better leaders. First we shift from a focus on leaders to leadership. With this shift, firms create the institutional systems and processes that sustain the next generation of leadership, not just the current individual leaders. Second, we want to shift from a focus on leadership to leadership brand. Leadership brand galvanizes leadership around processes that are distinctive, distinguishing that company's leadership from its competitors' and increasing the value of the firm. By focusing on external customers and investors, current and future leaders demonstrate attributes and deliver results that matter most.

2

The Case for Building
a Leadership Brand

SOME EXECUTIVES JUST DON'T GET IT. They may say they believe in leadership, but they don't act like it. When times are good, they invest in leadership and proclaim themselves good corporate citizens, but in tough times, leadership investments are one of the first budgets they cut. What they really need is to understand how an investment in leadership will help them reach their own goals and their company's strategies—and how lack of leadership inhibits growth and confidence and diminishes value.

Executives who do get it not only say leadership matters, they demonstrate their commitment in action that is consistent through good times and bad. This chapter builds on chapter 1 to further explain why leadership brand matters, and details how to demonstrate the value that leadership brand creates. This is an important first step in the development of a leadership brand, because it makes the rest of the process more durable. Knowing the why makes it easy to accept the what; when everyone knows why leadership will help them, they accept what they need to do to make it happen.

The case for leadership brand has a very simple proposition: leadership helps make strategy happen. Without the right leaders at all levels, an organization can't deliver on its brand promise to customers, its financial promises to investors, its social promises to community stakeholders, or its cultural promises to employees. At times, executives get it and stipulate that leadership matters. At other times, they need to be coached on how leadership brand helps them reach personal and corporate strategies. In this chapter, we look at how to build a case for leadership brand whether you have a growth or a value strategy, linking the development of high-quality leaders to growth and increased stake-holder value and confidence.

Case for Growth and Leadership Brand

A recent example (kindly disguised here) illustrates these ideas:

Growing into a Brick Wall

All the major business magazines have put CEO "Buzz Nielsen" on the cover to celebrate his firm's approaching global dominance, which looked likely to extend for many years into the future. Nielsen was humble but proud of the growth rate and profit-ability his firm had accomplished. In interviews for TV and magazines, he attributed his success to people and culture—the factors that make his stores unique.

Suddenly, a crack appeared. For the first time in history, a start-up unit in a major metropolitan area was still floundering after seven months of intense effort. Nielsen initiated an after-action review to determine what contributed to the failure. All the analysis pointed to the same problem—the unit manager.

It turned out that the firm had run out of internal candidates at the unit manager level and begun to hire leadership talent from outside the company for new operations to maintain the pace of growth. This particular candidate looked good on paper and interviewed well. She had the technical skills necessary, but it was soon evident that she did not fully grasp or demonstrate the culture. She quickly alienated longtime employees in key positions; and when that small group left, morale began to plummet. From that point on, the unit's failure was just a matter of time.

Nielsen faced some hard choices. Should he deliberately slow down business growth and stick with hiring people from outside the company who appear to be able to deliver the right results the right way? Or should he invest in a process to develop the leadership brand and build the right kind of leaders from inside the company? It seemed by no means certain that the second approach could be made to work: if he were to choose the leadership brand development route, could he really build the right kind of leaders fast enough?

A gap in leadership bench strength is a real problem for any company; it is a crisis for one that's growing fast. Strategy points the direction and promises results to employees, customers, communities, and investors. Leaders at all levels have to find ways to deliver those results in a sustainable way. If there aren't enough of the right kinds of leaders, the strategy simply cannot be implemented. The supply of leadership talent is often a primary governor on business growth.

To decide how much to invest in leadership brand, Nielsen can gather information in advance that spells out the connection between quality of leadership and desired results. Armed with accurate information, Nielsen and his executive team could make informed choices about what they can do to increase quality and quantity of leadership. This means that the strategy must be understood and made operational in terms of leadership needs.

Six rationales justify investing in leadership brand to deliver strategy (presented in more detail in table 2-1).

TABLE 2-1

Making the connection to strategy

Challenge	Case for leadership brand because of growth strategy
1. Workforce planning	We have to develop enough leaders who will help us grow in the future; growth won't happen without high-quality leadership. Leadership brand matters because having enough leaders ready to grow the business the right way is a business necessity.
2. Right results the right way	We have to have leaders whose behavior demonstrates customer expectations. Leadership brand matters because when leaders' actions demonstrate what really matters most to customers and transfer those expectations to employee behaviors, customer commitment rises.
3. Strategy shifts	As we move from strategy A to B, we need to evolve leaders who can deliver on the new strategy. Leadership brand matters because it promulgates leadership capabilities that will help make new strategies happen.
4. Geography	As we move to new parts of the world, we need leaders throughout the organization who have competencies to adapt to conditions there. Leadership brand matters because it identifies and develops leaders who more readily adapt to local conditions and transfer knowledge from one area to another.
5. Mix of M&A and organic growth	Future leaders must have the competencies to successfully deliver on both acquisitions and organic growth. Leadership brand matters because it creates leaders who have the capabilities needed to ensure successful merger integration as well as profitable organic growth.
6. Critical jobs	Certain critical leadership jobs will be put under tremendous stress during growth. Leadership brand matters because it creates processes that actively manage and match high-potential leaders with critical jobs.

- Workforce planning

- Right results the right way

- Strategy shifts

- Geography

- Mix of mergers and acquisitions and organic growth

- Critical jobs

Workforce Planning

Both quantitative and qualitative factors influence the kind of leadership brand a company needs to build. In Nielsen's case, the quantitative information he needs can be found by doing thorough workforce-planning analytics. He has told the market that he intends to double the number of units in the next five years.

A few years ago, when the company was smaller, this kind of growth was much easier. As the company has grown above a billion dollars, doubling gets increasingly more difficult because the numbers of people and the complexity of the business grow exponentially. To grow revenue from $100 million to $200 million over five years is an important feat, but to grow from $3 billion to $6 billion is far more difficult and complex.

To understand the size of his challenge, Nielsen must get the answers to some important workforce-planning questions:

- Given current turnover rates (retired, fired, or otherwise departed), how many leaders at which levels (assistant managers, managers, regional directors, and executives) must be hired each year to meet the forecast demand for leaders?

- What assumptions do we make about the quality of our current leaders as we move to the future? How many of our current leaders who are now high performers will be high performers in the future? This gap analysis is revealing: for example, given a grading of leaders as "A," "B," or "C" versus future needs, how will the distribution compare with the needs of the organization at $6 billion in revenue versus $3 billion?

- What are the implications of alternative structure, delivery, and technology on managerial capacity needs? What changes are likely to shift the balance of leadership resources?

Our experience is that many senior executives have an intuitive sense that this kind of workforce analysis is important, but find it hard to locate the requisite information to do it well. Assembling this information helps create a case for leadership brand: just articulating the challenge of the numbers and competencies is usually enough to get the attention of even the most skeptical executive.

In summary, if leadership brand is to be built, there must be a thorough understanding of what the quantitative leadership challenge is in the first place. How many leaders do we need to build? At what levels will they be working? Where are they most likely to be needed? What is our current supply? How will we meet projected leadership demand?

Right Results in the Right Way

Beyond the quantitative case for change, the company needs to assess the quality of the leaders it will need. The case should establish the importance of having leaders at all levels of the company who get the right results (as defined by customers) and get these results the right way.

Starbucks offers an interesting example of this problem. Howard Schultz, chairman and chief global strategist of Starbucks, isn't just opening Starbucks stores as fast as possible; he is building a "third place experience" (home is first and work is second; the third is a community—a role that is served for some by a church and for others by a pub or a gym . . . or a coffee shop).[1] So at Starbucks it's not just about having enough *baristas* (people trained to prepare and serve coffee of the quality Starbucks maintains) to fulfill growth objectives. It is also about developing the right kind of managers for their stores—excellent baristas who also can run the stores so that customers have the third place experience.

A company growing as fast as Starbucks faces three possible outcomes:

- It is unable to achieve its desired growth rate because it can't build its leadership cadre fast enough; it either blows up or slows down.

- It delivers on its growth objectives, but the units don't deliver on the company's promise (for Starbucks, that would mean failing to deliver a third place experience or the mission statement to "establish Starbucks as the premier purveyor of the finest coffee in the world while maintaining our uncompromising principles while we grow," and the company becomes big and soulless.

- It delivers on its growth objectives and on its promise.

The implication for the case for leadership brand is that successful growth requires an explicit process to learn what the "right way" means and for reward and recognition processes to weight equally the "right way" and the "right results." The right way is about building the leadership brand, not just hiring or promoting random leaders. The right way begins by clearly articulating what customers expect when they interact with the firm. In Starbucks' case, what will ensure that Starbucks delivers on its mission statement of "maintaining our uncompromising principles while we grow"? How can leaders behave in ways consistent with these customer expectations? When most companies are growing very fast, it is easy for senior executives to be seduced into thinking that their leaders are somehow learning the core values of the company by osmosis. The desire to focus on growth without leadership investment is strong because rapid growth can hide the flaws in leadership. Non-investment will catch up. Investment at this stage is time-consuming but essential. Leadership brand is built when enough leaders at each level of the leadership pipeline know how to deliver the right (customer) results the right way.

Strategy Shifts

When an organization's future strategy differs from its past—as it so often does these days—the requirements for leadership brand must also change. Payless ShoeSource has found itself in this position. Over the last several years, the original Payless business model has been under increasing pressure. The original idea (sell lots of cheap shoes) was a huge success for decades. With big-box retailers adding shoe departments to their mix, competing on price alone wasn't going to cut it.

A new CEO, Matt Rubel—credited for turning the Cole Haan brand into a fashion powerhouse—brought a new vision to Payless when he joined in 2005. Under Rubel's leadership, the company implemented a new business strategy to democratize fashion, design, and innovation in the footwear/accessories category by offering authentic, original designs; to become a house of brands retailer by offering well-recognized brand names featuring the latest trends, technology, and quality at its traditional value price point; to elevate the shopping experience and reposition the brand image of Payless to attract new customers; and to extend its superior vertical integration to deliver great products at a great price. The new strategy entailed a shift of the Payless business model from a reseller of products purchased from other sources to identifying and interpreting trends and creating original designs.

Working with Jay Lentz, SVP of human resources, Rubel identified gaps in expertise in the leadership team. It was clear that the new business strategy warranted new expertise and leadership in important key roles. In 2006, Payless built upon its existing bench of leaders by adding more than two dozen new leaders at the director level and above in key areas including strategy, global sourcing, supply chain, creative, and design.

With new talent in place in key areas, Payless has made significant progress toward implementing its new strategy. Significant success points include:

- The first redesign of the company logo in twenty years

- The launch of a new store format, called "fashion lab," and a refresh of 11 percent of the Payless store chain in North America by year-end 2006

- The creation of a New York City Design Center, some of whose design staff had most recently served in design roles at Kenneth Cole, Michael Kors, and other luxe brands

- Alliances with key fashion designers and stylists and the launch of Payless's first-ever designer label, Abaeté for Payless, the most widely distributed designer footwear brand in America today

- The acquisition of American Eagle and the launch of the new Tailwind brand with partner Exeter Brands Group of Nike Inc. (these brands join Payless's expanded offerings along with Champion, Airwalk, Spalding, and Dunkman)

Following three years of negative performance, Payless registered eight consecutive quarters of positive same-store sales and enjoyed record sales in 2006 for the Payless concept.

Leadership brand can be adjusted as strategy changes. In 1963, IBM chairman Thomas J. Watson Jr. published *A Business and Its Beliefs: The Ideas That Helped Build IBM*, which lays out the foundation for how IBM leaders should lead. The book is based on the thesis that in order for an organization to survive and thrive it must have a sound set of beliefs underlying all its policies and actions, that the most important factor in corporate success is faithful adherence to those beliefs, and finally that if an organization is to meet the challenges of a changing world, it must be prepared to change everything about itself except those beliefs as it moves through corporate life.[2]

Watson—who had every reason to know—maintained that IBM needed three basic beliefs:

- Respect for the individual
- Customer focus
- Excellence in everything we do

These beliefs and the culture and leadership brand that followed worked for decades, and IBM became one of the world's premier companies, having its most profitable year in 1990. The culture of IBM manifested itself in the Big Blue image of dark suits, white shirts, and dark ties, and the stories that IBM stands for "I've Been Moved" that we all remember.

Over time, however, each of these beliefs had taken on layers of meaning that no longer fit with the external environment. *Respect for the individual* meant lifetime employment and never firing people. *Customer focus* meant telling customers what to do (particularly advocating the mainframe computer) in the face of rising interest in making independent choices (through the advent of laptop and portable computing). *Excellence in everything we do* led to a level of perfectionism that made it harder and harder to get new product innovations out the door.

By 1993, the computer industry had changed. Just three years after its earnings peak, IBM was looking at losing $16 billion and was on the watch list for extinction—a result of its size, insular culture, and the PC era it had helped invent. Then Lou Gerstner was brought in to run the company. Gerstner realized that the three classic beliefs and the leadership brand based on them had to be killed. And he was the one who was going to shoot them.[3]

Gerstner led IBM to identify a new leadership brand, based on supporting a new set of cultural values that created a new set of three primary beliefs for leaders at IBM—their new leadership brand:

- Win
- Execute
- Team

According to our colleagues at IBM during this time, this new belief system met no resistance; IBM leaders at all levels embraced it immediately because it fit their new reality. And almost at once, the company's fortunes were on the mend.

The implication for building a case for leadership brand at Payless and IBM is that strategy efforts that position a firm in a future state must be folded into the present through the evolution of the leadership brand.

Geography

Where you are physically located as an organization can have a major impact on how you plan for your future leadership needs. For example, Central Utah Clinic (CUC) is an independent physician professional corporation based in Provo, Utah; its president and chairman of the board is gastroenterologist Dr. Tom Dickinson. The region's health-care delivery is heavily dominated by Intermountain Healthcare, an in-tegrated health-care system, with its own physician division. Over the last several years, CUC has seen tremendous growth, despite its com-petitive relationship with Intermountain. It has grown from thirty physician partners with annual revenues of $28 million to a hundred physician members with annual revenues of over $100 million.

A few years ago, CUC hired Scott Barlow as CEO. Barlow has fo-cused on reducing physician practice costs by installing a state-of-the-art IT system, which provides central billing and administrative services. CUC has also invested in medical equipment that creates a profit pool for the group. In a payroll survey last year, CUC doctors, on average, were at the 90th percentile of national incomes. This is an extraordi-nary accomplishment for a group of doctors living in central Utah.

The question facing Dickinson, Barlow, and the physicians at CUC is whether or not to continue growing geographically. CUC has a strong culture, and both physicians and staff see it as a preferred em-ployer. If it continues to grow, it may see scale efficiencies begin to de-crease with the admission of new cohorts of doctors and the placement of new administrative leaders in these new areas—and current employ-ees and physician members reasonably fear that these increased costs will come right out of their pockets. On the other hand, if the group doesn't continue to grow, it may face concerns over sluggish growth and profits that would damage its work environment and culture.

In a recent meeting, the CUC executive committee and board exam-ined their options and decided to continue their growth by expanding into other proximate counties. They did this with a clear understanding of their options and the implications of these options on leadership and organization effectiveness. Their leadership brand was consistent with their geography, and recognizing this allowed them to grow.

The leadership brand case for geography is to ensure that your organization understands the implications of moving into new regions and to ensure an effective process to manage all the leadership challenges that can be reasonably anticipated. Most large companies today talk about geographically expanding in areas like China, India, Russia, Brazil, and Indonesia—a much more complex expansion than CUC's expansion into proximate counties in Utah. These countries are seen as the future because of their burgeoning populations and economic growth. Workforce-planning tools can be used to identify the numeric leadership needs in a region. However, this is not enough. If countries like Brazil, India, Indonesia, Russia, and China are the future, then future senior leaders will need experience working in these cultures so they know how to operate effectively there, and leadership processes will need to be adjusted. Defining the leadership brand, assessing future leaders, building development programs, offering career paths, and using local versus global talent will all need to be addressed to build geographically adapted leadership brand. Without attention to these elements reflected in leadership brand, an expansion strategy can quickly fail. For example, Wal-Mart has left Germany in part because it was not able to adapt its practices to the German setting.

Mix of M&A and Organic Growth

If you eat too much or too fast at the dining table or the negotiating table, you can get into trouble. The suffering and recovery of Citigroup—a $90 billion-a-year financial services powerhouse that is consistently one of the most profitable companies in the world (Exxon-Mobil challenges it, depending on the price of oil)—illustrates the force of this warning. The present Citigroup was formed in 1998 when legendary Travelers Insurance CEO Sandy Weill merged his company with Citicorp. Over the next few years, Weill led a series of acquisitions that grew Citigroup into a highly decentralized group of financial services businesses including Smith Barney, Banamex, CitiFinancial, The Associates, and Primerica. When Weill stepped up to the chairmanship in 2004, his successor as CEO was Chuck Prince, who at the time was chief legal counsel. The expectation was that Citigroup would continue to grow primarily through mergers and acquisitions.

This changed in 2005 as Citigroup experienced a series of setbacks. Citigroup's Private Bank division was kicked out of Japan by regulators for not following protocols. This had an immediate market value hit of about $12 billion as investors lost confidence in Citigroup's near future. Things went from bad to worse when a loss of customer information was not reported for several months in Singapore (after a box fell off a truck). To add additional bad news, the German government sued the company for alleged unethical trading practices in London. During this period, global regulators banded together to forbid Citigroup from making further acquisitions until it figured out how to control what it already had.

Rather than focusing on continued growth, Chuck Prince was in a situation where he had to demonstrably change internal priorities quickly and effectively. Prince responded by clarifying and forcefully disseminating the Citigroup leadership brand. He did this by creating what he called the Five Point Plan, which encompassed a strategy for aligning organization practices with ethical leadership practices and included powerful cases based on Citigroup's lessons learned. Over the next two years, Prince managed to set a direction based on a leadership brand that balanced Citigroup's Shared Responsibilities (responsibility to the franchise, to the customer, and to each other) with Citigroup's vaunted prowess in delivering results. As the firm demonstrated—internally and externally—that it was a company that wanted the right results in the right way, regulators responded favorably by eliminating restrictions on Citigroup's acquisition activities, analysts' jitters subsided, employee confidence was restored, and customers regained confidence that their financial partners were uncompromising. Interestingly, Prince is now pursuing organic growth as a preferred emphasis for the future and this year has shifted the focus from "franchise responsibilities" to an emphasis on building customer commitment and growth.

The case for leadership brand for both acquisitive and organic growth is to articulate the implications on leadership of each growth option. A good strategy will make this explicit. If the company primarily pursues an M&A approach, then leadership brand must be actively and thoroughly inculcated into the newly acquired companies. Such leadership integration means moving leaders into the new company but also articulating and investing in the leadership brand within the acquired company. In a primarily organic-growth mode, leaders have to know how to build—and be committed to (and rewarded for) building—leadership brand in their organizations or divisions around shared values, collaboration, culture, and talent. Companies engaged in a mix of M&A and organic growth should build future leaders who have experience in both arenas so that they have a perspective on the challenges entailed by each option.

Critical Jobs

Planning for critical jobs (or positions) in companies without a leadership brand usually focuses on individual senior executive issues at the expense of a broader and deeper approach to leadership brand. As you develop a case for leadership brand development, it's important to look at leaders throughout the organization. Any strategy places a greater demand on certain leadership positions than others as the strategy is successfully implemented and growth is achieved. Identifying these "critical jobs" and the impact they will have on the success of the organization's strategy is a critical component of developing the case for leadership and identifying where to focus leadership attention for the future.

Lowe's provides an example of the importance of this issue. A direct competitor to Home Depot, it is expanding its operations very quickly. Any company that grows at this rate will experience leadership stress in every function and at every level. However, what level will receive the most stress? And even more important, if Lowe's is to be successful, which leaders will have the most impact on the successful execution of the strategy? Our guess is that store managers hold the most critical jobs for the future of the company.

As part of the case for leadership brand, it is necessary to review a strategy through the lens of identifying which jobs are most critical for successful implementation of the strategy. This is likely to involve a review of the current structure as well as some forecasting about likely structural changes in the future. This analysis is very useful in focusing where to invest development resources. Knowing how and where the strategy will build a demand for the leadership brand differentiates successful from unsuccessful strategies.

Case for Value and Leadership Brand

A second approach to preparing a case for developing a leadership brand is the impact of leadership quality on value. We have discussed elsewhere that value is defined by the receiver more than the giver, which means that the value of a leadership brand should show up:[4]

- For investors

- For customers

- For employees

Table 2-2 summarizes the way this works.

Leadership Brand Creates Value for Investors

Warren Buffett is one of the world's greatest investors, and his firm consistently ranks toward the top of the *Fortune* survey. What Buffett looks for before he invests basically comes down to two factors: (1) he wants to invest in businesses he understands, and (2) he bets on the quality of leadership teams. If he believes in the leadership, he believes in the company.

Most savvy investors decide to invest in one company over others because they forecast that the future of one company will be better. Knowing the leadership team—their track record, how they have dealt with problems before, how they have attracted capital, and the like—is a strong indicator of the likelihood of future success. In *How Leaders Build Value*, we explored how intangibles like leadership increase or decrease confidence in the future.[5] A yardstick for this performance is the price-to-earnings multiple. When we compare companies in the same industry, a higher multiple indicates greater investor confidence for the future. As we shared in chapter 1, the P/E ratios within an industry may vary up to 50 percent. While short-term fluctuations may be due to a host of factors, long-term premiums or discounts begin to reflect investors' trust in the quality of leadership.

TABLE 2-2

Making the connection to value

Opportunity	Case for value derived from leadership brand
Investors	A strong leadership brand increases investor confidence in future earnings and shows up in investor intangibles. Leadership brand matters because it builds market value.
Customers	As customer needs and tastes change, leadership brand must adapt to continue to ensure sustainable value propositions that matter to customers. Leadership brand matters because it increases customer share.
Employees	Leadership brand ensures ongoing value created for customers by building employee commitment and engagement. Leadership brand matters because it affects employee competence and commitment, which are strongly correlated with customer retention and satisfaction and, in turn, financial returns and market value.

Investor confidence may go up or down depending on investors' collective confidence in the leadership depth in the company. Current examples of firms where leadership brand has created intangible value that is reflected in the price-to-earnings multiple include Pfizer's high investor confidence ratings in pharmaceuticals, Herman Miller in office furniture, Toyota's preeminence in the auto industry, and the way the relatively low revenues of Southwest Airlines support market value so much higher than that of their competitors.

Leaders also destroy brand value when they act in ways contrary to the best interests of shareholders. Like most readers, we followed the trial of Jeffrey Skilling and Kenneth Lay, former CFO and CEO of Enron, with morbid fascination. Prosecutors held Skilling and Lay primarily responsible for the decline of Enron. In this process the two have become famous as leadership pariahs—they represent all that is the opposite of effective leadership brand building. Lying and manipulation of a company's state of affairs may boost current confidence with stakeholders, but it's a recipe for disaster when it eventually comes to light. A more routine example of how leadership brand can destroy investor value comes from Pfizer's leadership change, whereby the departure of Henry McKinnell and the appointment of Jeffrey Kindler resulted in a drop in share price as investor confidence in the future fell when the board replaced a known and successful CEO with a relative newcomer with little pharmaceutical experience.

Leadership brand must be sustainable over time to create investor value—it cannot be built on empty promises and false premises or on unexpected and unknown leaders.

Leadership Brand Creates Value for Customers

As we write this, the media are talking about the demise of General Motors as almost a foregone conclusion. But is it really? Experts tell us that GM does not know how to build cars that its customers want to buy, so customers are turning to Toyota, BMW, and Mercedes. They point to GM's raft of problems, especially the high legacy costs it endures (every active U.S. employee supports 3.2 retirees, amounting to $1,500 per vehicle of cost and destroying profits on all but the most expensive cars).

In spite of this, we have confidence that Rick Wagoner, GM's CEO, is up to the task of restoring GM's luster for the future. Over the past year, one of GM's top priorities has been to improve their business in North America to position GM for sustained profitability and growth in the long-term and to achieve competitiveness on a global level. In 2005, GM announced a historic agreement sharing health-care costs with the United Auto Workers, which reduced GM's U.S. retiree health-care liabilities by $15 billion. This is just one of the many actions the company has taken to become more competitive and address their legacy costs. In the meantime, GM is selling off factories and offering packages to its entire North American hourly workforce. It's also shedding assets—including a 51 percent stake in GMAC Finance, sold to a private equity firm for $14 billion. And in non–North American markets (Europe, Asia, and Latin America), GM is profitable.

But Wagoner isn't content to just reduce costs as his legacy for the GM leadership brand. In 2001, Wagoner brought in Bob Lutz—renowned for his work at Ford with cars like the Mustang—to head the revival of its product line. Lutz is seen as a leader who *can* design cars that customers want to buy, and he seems to be on track at GM. *Time* magazine described four new cars as candidates to restore GM's profitability because of their connection to target customers:[6]

- *Saturn Aura:* "Its German design is a bid to win back buyers who have split for VWs, Hondas, and Toyotas."

- *Buick Lucerne:* "Earning high marks for an excellent ride, crisp handling and a quiet cabin."

- *Chevrolet HHR:* "Is winning buyers drawn to its good fuel economy and spacious interior. GM had to increase production . . . and it looks like a PT Cruiser."

- *Chevrolet Tahoe:* "Folks who just gotta have a big SUV love its family-friendly design, as long as they can handle the pain at the pump (and dirty looks)."

Finally, GM now resonates with Chinese customers—a huge and potentially company-saving market. GM is investing in China, not downsizing, as GM vehicles are selling at a premium because of their cachet. With these new product launches, GM leaders like Wagoner and Lutz have shown that GM is working to create a more customercentric leadership brand.

Leadership Brand Creates Value for Employees

Employee attitude inside the firm (often referred to as engagement or commitment) is linked to customer behavior relative to the firm (customer satisfaction and retention). There are several key ways this link has been established.

Sears did research that showed that employee attitude was a lead indicator of customer attitude and financial performance. It found that a 5-point increase in employee attitude corresponded with a 1.3-point increase in customer satisfaction and a 0.5 percent increase in profit growth.[7]

In addition, each year *Fortune* publishes a feature called "Best Companies to Work For." This study rates companies on pay, turnover, diversity, and employee morale. In conjunction with the study, *Fortune* examines how these companies perform on a financial basis, and it's clear that companies that are great to work for also make great investments.

Figure 2-1 shows that "had you bought the public companies when the 1998 list came out, and reinvested in the new list each year, you would have earned 10.6 percent annually. That wallops the S&P 500's 5.7 percent annual return over the same period. These numbers assume a market-cap-weighted index: weighing each stock equally would have provided an even more dazzling 18.2 percent return annually."[8]

It's worth noting that Enron made the "Best Companies to Work For" list in 1998, 1999, and 2000. One explanation for this surprising fact is that Enron employees, like investors, were duped by management. Enron did not appear on the 2001 list.

What is it about a company that earns a place on this kind of list that also drives investor returns? The secret is not about pay and working conditions and creating a country club environment. What truly motivates people are factors like challenging jobs, opportunities for growth and development, and relationships with others in the work group, especially the leader.

Leadership brand creates value for employees when leaders create the conditions for high performance. High performance drives employee commitment. People who feel they are part of a winning team, and that their team is making a difference and recognizes them for their contributions, are willing to invest discretionary effort to deliver ongoing results. Costco has a reputation for not only meeting customer needs but having employees who are engaged and committed. Its em-

FIGURE 2-1

Stock market return on *Fortune*'s "Best Companies to Work For"

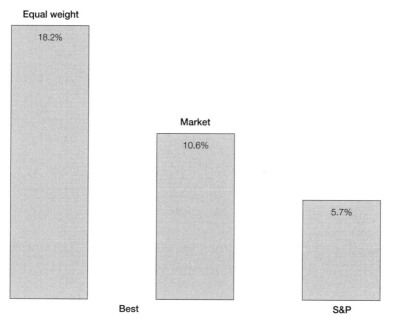

Equal weight

18.2%

Market

10.6%

5.7%

Best   S&P

Source: Fortune, May 27, 2002, p. 162.

ployee turnover is one-third less than competitors', and while it pays more, its productivity is 20 percent higher than the industry average (sales per employee).[9]

Conclusion

In the quest to build leadership brand, building a case for leadership brand is the step most frequently skimmed over. We may see this unusually often because people don't talk to us unless they have already decided to do something. However, skipping this step is a precursor to building a "sunny days" leadership brand process, or one that lasts when profits are good. An explicit business case for leadership brand is the only way to ensure ongoing and sustainable investments in leadership brand building. What seems like an obvious investment today may

Leadership brand commitment index

Circle the number that corresponds to the extent to which each statement applies to your organization's case for investment in leadership brand.

	To what extent . . .	Low High
1. Workforce planning	Do we have a clear picture of how many leaders we need, what skills they have, and where we need them to sustain our business strategy and growth objectives?	1 2 3 4 5 6 7 8 9 10
2. Right results the right way	Is there a process in place to ensure a continuity of our desired culture and values as we bring on new leaders?	1 2 3 4 5 6 7 8 9 10
3. Strategy shifts	Do we have a systemic process to ensure that our leaders have the right technical and social competencies to deliver on changing strategies and challenges?	1 2 3 4 5 6 7 8 9 10
4. Geography	Do we have an explicit process to give leaders at all levels experiences in geographies that represent our future strategic portfolio?	1 2 3 4 5 6 7 8 9 10
5. M&A or organic	Do we provide job assignments to develop leadership competencies consistent with how we plan to grow—acquisitions as well as organic growth?	1 2 3 4 5 6 7 8 9 10
6. Critical jobs	Have we identified and prepared leaders in jobs that will be under the greatest stress as we grow?	1 2 3 4 5 6 7 8 9 10
7. Backups	Are there enough backups for our senior executives as well as for our critical jobs?	1 2 3 4 5 6 7 8 9 10
8. Investor value	Have we created investor confidence about the quality of our leadership brand?	1 2 3 4 5 6 7 8 9 10
9. Customer value	Do we have leaders capable of building an organization that consistently meets or exceeds customer expectations?	1 2 3 4 5 6 7 8 9 10
10. Employee value	Do we have leaders who are able to attract, retain, and engage high-performing employees?	1 2 3 4 5 6 7 8 9 10
	Total	

Key:

Over 75: You have already built the case for the need for leadership brand and can move on to the steps recommended in chapter 3.

Between 40–75: You have built a partial business case for leadership. Use your low scores to identify ways to build a stronger case.

Under 40: You need to do your homework and build the business case for this important investment.

be an easy target for cost reduction without this clear case. Building the case for change avoids leadership shopping and loss of leaders.

If you are a leader or an individual responsible for developing leadership in a company and your senior leaders get it—*they not only say leadership matters, they invest personal and corporate resources to make it happen*—this chapter only confirms the work you have done. But if you're dealing with a commitment to leadership that is only a thin veneer, you can use the arguments in this chapter to help build the case for investing in leadership. Take the survey in assessment 2-1 and invite others to do so, and it will underscore the point that an investment in leadership brand is one of the most significant investments anyone can make for their own success and for the future success of their company.

3

Creating a Leadership Brand Statement

WHEN WE POLL workshop participants about what makes an effective leader, we generally get generic answers: effective leaders have integrity, passion, and courage; they know how to set goals, build teams, and engage employees. That's all true, of course, and it shows that our participants have internalized the generic leadership code that we introduced in chapter 1. The "right stuff" for leaders is embedded in this code but it is not enough to fully explain leadership effectiveness.

As noted in chapter 1, because the leadership code may explain 60–70 percent of leadership, it is necessary but not sufficient for effectiveness. Leaders who master the code have a higher probability of becoming effective. But unless they can adapt the code to their particular setting and then also create differentiation by seeing their internal leadership through the eyes of external customers and investors, they will remain generic leaders. In small and large companies, successful leadership goes beyond the leadership code to a statement of leadership brand that includes both the code and the differentiated leadership required to shape it to that specific business: the *leadership brand*.

To revisit the automotive analogy, just as all cars have similar internal systems—suspension, chassis, braking, fuel, and so forth—all companies need the basic elements of the leadership code. Likewise, just as, say, the suspension system will be different in an SUV from the one in a sedan (and different again within either model branded "Lexus" or "Toyota"), the performance management system in a microelectronics firm will be different from the one in a petrochemical giant—and different again between one firm in each industry and others in the same industry. That is, the expression of leadership in a short-term, rapidly changing industry will differ from that in an industry focused more on long-term stability, and differ again according to the particular value proposition the firm in each industry maintains. Leaders in all of them must be personally proficient, strategists, executors, talent managers, and human capital developers, but these abilities will find somewhat different expression in each context. As we've said, mastering the general principles implied by the leadership code explains about two-thirds of effective leadership. The rest comes from adapting those principles to a specific context and then building a differentiated identity that connects the outside to the inside, what we call moving from leadership to leadership brand.

While sedans and sports cars have differing systems, the various makes of each type also have unique product and service features that distinguish and position each brand. Likewise, even after leaders master the code, they must then adapt the leadership brand to help their organization distinguish itself from others. This differentiation—the creation of the firm's leadership brand—is the connection between the customer views of the organization (firm brand) and the employee views of the organization (culture). Leadership brand becomes the process whereby the identity of the external customer translates to the behavior of the internal employee and organization processes. When this connection of the outside and inside is made real (in terms of both rhetoric and action), we call that a *statement of leadership brand*.

The bridge image helps capture this construct. The island at one end represents the firm's brand, its identity in the mind of target customers, or the experience customers have with the firm. The firm brand positions the organization in the marketplace, creates a reputation, and gains customer loyalty over time. The other island represents the employee behaviors inside the firm based on the firm's culture, or how employees work—with each other and with customers. When the culture inside bridges the firm brand outside, employees understand how their behaviors lead to customer share, and customers see employees as having their interests in mind. The bridge connecting the inside culture and the outside firm brand is the leadership brand. Leaders translate customer expectations into employee behaviors. They make sure that marketplace demands show up as workplace actions. They make the firm identity real through policies and practices inside the firm. A statement of leadership brand becomes the connector of customers and employees.

A firm brand statement requires thoughtful and thorough analysis of what customers should know the firm for, and it results in a simple statement that captures this message. A brand complements vision, mission, and value statements. Vision statements explain why a company is in business; missions define what business they are in; values describe internal expectations about employee behavior. Too frequently, such statements focus on what companies expect from their internal constituents; and too often, they generate cynicism because they have little grounding in reality or action. A brand, on the other hand, connects a firm's reputation with customer needs and investor hopes. When a leader's behavior is shaped by customer expectations, it is rooted in an external reality larger than the individual. The brand expectations in the marketplace become criteria for employee and organization behavior in the workplace. The brand logic rechannels vision, mission, and value statements to an outside-in focus. Rather than what *we* want to be known for, the brand emphasizes *what we want customers to know us for*.

Likewise, a statement of leadership brand begins with an alignment of the leadership (both attributes and results) with the firm's customer identity and subsequent strategy, but then goes from that alignment to a simple statement that is the basis for a set of expectations and standards for leadership. For example, 3M wants customers to know it for its ability to innovate, and so executives communicate their dedication to innovation in reports to investors, customers, and employees. The firm measures leaders and divisions by innovation, or the percentage of new products created in the last few years. Innovation as a firm brand becomes a leadership brand when leaders at each level of the firm are aware of the firm's innovation identity and align their personal behaviors, results, and ultimately their own identities with the need to innovate. HR practices, through the criteria used in hiring, promotion, and compensation decisions, reinforce innovation as a leadership brand. Innovation becomes the standard for leadership and is woven into leadership development practices. A statement of leadership brand states what leaders are known for that reflects customer expectations and employee and organization behaviors. This statement of leadership brand is then embedded into practices that shape leaders throughout the organization.

Creating a Leadership Brand Statement

At its simplest level, creating a statement of leadership brand simply requires turning the descriptors in a firm brand into leadership behaviors. A firm brand defines what the company is known for by its best customers. Apple wants to be known for innovation; General Electric, for invention; Marriott, for service; Wal-Mart, for cost. These external images then need to be turned into leadership behaviors. A leadership brand model at Apple would require leadership behaviors that encourage innovation (e.g., risk taking, experimenting, and encouraging debate and dialogue). In contrast, the leadership brand model at Wal-Mart would emphasize behaviors that reduce costs (e.g., doing process re-engineering, contracting aggressively with suppliers, and managing to a budget). Whereas at Marriott, the leadership brand behaviors would be consistent with service (knowing customers, listening to customers, responding to customers, and so forth). While the leadership code suggests that all leaders in all companies will require mastery of the basics, the leadership brand enables companies to tailor their leadership to external requirements.

While this process is simple, we have identified six steps to creating a statement of leadership brand that differentiates leaders according to the identity the firm wants to establish among targeted customers. Creating such a leadership brand statement builds on traditional competency models by aligning competencies with the firm brand, by focusing on the future instead of the past, and by defining the results that should occur—instead of just the competencies that differentiate high and low performers. This approach to leadership brand begins with an understanding of customer expectations and how they shape the strategy, shifts to defining the firm brand, and then tailors a leadership code and anticipated results. It integrates these items into a statement of leadership brand and then elaborates standards to evaluate leadership. This is a logical, linear process that enables executives to create a leadership brand statement that works for the firm (see figure 3-1).

Step 1: Start with Strategy

Many terms are used to describe how an organization positions itself for future success. In general, a vision defines why we are in business; a mission, what we do; a strategy, how we win; values, what matters most to us; and goals or objectives, what we will do that we can track and

FIGURE 3-1

Creating a leadership brand statement

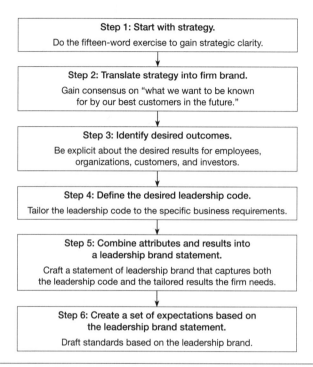

> **Step 1: Start with strategy.**
> Do the fifteen-word exercise to gain strategic clarity.

> **Step 2: Translate strategy into firm brand.**
> Gain consensus on "what we want to be known for by our best customers in the future."

> **Step 3: Identify desired outcomes.**
> Be explicit about the desired results for employees, organizations, customers, and investors.

> **Step 4: Define the desired leadership code.**
> Tailor the leadership code to the specific business requirements.

> **Step 5: Combine attributes and results into a leadership brand statement.**
> Craft a statement of leadership brand that captures both the leadership code and the tailored results the firm needs.

> **Step 6: Create a set of expectations based on the leadership brand statement.**
> Draft standards based on the leadership brand.

monitor. A strategy for winning may be explicated at any of many levels within an organization. Strategy is about allocating resources to win in the marketplace. For the multidivision corporation, the strategy is a statement of portfolio investments so that a firm manages a mix of businesses to win. The overall firm brand permeates each division brand so that value is added for customers. For example, the Marriott brand of exceptional customer service is added to divisions to increase consumer confidence: Fairfield Inn by Marriott, Courtyard by Marriott, Residence Inn by Marriott. At a division level, a strategy may be created to figure out how to gain customer share for targeted customers. A customer-focused strategy ensures that investments are aligned with customer expectations. Courtyard, for example, focuses on business travelers making short stays and makes sure that room amenities are aligned with what business travelers prefer (Internet hookup, cable TV, coffeemaker), while Residence Inn focuses on extended-stay travelers by offering larger rooms, kitchenettes, and conversation areas.

Likewise, firm brands at all levels should be crafted to be consistent with the overall strategy. This means that they should all reflect the corporate firm brand but also be adapted to the division or subunit brand. One of the exercises we often use is to ask, "How much of the leadership brand should be firmwide instead of business-specific?" Depending on the influence of the corporate identity, the response may range from 50 percent to 80 percent shared across the corporation. Beyond that, every unit with its own business strategy needs a statement of leadership that aligns with both the corporate brand and its own specialized requirements.

Numerous approaches exist to clarify strategy. A strategy often combines a desired image of the future (vision, mission, values) with specific allocation of resources to fold the present into the future (goals, objectives). A brand lens on the vision and goals focuses them on the outside in: are these the things that we want customers to have of our desired image and goals? Strategic clarity simply means that the executives have articulated a point of view about the future that is shared with employees inside and customers and investors outside the organization. Here's an exercise we've used to help businesses test for and build strategic clarity:

- Have each member of a leadership team (at any level where strategy work is performed—corporate, division, function, plant, business unit) write the strategy of their unit in fifteen words or less.

- Compare statements and look for similarities.

- Discuss similarities and differences as needed, and develop a shared strategy statement.

- Test this strategy statement with those outside the firm—for example, customers and investors—to find out whether it reflects what they want you to be known for.

If strategic clarity already exists, this exercise quickly confirms it. On the other hand, if team members turn out to have radically differing views of their unit's strategy, simply becoming aware of that difference is the essential first step toward developing a unified approach.

Bear in mind, however, that it is much easier to draft a strategy than to deliver one; to espouse what should be than to exhibit by action what actually is; to form a strategy than to implement one. This exercise will show its real value only as the strategy becomes linked to a firm brand outside the firm and embedded in employee actions and organization practices inside the firm.

Step 2: Translate Strategy into Firm Brand

A strategy is an aspiration statement about how to position an organization in the future. It leads to allocation of resources to realize the position. It should also lead to a firm brand that meets the ten criteria outlined in appendix A:

- Do the basics well.

- Start from the outside in.

- Communicate in customer terms.

- Evolve along with customers.

- Tell a story people want to hear.

- Spread the word.

- Have staying power and endurance.

- Make it work.

- Keep it relevant.

- Sustain price and value.

That is, a brand needs to communicate the reputation, image, and character of the firm to those who use the firm's products or services. It is generally captured in a simple statement but validated by behaviors congruent with that statement. It guides investments in advertising, customer relations, marketing, and promotional materials. It is tested with market research and evolves as customers change. It communicates the promise of the firm to its customers. It has efficacy when this promise is fulfilled. It endures over time and evolves with new customer requirements.

Sometimes, firms have an existing identity that needs to be continued. Consider the Olympics. The five Olympic rings stand for the major geographical regions of the world: Africa, the Americas, Asia, Europe, and Oceania. The colors represent the flags of the countries that participate in the Olympics, all of which include at least one of the ring colors:

blue, black, red, yellow, and green. The connection of the rings sym-
bolizes the international collaboration as the countries come together
at Olympic events. This brand image has been nurtured since the 1912
Olympics with consistent communication and Olympic branding efforts.

Few firms have the kind of stability reflected in the constant
Olympic brand. Most need to either clarify or update their brands from
time to time. Firm brands should evolve as customers evolve. We have
found a simple exercise that helps shape the desired identity of the firm.

A leadership team should ask itself one question: What are the top
three things we (our organization) want to be known for by our key
customers in the future? The responses will help identify the extent to
which a shared identity already exists among the management team members who answer the question and provide the basics for creating a shared
identity if one is still needed.

A firm brand is legitimate if the answers given by the management
team match the answers customers would give. For example, the CVS
pharmacy chain is known for *customer, value,* and *service* by its management team (as the name of the company implies)—and its customers
know it for the same values. Saudi Aramco has worked to become known
as a reliable source of energy both by its customers and by its senior
management team. McDonald's core values of quality, service, cleanli-
ness, and value resonate not only with the management team but also
with customers, who see these values as part of the McDonald's brand.
Southwest Airlines has become known for fun, on-time delivery, and
low prices both among senior managers and among customers. When the
brand outside the firm reflects the desired culture inside the firm,
the brand and the culture have staying power. The brand translates to
employee behaviors, and the culture becomes less an abstract set of
ideas or values and more a living identity that will lead to customer
commitment. The justification for a firm brand is clear: strong brands
command a premium in the marketplace. In workshops, we often have
a delegate stand with his hand over the logo (Polo, Ralph Lauren,
Eddie Bauer, or others) on his shirt, and we ask, "What would you pay
for this shirt?" Then we have him remove his hand and reveal the logo,
and ask, "What would you now pay?" This simple exercise shows that most
of us recognize the power of a brand for capturing consumer confidence in revenue generated.

A firm brand in the mind of customers may be brought inside by
shaping an assortment of HR practices: hiring, training, and rewarding

employees who embody the brand; aligning performance management practices with the brand; or creating a structure that reflects customer expectations.[1]

We have often seen leaders make the mistake of separating culture inside the firm from customer expectations outside the firm. This mistake often builds cultures based on personal values rather than customer expectations. The resulting cultures tend to last as long as the current leader espouses and pursues them, but a new leader may change the cultural values again. When the focus is on customers, the internal culture has staying power because it shows up in increased revenue and customer share. Consistent with the shift in leadership from individual leaders to leadership brand, the cultures tied to customers, more than one manager's value, become institutionalized and endure. Culture may change as customer expectations change. The rotund Pillsbury Doughboy slimmed down as society recognized the health risks of obesity.

Some firms with worthy and noble value statements that have taken enormous time on the part of their executive teams see very little impact for all their work. The statement looks great in its rosewood frame but can't seem to reach outside it. Fortunately, the work isn't wasted; it is possible to turn these internally focused value statements into firm brands by going to key customers with these statements and asking three questions:

1. *Are these the values you want us to be known for?* This question lets the firm find out whether the values espoused in the statement are really the ones that customers are interested in. Generally, the answer is yes, since most value statements contain noble values. But we have found that this question may force rethinking of the values. One firm had a value "to be the most profitable in our industry." When we asked what would happen if customers were to assess this value, its sponsors—realizing that few customers would endorse a value that came straight from their own wallets—soon refocused their values away from a primary focus on the firm's financial goals.

2. *If these are the values that we should espouse, what do we have to do to demonstrate that we live them better than our competitors do?* This question now shifts the behaviors associated with the espoused values from inside-out to outside-in. If and when customers can describe what an organization can do to be

innovative, customer focused, ethical, changeable, talent rich, responsive, team focused, or other values, these customer expectations then set the standard for how the firm can demonstrate that it has delivered its firm brand. This question moves values from generic and perhaps esoteric ideals to specific behaviors that have meaning for customers.

3. *If we demonstrate that we live these values, would you be willing to do more business with us?* Now the questions lead to business results. The purpose of values is not just to have a set of beliefs, it is to have a set of beliefs that make a difference in customer share and revenue.

These questions and exercises help shape a firm brand and build an identity that is real to customers and to employees. But we believe that to sustain this identity, leaders must also translate the expectations customers have of the firm to employee and organizational behaviors.

Step 3: Identify Desired Outcomes

Obviously, leaders must deliver results. In our previous work, we have identified four domains of results that leaders must deliver according to the stakeholders they serve.[2] To investors, leaders must deliver financial performance today and intangible confidence about the future, which shows up in market capitalization. To customers, leaders must deliver products and services with reliability, consistency, and value, resulting in improved share of target customers. To employees, leaders must deliver working conditions and opportunities that show up in employee competence and commitment. And to the organization, leaders must deliver a set of capabilities that become an enduring culture—a culture not tied to any one leader or practice but maintaining an organizational life of its own. Figure 3-2 shows some of the results that leaders might deliver. A leadership challenge is to prioritize and tailor the results delivered to stakeholders.

These results can be defined in two ways. First, leaders can simply say that given the strategy and firm brand, a set of results should follow—as identified through a strategic map where investor and customer goals turn into organization processes and employee actions.[3] To take this approach, it's useful to begin by brainstorming and prioritizing measurable goals that would align with the firm brand, and then saying, "If we had this firm brand, how would we know? What would we see

FIGURE 3-2

Generic leadership results

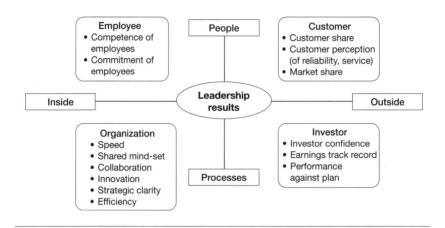

more of or less of?" These questions elicit dialogue that helps the group frame measurable goals and drive leadership results. This free-flowing type of discussion often works with management teams who have worked together long enough to feel comfortable, who have great experience with the desired strategy and firm brand, and who have the ability to turn abstract ideas into concrete actions.

Alternatively, the leadership team can simply pick three or four results from the leadership results grid in figure 3-2 as a way to define and prioritize their goals. This exercise asks each member of a senior team to select three or four results that leadership should focus on given the strategy and firm brand, and then discuss the individual selections until reaching consensus on a final list. The generic results derived then need to be restated in terms consistent with the organization language and culture.

Either approach allows the development of a tailored list that defines what the firm's results should be, given the strategy and firm brand.

Step 4: Define the Desired Leadership Code

The firm brand endures when it shows up in leadership action. It is all very well to proclaim a firm brand of reliability and trust, but high turnover among leaders or toleration of leaders who don't create trust among employees will rapidly erode the brand. Leaders model the brand by their example: they demonstrate the brand by their decisions and they live the brand by their behavior.

A solid firm brand forms the core of a statement of leadership brand. Once the brand establishes "what we want our firm to be known for," it becomes possible to translate those customer requirements into leadership brand expectations. Returning to 3M, it wants its customers to think of it as a source for innovation, so it must have leaders who demonstrate the behaviors of innovation (taking risks, thinking of novel approaches to old problems and also of novel problems, experimenting, continuously improving, challenging the status quo, and so forth). Likewise, Continental Airlines wants travelers, and especially frequent travelers, to know it as a source of consistent on-time arrivals, so it encourages leaders who act with discipline and rigor—and who meet commitments.

Alternatively, you can use a critical-element process like the one suggested for firm brand to define the desired leadership code. Ask leaders to examine the five categories of leadership code (see figure 3-3) and select descriptors in these generic categories that would be most important to them, given the organization's strategy and firm brand, and then develop a consensus list. If a firm's desired brand is focused on managing cost, the team might pick items like *building efficiency* or *change disciplinarian* descriptors. If an organization is focused on growth, the leaders might define items such as *pioneer* and *innovator* as the most critical parts of the leadership code. Then the team should tailor these generic descriptors to specific words, phrases, or images that capture the uniqueness of the firm. When a global hospitality company worked to become more consistent in customer service, its leaders focused on the leadership behavior of *change disciplinarian*, but then they talked about what this meant for them and evolved the image of "magic," which had the unique meaning for them of being able to deliver customer expectations on time, every time. In particular, this magic was translated into leader behaviors related to change that customers would experience. Customers would experience service when leaders responded to their concerns within twenty-four hours, when employees were empowered to make immediate judgments about customer service (e.g., room upgrades), when leaders knew frequent customer preferences (according to a customer database) and met those needs before customers requested the service. These leader behaviors define how leaders can change in ways that meet customer service expectations.

FIGURE 3-3

Generic leadership code categories

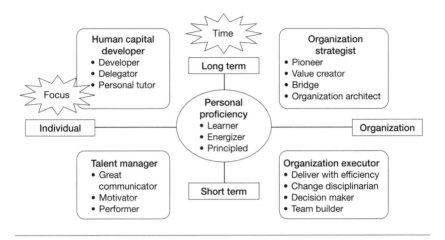

Whether the leadership team goes from the firm brand directly to the leadership code or through the descriptors of leadership we have proposed, the goal is to establish a critical subset of tailored attributes that leaders must demonstrate inside the organization to deliver on the firm brand promise outside the organization. The elements of generic leadership are thus defined and tailored according to the expectations of the customers of the firm. What this means in practice is that while most companies have developed leadership competency models, these models have not been tested, refined, and aligned with customers or investors. We have worked with a number of companies to take their internally derived competency model to external customers and investors and to find out if the stated competencies will give external stakeholders more confidence in the firm. If not, customers or investors might tailor, add, or delete items; in general, we find that about 30 percent of a competency model may be tweaked by engaging customers and investors in shaping it.

Step 5: Combine Attributes and Results into a Leadership Brand Statement

A statement of leadership brand is neither the leadership code nor the promised results alone; it is the combination of the two: a statement of what leaders should know and do to be consistent with the firm brand (leadership code) and what they should deliver (leadership results). We have found that adding the phrase "so that . . . " helps turn a set of attributes into results. Leaders may be working hard, delegating to others, communicating well, and acting with integrity, but these attributes on their own—without results—are not a leadership brand. The "so that" query turns an attribute into a focused result.

Teva Pharmaceutical Industries, the world's largest generic pharmaceutical company, has grown rapidly in the last few years through acquisitions. To ensure consistency across the growing organization, the leadership team articulated a strategy of continued growth and profitability. The leadership team then worked to capture the elements of their identity or firm brand that would resonate with customers. They decided that at Teva they wanted to be known for:

- *Innovation*, as characterized by flexibility and assertiveness

- *Global reach*, as defined by serving customers worldwide

- *Partnership*, as defined by professional service and one-stop shopping

- *Integrity*, as defined by living ethically and reliably meeting commitments

- *Affordability*, as defined by being the low-cost provider

Teva leaders then worked to turn this desired external identity into a leadership brand that would set expectations for leaders and shape the culture for employees. They derived the dimensions of their leadership brand, shown in table 3-1. Teva leaders would be known for these attributes as evidenced by behaviors customers would experience from Teva leaders.

The Teva executive team felt that these five descriptors and customercentric behaviors, if practiced by leaders throughout the company and if woven into the practices that create and sustain leaders, would communicate their desired brand to their external constituents and create the internal culture that would affect employees *so that* they would produce sound, innovative, and affordable products with global reach.

Table 3-2 shows other firms and what they want their firm brand to be and their subsequent leadership brand.

These leadership brands become the bridge between the external identity of the firm—what its customers know it for—and the behavior of its employees. Each year, *BusinessWeek* identifies the world's most

TABLE 3-1

Teva's leadership brand

Attributes	Behaviors customers will experience *Customers will experience Teva leaders who . . .*
Global mind-set	• Can operate in regions around the world • Can help meet customer demands anywhere in the world • Have sensitivity to local cultures yet envision global solutions
Aggressive execution	• Deliver products and services on time every time • Fulfill promises even when things go wrong • Set high standards for performance on dimensions that matter to customers
Ability to lead change	• Adapt quickly to changing customer views • Understand trends in the industry and come to customers with innovative solutions • Have flexibility in how to respond to unique customer requirements
Management of complexity	• Can work with multiple levels in the customer organization (e.g., purchasing, R&D, manufacturing, distribution) • See alternative solutions that may not be as visible at first • Tolerate ambiguity
Bringing out the best in people	• Have world-class skills and expertise in their functional area • Offer insight and counsel to customers on areas where customers may be less qualified • Work well in teams and as collaborators to solve problems

valuable brands (see table 3-3). We believe that firms with this level of brand value can and should turn their firm brand images into a set of leadership requirements, as we have indicated in the right-hand column of the table.

Step 6: Create a Set of Expectations Based on the Leadership Brand Statement

With a statement of leadership brand that reflects the firm brand, you can set standards for leaders consistent with the leadership brand. These standards translate the leadership brand into specific knowledge, skills, and values that leaders should demonstrate, as well as results leaders must produce. These standards make the firm brand operational as the leadership brand. These standards are the basis for assessing leaders

TABLE 3-2

Firm brands and leadership brands

Firm	Firm brand *What we want to be known for by our customers*	Leadership brand *What we want our leaders to be known for*
Saudi Aramco	A reliable source of renewable energy	Reliability defined through consistency, operational excellence, and consistent delivery on promises
3M	Innovation in products and services	Creativity and ability to think and act in unique ways as demonstrated by the way they generate new ideas, experiment, take appropriate risks, and learn from successes and failures
Nordstrom	Best-in-class service and fashion design	Identifying and exceeding expectations of target customers; demonstrating a commitment to fashion by both decisions and personal style
Lexus	Relentless pursuit of perfection	Doggedly seeking to improve the design and manufacture of vehicles and service to customers
Microsoft	Domination of the market	Competitive aggressiveness and unmatched technical and raw intelligence
Novell	Innovation and integrity to be number one in networking	Uncompromising trust, technical competence, and drive to forge relationships

against the firm brand (chapter 4) and for holding leaders accountable for the results of the brand (chapter 6).

To help delineate these leadership brand attributes, we have found it helpful to use metaphors, as suggested by our colleague Bonner Ritchie. In our conversations, Ritchie has taught us that metaphors may be used for a variety of purposes, including enhancing understanding, communicating values, justifying behavior, simplifying complex ideas, providing a shortcut to understanding, avoiding direct comment, motivating, and confusing. We would like to add to his list the point that metaphors can also help people set clear standards in a compelling way.

We are all familiar with metaphors that describe the organizations we work in and the people we work with. Here are some of the most common metaphors used in business:

Knights: "Earn your spurs."

Cowboys: "A Smith and Wesson beats four aces."

TABLE 3-3

World's most valuable brands and their leadership implications

	Firm brand *Statement and subsequent values*	Leadership requirements *What it takes to deliver on the brand promise*
eBay	The power of all of us.	Leaders who work collaboratively.
UBS	You and us.	Leaders who work well in relationships and with teams. Team building and talent management would be their key skills.
Morgan Stanley	One client at a time.	Leaders who relate to the people. Human capital development and talent management skills are key.
HP	Everything is possible.	Leaders who envision the future. Organization strategist skills are going to be the most important.
Coca-Cola	Refresh the world in body, mind, and spirit.	Leaders who "refresh" inside: innovative, lifetime learners, looking for new ways to do things.
Microsoft	Where you work is entirely up to you; company mission is to help people and businesses realize their full potential.	Leaders who give employees enormous autonomy but maintain the focus on work. They also engage people to develop and learn and grow to reach their full potential.
IBM	IBM helps you meet real-time demand and add some life to your supply chain. "At IBM, we strive to lead in the invention, development and manufacture of the industry's most advanced information technologies, including computer systems, software, storage systems and microelectronics."	Leaders who are good at organizational execution, make things happen, and are inventive in what they do.
Intel	Advancing life through technology—to focus on what people around the world can accomplish when they have access to uncompromised technology and the means to use it.	Leaders who push the future by focusing on what the organization and employees can do next.
Nokia	Connecting people. "By connecting people, we help fulfill a fundamental human need for social connections and contact. Nokia builds bridges between people."	Leaders who can be connectors and team builders. Their focus is on social and interpersonal skills and contacts.
McDonald's	"I'm lovin' it."	Leaders who create a community where employees feel engaged and committed to work.

Sports: "We need to win this one!" "Remember, we're in a marathon, not a sprint."

Military: "Take back the streets." "Crush our opposition." "Attack the problem."

Parenting: "We will take care of you." "We want you to feel part of our family."

Ritchie has shown us that metaphors communicate values and shape behavior, and that leaders who demonstrate their commitment to the leadership brand around a meaningful metaphor are more able to clarify the specific behaviors they must demonstrate. For example, the cowboy metaphor would be useful if the firm brand had to do with independence, individual responsibility, and the intent to ride roughshod over the world (somewhat akin to Microsoft's firm brand). The sports and military metaphors are helpful to organizations that define their industry as a win-lose game. The military metaphor adds a life-and-death element and thus fits an environment of regimentation and control (Teva focuses on disciplined processes). The parenting metaphor encourages connection and relationships (Nokia).

Fortunately, Ritchie has also identified other metaphors that seem more in sync with a global environment where collaboration is more important to success than independence:

Nature: "This will have a tsunami effect!" "It's a breath of fresh air."

Music: "Playing off the same score." "Marching to a different drummer."

Art: "The world is your canvas." "This is an art, not just a science."

These metaphors are richer for most global organizations, as nature metaphors are useful to a firm seeking equilibrium or radical change, music metaphors search for a world of harmony, and art metaphors are about creativity, problem solving, beauty, and love.

Each of these metaphors creates a set of images about what leaders should do to enact the metaphor. Table 3-4 lists these metaphors, along with behaviors consistent with each one.

Metaphors of this type allow you to compare leadership attributes with your brand standards, looking for alignment or harmony between the strategy, the firm brand, and the leadership attributes. With these metaphors, the leadership brand can now be turned into a consistent

TABLE 3-4

Leadership metaphor, behaviors, and brand

Leadership metaphor *Our branded leader will act as . . .*	Consistent leadership behaviors	Derived leadership brand *Therefore, we have leaders who are known for their . . .*
Cowboy	• Independent • Autonomous • Act with limited information	Inward orientation without regard to the external world around them
Coach	• Directive • Motivator • In charge	Ability to compete to win and beat the competition
Military officer	• Orderly • In charge • Aggressive	Desire to control and dominate the company and the industry
Parent	• Nurturing • Connecting • Helping	Desire to build relationships and connections within the community
Part of nature	• Collaborate • Build support	Ability to create equilibrium and balance among competing forces
Musician	• Creative • Complex • Improvisational	Ability to achieve harmony and balance
Artist	• Observant • Creative • Integrative	Ability to create patterns among disparate areas and form new relationships; consistent with innovation

set of specific leadership standards that support the brand criteria laid out in chapter 1, including both the tailored leadership code and the differentiated leadership results. Thus the theory of leadership within the firm communicates what leaders should be known for to fold customer and investor expectations into employee actions.

Conclusion

Many executives proclaim that they have great employees and leaders, but they don't explain why. *Why* comes from the statement of leadership brand. It is what separates leaders who understand it from leaders in other firms. It captures the essence of leadership within the firm because employees can see that their leaders know and do things that are important to the firm because they are important to key customers of the firm. They absorb the culture of a firm when it is reflected in leader thought and deed and tied to customer expectations framed by the firm brand.

A statement of leadership brand offers a unifying framework that allows the development of leaders devoted to a common outcome, branded leaders across the company. The statement of leadership brand describes this overall purpose. A company's mission statement positions the company to win in its chosen market. Likewise, a company's statement of leadership brand positions leaders as the bridge between customer expectations and employee behaviors.

We have found that the following questions test the extent to which a firm has a viable statement of leadership brand:

1. Is there a clear, simple statement of what we want our leaders to be known for?

2. Is it consistent with what we want our products, services, and firm to be known for?

3. Does it meet the criteria of the brand as outlined in appendix A?

4. Is it flexible for the future?

5. Does it lead to a set of standards and expectations for future leaders drawing on metaphors for describing leadership?

When you can answer yes to all five, you are well on your way to branded leadership.

4

Assessing Leaders
Against the Brand

ONCE YOU'VE CRAFTED a statement of leadership brand, how can you tell whether you and your fellow leaders at all levels are living up to it? You don't have to hope and guess; the tools presented here will allow you to assess your leaders and your leadership in terms of your desired leadership brand. The resulting information can be used for leadership brand improvement, development, and evaluation.

Assessment is not new to any of us. We constantly assess relationships in our daily lives. Sometimes we do the assessments intuitively.[1] Other circumstances need more thought, because the implications of a poor assessment have long-term consequences. Obviously, some people do a better job of assessing and choosing among alternatives than others. What is the secret to good assessment? What can we learn from those who do this well? And how do these general principles apply to assessment of leadership brand? These are the questions for this chapter.

Lessons of Assessment

Assessment requires a standard against which to judge actions. Senior executives must have a point of view about what good leadership is and then be explicit about it. Without an explicit, organization-wide statement of leadership brand to use as a standard, people will make up their own standards, so it's well worth going through the six steps outlined in chapter 3 to come up with a sound and relevant statement of leadership brand. Absent such a standard, a glib or charming individual may seem to be a gifted leader without being able to either demonstrate the leadership code or deliver the leadership results customers and investors expect from the organization.

Assessment requires a broad base—self-assessment or assessment by a supervisor is never enough. For example, one company we worked with did a survey of how employees rated the company's ability to manage and respect differences and diversity in the workplace. The ratings from the all-male senior management team averaged about 4.6 on a 1-to-5 scale. But when they looked at ratings by women, scores dropped; with minority women, they dropped again; with minority women with children, they dropped again; and with minority women who were heads of households, they dropped still further—the more employees differed from the top management group, the less successful the company's diversity efforts were in their eyes. The conclusion was that leaders were so removed from the realities of some of the subgroups of employees that they could not grasp the ways their company was performing.

It turns out that assessment works only if the person being assessed is interested in using the data. Even the best data—based on relevant (and not merely easily measured) behavior, well quantified, and drawn from multiple viewpoints—will have no effect if someone receives feedback before being open to change. In this respect, leaders resemble consulting clients; just as consulting is apt to fail without a contract putting the client on record as being willing to change if the diagnosis and analysis shows things that need to change, leadership assessment depends on a leader's commitment to take the data seriously and use it to shape future behavior.

Even for a prepared audience, successful assessment requires shaping data into a few key themes or stories. Individual incidents are not necessarily diagnostic—anyone can have a bad day—so it's useful to go from the data to a few themes. Look for patterns. Ask what the patterns mean, and shape them into a brief, cogent "elevator speech" that highlights the action indicated.

Assessment also requires follow-up. Very few people can change their behavior on their own, but most can eventually do so if they're supported by follow-up and feedback on how they're doing.

The best assessment efforts focus on building on strengths. Rather than just trying to improve weaknesses, it's better to use strengths to minimize the impact of weaknesses. Building on strengths also has a halo effect—excellence in a few areas tends to improve a leader's reputation across the board, making weaknesses seem less important.

With these general observations on assessment as background, we can move on to the assessment of leadership brand in particular. You need to track three aspects of leadership brand—the extent to which leaders throughout an organization have:

- The *right stuff*
- At the *right stage*
- Delivering the *right results* in the *right way*

The Right Stuff

The right stuff is the extent to which leaders live the statement of leadership brand. To figure out who has the right stuff for the next leadership position, you can assess people's predisposition toward the leadership brand, and you can look at behavioral feedback from their bosses, peers, direct reports, and clients or customers.

Predisposition to the Brand

An organization sources its next-generation leaders by promoting individual contributors, recruiting from the outside, or inheriting leaders as part of a merger or an acquisition. In each case, it is both possible and desirable to assess candidates carefully before moving them into a specific role. Nonetheless, though everyone knows how important rigor is here, few companies are as consistent about selection as they should be—even though poor selection of leaders is a very costly mistake. The secret to success is not in being sophisticated about assessment but in being rigorous and consistent. The following ideas have proved effective.

First, translate the statement of leadership brand into leadership behaviors and character traits, so that it's clear what you are assessing for. For example, if your statement includes a word like *savvy*, break it down (define what constitutes savvy) in terms of behaviors and character attributes that have meaning to customers, like these:

- Knowledgeable about the target customer
- Able to apply knowledge via good presentation and interpersonal skills
- Confident enough of this knowledge to remain calm in difficult situations

With a clearer idea of what is desired, you can use behavioral event interviewing skills to talk with candidates about times in their career when they have faced situations where they needed to be savvy and to see how they actually behaved.

In behavioral event interviewing, remember to let the candidates do the talking. The role of the interviewer is to get candidates to talk in depth about their approach to specific events related to the behavior or characteristic in question. Saying, "Tell me about a time when you were faced with an ambiguous situation and everyone seemed confused about what to do" will evoke a useful response, but then you need to go further and focus on behaviors. With a specific event or situation in mind, then ask the candidate to tell what was done and why.[2]

Another approach to interviewing is to use psychological tests. Psychologists have developed and applied leader assessment, selection, and development tests and techniques in a wide range of settings for many years. Look for tests and procedures that are both empirically derived and field-tested. Or more customized tests can be designed and validated that assess a potential candidate's ability to demonstrate the desired leadership brand. A good approach includes an analysis of leader task and temperament requirements and identifies the quality of the fit between potential future or current job requirements and each candidate's skill set and temperament. The test battery addresses major job-related constructs and produces reliable and valid indications of a leader's scores relative to current or potential future job demands. Tests like these have their weaknesses (they're one-time events, and candidates can try to game them or fudge on responses), but a good test can still be used to show predispositions.

These techniques, which have been refined as a result of the testing of thousands of leaders, can be used to identify candidates with the highest potential for future promotion and fit with the brand. The process identifies a candidate's strengths and weaknesses relative to current and future job requirements. When professional experience is incorporated into specific feedback tailored for each candidate according to individual test results, the feedback is discreetly provided in positive and developmentally oriented one-on-one sessions designed to promote growth and improvement in areas requiring such and to reinforce individual strengths identified.

Behavioral Feedback

Another assessment tool that we have found to be effective for in-house and inherited M&A candidates to assess leader brand development is to combine the individual test assessment with a 360-degree assessment that includes input from each candidate's direct reports, peers, superiors, and customers or clients. This combination produces reliable behavioral information about each candidate that is then used to create individual action plans. The 360-degree instrument must be adapted to measure both behaviors associated with the organization's leadership brand and those reflecting the leadership code.

When you're using 360-degree feedback in hiring, select the respondents carefully. Make sure that they represent the right mix. (Most of us would like to have our mothers fill out the 360-degree rating sheet.) It can work well to have the candidate pick half and have the rater pick the other half.

In addition, consistent with brand ideas focusing outside, not just inside, the company, we have found that the 360 may be turned into a 720. A 720 solicits observations from those outside the candidate's organization, including suppliers, customers, dealers, financiers, government agents, community leaders, or others. A board of directors did a 720 on a CEO and found that while he managed his direct reports well and had earned their confidence, he had not sufficiently earned the confidence of the customer community. Targeted customers were able to report that his behaviors were not consistent with those they would most like to see in a CEO in his role. While he should not overreact to this data and minimize his internal executive responsibilities, he should be aware of it as he tries to build relationships with targeted customers. The 720 assessments may not be for everyone, but for those who deal with external stakeholders, these stakeholders' views can be added value in assessing leaders' overall performance.

At the Right Stage

Most assessments of the leadership pipeline are optical illusions. Companies spend significant time and effort evaluating succession candidates, projecting leadership "depth charts," and creating next-in-line scenarios. Too often, what they end up with is a portrait of "managership" or "promotionship," not leadership. In other words, such assessments are heavily biased toward candidates who walk, talk, dress, act, and appear to be management material, or corporate promotables. Whether they will be able to demonstrate the truly desired leadership brand is another question. What's worse, the assessments' singular focus on *formal* leadership positions typically ignores a large cadre of people throughout the organization who are providing crucial *informal* leadership. Finally, an ideal assessment helps us understand not only individual leaders but also leadership brand as an organization capability.

A pattern of leadership behavior can be exactly right for one job and dead wrong for another—and when it's dead wrong, it undermines the leadership brand. There is a fundamental and simple equation for leadership effectiveness:

$$\text{Leadership effectiveness} = \text{Efficacy} \times \text{Awareness}$$

Too much emphasis on the "awareness" (or "appearance") side is dangerous. Over the course of a career, individuals who looked like high potentials or top performers can find themselves promoted into jobs where the very qualities that were once strengths can turn into derailers. Another case in point:

Give Me the Numbers!

Several years ago, we had an engagement with "Zack Petersen," CEO of a privately held global company. His company had grown very quickly in large part because its major customer had attained phenomenal growth and success. To all appearances, the future seemed promising.

Petersen prided himself on being a finance man. Everyone knew that when you went in to see him, Petersen would ask for a "return on investment" before he would agree to support any initiative. For the most part, this worked. However, he asked for hard numbers on everything, including initiatives that were very difficult to quantify. And if something could not be quantified, he would not support it. Over time, this meant that he did not invest in intangibles such as leadership development, culture, talent development, and ensuring collaboration across departments. In spite of his speeches to the contrary, Petersen nurtured a competitive, cutthroat environment among his direct reports and throughout the company.

As a result, direct reports tended to leave him after a few years. When they left, they described him as *too competitive, a micromanager, lacking a strategic vision, abrupt*, and so on. Over the years, his company attracted talent because of its ability to pay good salaries and because of its interesting business challenges and opportunities, but it did not know how to keep people around for the long term, especially at the most senior levels. In particular, it had not been able to keep a CFO for more than a year.

Petersen's story is repeated thousands of times a year, all over the corporate world. Petersen's leadership skills were an optical illusion; the assessment process that led to his being placed in the top job was flawed. He had the skills to be a strong player in a narrow specialty function but lacked the depth, breadth, and wisdom to succeed as a CEO. In effect, he became a one-man can of leadership repellant, driving talent from the organization and weakening the confidence of external stakeholders.

To understand what is going on with Petersen's case, we need a framework that describes the performance of leaders and leadership in a way that is not hierarchical, because hierarchy too often obscures rather than clarifies our view of leadership. Our proposed framework challenges many preconceptions people have about development and the assessment of talent. Despite living in the Internet age, when information flows freely in all directions (not just down from the top), and regardless of the continual waves of downsizing and flattening in organizations, most people fail to question their outdated, hierarchical assumptions about leaders:

- The best manager is the highest-performing worker. (Who else would you pick?)

- People in senior positions (at least, nonelected senior positions) must have the skills and experience to do the job well. (How else did they get there?)

- As people get older, they accumulate the type of knowledge, wisdom, and perspective that helps them do more complex jobs. (We pay them more as they gain seniority, so why would this not make sense?)

Plausible as they seem, research in leadership development shows that these assumptions are tottering on shaky foundations. Our examination of assessment strategies for leadership brand will topple these assumptions and uncover Petersen's development gaps as a senior executive as well as uncover critical needs for his entire organization.

All the World's a Stage

In many of the successful companies we have worked with, the "four stages" logic originally introduced by Gene Dalton and Paul Thompson during the 1970s is the foundation of leadership development and provides a compelling way to do leadership brand assessment.[3] Originally, the four stages logic was used to help individuals improve their performance and contribution, but in the context of leadership brand it provides a framework for understanding the developmental progression of the pipeline of talent throughout an organization and identifies any developmental gaps through the lens of each stage. The stages framework breaks up the talent pipeline into four discrete development stages. This allows assessment at each stage and at transitions between each stage about desired performance and contribution factors. In addition to focusing on individual talent development, the stages logic provides an organizational perspective about the desired developmental level of leadership at each stage in order to execute the business strategy. Development gaps within any of the stages or at transition points between stages delineate leadership brand challenges to deliver value and implement the strategy described in our case for change in chapter 2. This is a unique tool for assessing leadership brand as an organization capability, not just as an individual competency.

The framework is simple and helpful because it casts a bright light on both individual and organization implications of leadership brand building, especially concerning the development gaps that should occur as individual contributors become supervisors, supervisors become managers/leaders, and managers/leaders become executives. Kurt Sandholtz, our colleague at The RBL Group, has spent years applying these ideas to leadership development, and we have borrowed liberally from his ideas here about how to apply them to leadership brand.

A bit of history may be instructive. The research began with an examination of the performance rankings of both managers and nonmanagers, correlated with their years of experience. Dalton and Thompson were troubled by the trend: people's performance rankings tended to peak around midcareer and then decline steadily until they retired. (Nearing midcareer themselves, they certainly didn't like the writing on the wall.) The overall trend held true for managers and nonmanagers alike.

Yet when the researchers looked more closely at the performance data, they discovered the "optical illusion": while the experience-group averages seemed to show a general decline in performance with experience, there were significant numbers of top performers in *every* experience category. In fact, the performance differences were more dramatic *within* experience groups than across experience groups. Some mid- and late-career professionals were rated as highly as the "young stars" in the data set. Their goal became to discover what differentiated these "mature stars" from their below-average age cohort.

Employing proven "grounded theory" methodology from the social sciences, the researchers next interviewed hundreds of managers, asking them to describe what characterized their top performers (regardless of age). The responses seemed almost random: one manager would describe the high achievers as technical whizzes, while another described the top performers as interpersonally skilled. Some managers praised detail orientation, others the importance of "big picture" or systems-level thinking. All told, the research turned up more than a hundred conflicting descriptors of high performance. Instead of getting closer to an answer, the research seemed to be getting further away from pinpointing what "top performers" look like throughout their careers.

The light bulb moment came when the researchers stepped back from the data and looked for patterns. Where, they asked themselves, do we find bundles of descriptors that hang together, even though the overall data set is a confusing mess? This simple question led them to a profound insight: the way high performers "show up" is markedly different at different stages of an employee's development (see table 4-1). Most germane to our discussion here, leadership brand—especially the way it is demonstrated and the scope of its impact—is one of the key dimensions on which these four stages differ.

Importantly, this research that began with engineers in Boston has since been replicated in nearly all functions and at all levels of large organizations, including numerous organizations in western Europe and the Asia-Pacific region. With minor cultural variations, the four stages model has proved a robust descriptive framework for leadership growth and employee performance in organizations around the globe.

The stages framework also works well as an assessment tool, for two reasons. First, its genesis as a descriptive model frees it from the normative or "prescriptive" overtones of so many leadership models. Rather than pronounce what leaders *should* do, the stages merely reflect what organizations tend to value and why—again this is very helpful in assessing whether the leadership brand is "taking" and what might be

TABLE 4-1

The Dalton/Thompson stages model, applied to leadership development

	Stage 1: Apprentice	Stage 2: Contributor	Stage 3: Local leader	Stage 4: Global leader
Central activities	Performing tasks under close supervision	Establishing distinctive competence; in-depth, problem-solving work	Leading and developing others; interfacing across functions, businesses, or areas	Shaping the organization's direction; focusing on competitive advantage
Keys to success	• Earn trust by delivering on commitments. • Do the grunt work willingly and well. • Absorb the organization's culture. • Seek and accept direction from others.	• Become one of the best in the organization in your specialty. • Rely more on colleagues and less on your manager for direction. • Pull your weight on the team. • Don't be a lone wolf; keep others in the loop and provide regular updates on your work.	• Broaden your perspective to include other functions and disciplines. • Deliberately extend your network of relationships inside and outside the organization. • Give up your need to be the subject matter expert (SME). • Spend time developing others through mentoring, coaching, and job assignments.	• Focus externally and think long term. • Exert power and influence for the benefit of the organization. • Become a bridge, representing the organization to external stakeholders and translating their needs into organizational behavior. • Identify and sponsor a diverse set of promising people for future leadership roles.
Leadership brand implications	Learn the brand: get to know the fundamental competencies and unique features of your organization's leadership brand.	Demonstrate brand efficacy: build a solid track record of expertise and results consistent with the leadership brand (i.e., right results, right way).	Build the brand in others: foster the development of "branded" leaders at all levels through one-on-one interaction. Get branded results by ensuring integration across organization silos.	Perpetuate the brand in the organization: create systems that will ensure the selection, assessment, development, and rewards for the right kind of leadership now and in the future. Demand that all leaders deliver the right results, the right way.

done to cultivate it. Second, the stages apply equally to formal and informal leadership, thus avoiding the traps and "optical illusions" mentioned earlier. Whether an individual is a midlevel manager or a senior engineer (with no direct reports), he or she needs to be demonstrating stage 3 leadership—and the organization needs a way to recognize, assess, and develop such leadership.

The stages framework excels at illustrating leadership transitions. Just as a reptile sheds its skin in order to grow, leaders must stop doing much of what made them successful in earlier stages and add new skills, experiences, and perspectives to be effective in successive stages. These new skills, experiences, and perspectives determine the extent to which a leader is able to deliver the right results *the right way*. This will become more apparent as we examine each stage in greater detail.

STAGE 1—APPRENTICE: LEARNING THE BRAND. Newcomers to any social system—be it a neighborhood playgroup or Google—have to do certain things to demonstrate that they fit in. This is a big part of what happens in stage 1: new entrants get socialized in the norms and values of the organization, at the same time earning the trust and respect of their manager and colleagues. This is akin to "learning the brand"—learning what the organization stands for, how it delivers value to its stakeholders, and what leadership means.

Because they are on the receiving end of the process, high performers in stage 1 need to be willing to work under relatively close supervision and direction. Their work is rarely entirely their own but rather part of a larger project. Predictably, they do a lot of the routine or detailed work. They haven't been hired to redefine the brand (at least not yet). First they have to internalize and get comfortable with the organization's leadership brand. A story may illustrate the point.

Kill Bill

Bill Watrous joined a multinational oil company shortly after graduating with his MBA from a respected Ivy League school. With an engineering undergraduate degree, he was seen as a high-potential employee and treated accordingly. After eighteen months in the company's leadership training program (including three six-month stints in different jobs and locations), he accepted his first "real" job at a natural gas processing plant in southwestern Louisiana.

Eager to demonstrate his prowess and potential, he spent a week getting to know the operation and then scheduled an appointment with the plant manager, a seasoned veteran of the oil and gas business who had no formal education beyond high school. In this meeting, Watrous reviewed his list of "10 Things We Can Do to Run This Plant More Effectively." The plant manager listened intently, responded courteously, and thanked Watrous for his efforts. After Watrous left the office, the manager picked up the phone, dialed headquarters in Houston, and said, "Get this weenie off my staff before I shoot him!"

Perhaps the plant manager overreacted. Still, the story illustrates the dangers of stage/role dissonance. In his mind, Watrous was ready to play a stage 3 or stage 4 leadership role. He was doing things, he thought, that would make him look like a high performer. In the supervisor's mind, however, Watrous hadn't earned any credibility yet. Watrous's naive "presumption of leadership" was premature and actually made him look like a "lo-po" instead of a "hi-po." He needed to first build a foundation of relationships and expertise, and then begin to exert more directive leadership at the plant. Following comes before leading. Watrous should have spent time learning the leadership brand required to succeed in his operation. This would have meant soliciting and interpreting customer expectations for the operation, recognizing how leaders responded to those expectations, and learning the expected behaviors and norms that sustained those expectations (like not telling a seasoned boss how to operate the business with little or no experience). Without learning the present leadership brand, Watrous will never be trusted to move to areas of greater responsibility and have a greater impact in the future.

Future leaders who are impatient or arrogant often fail to grasp the significance of stage 1. This is particularly true for experienced hires. Even if someone has been a vice president or director at a previous firm, he or she needs to spend a few days (perhaps even weeks or months) doing the stage 1 drill: figuring out "how things work around here." It's not about dues paying; it's about investing in their own leadership portfolio by figuring out the features and attributes of the organization's leadership brand. Such an investment almost always pays generous returns over the long haul.

We should also recognize that successful companies provide a myriad of leadership experiences as their people move through these development stages. For example, by the time someone reaches stage 3, she should have had a P&L experience, a functional experience, an experience in a new culture (country), and perhaps a turnaround or an M&A experience. These "experience sets" allow leaders to adapt as today's expectations change, either as the existing customers evolve or as new customers enter the market. With changing customer expectations, leader reputation and identity must also evolve. Computer hardware firms like IBM and Hewlett-Packard have had customer shifts from product to services. With these shifts, the leadership brands in these firms also have had to shift. When leaders are provided with explicit, targeted opportunities to have business experiences consistent with their stage of development, they are able to more easily adapt to new leadership brand needs. In some cases, leaders must become more sensitive and responsive to service opportunities, not manufacturing efficiencies. Tomorrow's leadership brand may differ from today's because customer expectations may change. So firms that encourage more divergence among leadership brand experiences at all stages have a higher chance of meeting tomorrow's expectations.

STAGE 2—CONTRIBUTOR: DEMONSTRATING BRAND EFFICACY. Inherent in each stage are the seeds of its own destruction. As soon as a person masters the leadership characteristics of one stage, the organization starts to expect different characteristics. Stage 1 is a great (indeed, an inevitable) place to start, but it's a terrible place to stay. Once an individual has "learned the brand," he or she needs to start showing it. This is the essence of stage 2.

Stage 2 is all about demonstrating personal efficacy: being known as a competent, knowledgeable, results-oriented professional who fits the firm's leadership brand. High performers in this stage take on and "own" projects for which they are held personally accountable. They work independently or as equal members of a team; supervision is more distant and less necessary. In the process, they earn a reputation as experts in some core area of the organization's work. They develop their own signature strengths that will help them succeed and that others will come to rely on. They develop a grassroots feel for the business, the customer base, and/or the technology.

The scope of leadership brand in stage 2 is typically limited to self (managing one's own time and resources) and task (getting one's own work done, though often in the context of a team effort). Yet those who make the most of their stint in stage 2 gain tremendous "street cred" in the organization. Even more crucial to future leadership is the empathy they carry for the workers in the trenches. Having "been there, done that," they are less likely to alienate (or simply mystify) employees when they make bold strategic moves in the future.

Leaders at this stage begin to develop their personal brand (see chapter 9) to align with their organization's leadership brand. They gain personal credibility and reputation for doing their work well. When their personal brand aligns with the desired organization's leadership brand, they are likely to be successful in mastering the requirements of this stage.

STAGE 3—LOCAL LEADER: BUILDING THE BRAND IN OTHERS. Any brand will sink into oblivion without active management and promotion. Even a fortress like Coca-Cola (perennially the number-one brand in the world, according to the annual *BusinessWeek*/Interbrand poll) can be vulnerable in a crowded, competitive marketplace. If Coca-Cola were to quit advertising, change its formulation, stop investing in its distribution channels, and revamp its trademarked graphics, how long would it persist as a recognizable global brand? A year? A month?

The same holds true for leadership brand. As valuable as it is to have solid individual contributors who get the right results the right way, an organization's leadership brand will be diluted and eventually die out if no one is actively furthering it. Stage 3 leaders play a critical role in this process. Not only are they role models for the leadership brand, they're also on the front lines of building the brand in others. High-performing leaders in stage 3 have grown beyond independence to true interdependence. They've learned how to accomplish work that is larger than they could accomplish on their own. Most importantly, they have learned to gain satisfaction from seeing others grow and develop.

This ability to develop others doesn't necessarily mean that stage 3 people manage or supervise others. In fact, our experience and the research suggest that nonsupervisors vastly outnumber supervisors in stage 3. This perspective is critically important in leadership brand development. Because of most people's subconscious hierarchical bias (mentioned earlier in this chapter), they tend to see leaders as the ones in formal positions—and miss the fact that the greatest numbers of leaders lack formal titles. A leadership brand exists when the desired expectations of customers are embedded in the knowledge, skills, and values of employees throughout the organization. These stage 3 players make things happen across organization boundaries and influence what people do in critical ways—often despite their employers' development and incentive systems, which don't adequately recognize these contributions (or worse, actually hinder them).

Stage 3 leaders build the organization's leadership brand in several ways. First, they master the leadership code by having personal proficiency but also by being strategists, executors, talent managers, and human capital developers. Since these skills related to the leadership code are baseline components of the firm's leadership brand, stage 3 leaders serve as important role models for these attributes. Second, because of their more ample network, stage 3 leaders are critical "boundary spanners" and greatly aid the flow of ideas and information throughout the organization. By what they do and say, their leadership style demonstrates to others their organization's leadership brand. Finally, and most importantly, stage 3 leaders get involved in the development of people by providing feedback, mentoring, coaching, and job assignments that stretch and grow the talents of others.

This crucial role in the development of others can cut both ways. If a stage 3 leader buys into the organization's leadership brand, she will naturally try to build that brand in others; her developmental efforts will align with the organization's desired results and attributes. And remember, the key issue in building a future brand is understanding, aligning, and translating customer expectations into employee behavior. As customers evolve, so must the brand. On the other hand, if she is disaffected, cynical, or simply inadequately steeped in the organization's leadership brand (as in the case of an experienced hire brought in from the outside), she becomes in effect an "antimentor," infecting a cadre of protégés with values and behaviors that run contrary to the firm's intent. The result: brand confusion rather than brand unity.

STAGE 4—GLOBAL LEADER: PERPETUATING THE BRAND IN THE ORGANIZATION. If stage 3 leaders focus on developing other leaders, stage 4 leaders concern themselves with building *leadership*. Their unit of analysis is not the individual but the organization: its systems, processes, and resource allocation. They are not so much interested in cloning themselves as in creating a pipeline that will produce the right kind of leaders now and in the future. They are attuned to the needs of customers, investors, and other stakeholders; theirs is the critical responsibility of translating these external expectations into internal leadership behavior. High performers in stage 4 perform the following vital functions:

- *Decision maker:* They exercise significant influence over critical decisions in the organization.

- *Strategist:* They help shape the future direction of a major part of the organization.

- *Spokesperson:* They represent the organization in wide and varied interactions both outside and inside the organization.

- *Sponsor:* They create opportunities for promising candidates to prove themselves capable of filling key leadership roles in the future.

Stage 4 leaders typically are found in one of three executive-level roles. The most common of these is formal leader—vice president, general manager, CEO, and so on. Organizations certainly need their top managers to be functioning in stage 4, but unfortunately, not all senior execs are stage 4 players. Because they get promoted on the basis of the "optical illusion," some senior managers are functioning in stage 3 or even stage 2. We'll return to this idea later in the chapter, when we reexamine the case of Zack Petersen.

The second prominent stage 4 role is that of idea innovator or internal entrepreneur. These individuals are often quirky, iconoclastic, rough edged—and drop-dead brilliant. They see huge commercial opportunities where others see nothing, and they have the organizational savvy (and personal credibility) to turn their vision into reality. Art Fry, the legendary father of the Post-it note, played exactly this role at 3M.

The third common stage 4 role is "idea sponsor." Unlike the idea innovators, idea sponsors don't come up with the breakthroughs themselves. Rather, they stay close to external customers and internal researchers, finding products or services that match the needs of the former with the capabilities of the latter. At various times in his career, Steve Jobs has played this role masterfully—while simultaneously occupying a "formal" executive role (such as CEO). In the process, Jobs has established a clear and unique leadership brand at Apple.

While most stage 4 leaders manage large groups of people, a few idea innovators and internal entrepreneurs—usually in R&D or sales-related areas—have few, if any, direct reports. Yet these stage 4 non-managers are often icons of the leadership brand. They are worth many

times their weight in gold and should be retained, developed, and recognized for their contributions.

Applying Stage Theory to Leadership Assessment

With this understanding of the four stages, let's now return to the case
of Zack Petersen, CEO.

Back to Zack

We gave Petersen and his executive team a short four-stage self-
assessment to fill out. After about fifteen minutes, Petersen sat back
and said, "Interesting—this says I'm in stage 2!" It was a blinding
flash of the obvious—news to Petersen, perhaps, but to no one
else. His senior team looked at their shoes and nodded, as if to
say, "We know, we know." For Petersen and the company, this
self-insight was a watershed moment. He *liked* being a stage 2
financial expert. He wasn't cut out for and didn't enjoy the role of
the stage 4 executive. More to the point, he realized that the
leadership brand he was perpetuating—*too competitive, a micromanager, lacking a strategic vision, abrupt*—was diametrically opposed
to the brand of leadership the company needed. Over the next
year, he took himself out of the CEO role, brought in a stage 4
CEO from the outside (who did personify the leadership brand),
promoted himself to chairman of the board, and continued to
drive the finance people crazy with his projects and ideas.

Petersen's story illustrates several important ideas. First, the stage a
person is in is not related to age or position. Promotion does not magi-
cally change someone's skills and psychological orientation to fit the
new job. However, leadership positions do have expectations for a particular stage attached to them. We expect a CEO to be in stage 4 and to
think like a stage 4 person. Petersen, by contrast, was a hard-working
stage 2 entrepreneur whose business grew beyond his personal leadership reach. A stage 2 CEO makes it all but impossible for his or her direct reports to function in stage 3 or stage 4. And without stage 3 and 4
leaders, the brand lacks positive role models.

This dilemma—a boss in the wrong stage inhibiting the ability of
others to act up to stage—is not confined to the senior executive suite.

We expect a supervisor to coach, mentor, and develop direct reports like someone in stage 3, not to compete with them like a person in stage 2. Comments like "We lost a good accountant and got a lousy supervisor" are strong indicators that someone is suffering from a stage/position mismatch.

The stage-of-development logic provides a way to cut through the optical illusions when assessing the knowledge, skills, and perspectives of people in your talent pipeline. We have created a three-step process that is relatively straightforward and can lead to unexpected insights.

1. Determine the ideal "leadership stage distribution" for your part of the organization, given your strategic priorities.

2. Determine your actual leadership stage distribution.

3. Determine how you will bridge individual and organization gaps and overcome barriers to transition.

Ideal Stage Distribution

When we ask people to identify the ideal leadership stage distribution for their part of the organization, we often get rolled eyes. People think the answer is obvious: *we want all stage 4*, or *we just want people who will do what we tell them to do—all stage 1*. Neither of these extremes is a desirable outcome for delivering on the case for leadership brand discussed in chapter 2, and in fact neither is possible. Development does not happen by edict. The first step in effective development is clarity about outcomes (like desired leadership stage distribution given strategic priorities). The remaining part is providing guided experiences for people to develop, and rewarding those who are interested in developing in the direction the business needs. Everyone does not define career success as "moving up"—some people love their specialty areas and don't want to manage others; others will resist moving all over the globe to gain new experiences because they are rooted to a geographic area; still others want to balance their work life with their home life or a hobby.

Our experience suggests that a typical stage distribution for an organization that has not explicitly tried to mold it is as follows:

Stage 1: 20 percent

Stage 2: 60 percent

Stage 3: 18 percent

Stage 4: 2 percent

As people learn about the implications of this distribution pattern, most conclude that they need more stage 3 people. They come to this conclusion because stage 3 people are able to direct the work in a more strategic fashion, and (given their broader perspective and ability to cross boundaries) they are able to make desirable results occur. Implementing strategy and delivering value to stakeholders gets easier with more formal and informal stage 3 leaders.

Other stage distributions become more obvious given different ways of competing. In our consulting firm (The RBL Group), we compete on the basis of our thought leadership and our utilization of former senior executives with a great deal of applied experience. For us, a desired leadership stage distribution looks like this:

Stage 1: 5 percent

Stage 2: 15 percent

Stage 3: 65 percent

Stage 4: 15 percent

Note that we are not trying to eliminate any stage, including stage 1. We regularly hire new people to cover administrative and clerical tasks, and recently hired an intern from the local university. We hope that our people in support roles will grow into stage 2 independent contributors, requiring little supervision and deepening their expertise in their respective areas. We also work hard to outsource work that is not central to our purpose. Realistically, however, we can't outsource everything that involves the ability to follow procedures and get the details right. We will always have a small percentage of stage 1 work to be done.

Actual Stage Development Distribution

Identifying your ideal leadership stage distribution is primarily a conceptual exercise. Figuring out what you actually have takes more work. Getting the right answer is a huge step because clarity about development needs is tremendously useful. Two approaches have worked well:

• Index cards

• Talent management software

INDEX CARDS. This exercise produces amazingly consistent results. It takes about half an hour for the manager or executive of an organization of about a hundred people. We recommend that you do this separately with two or three senior executives in the same organization. Follow these steps:

1. Take about ten minutes to explain and discuss the four stages, and then give your contact a copy of table 4-1 to use for reference while completing the rest of the exercise.

2. Write the name of each person to be assessed on a separate 3×5 card, and hand your contact the deck of cards.

3. Tell your contact to sort the names into four piles—one for each leadership stage.

Once you have done this with a few executives, you will have what you need—a leadership stage distribution for this organization. As you analyze the results, look for issues like these:

- What are the biggest gaps between ideal and actual stage distributions?

- Are there individual examples (or trends) of stage/job mismatches?

- What are the surprises?

In our experience, you will find that most knowledge worker jobs have a range of appropriate leadership stages—from stage 1 to stage 3. Formal leadership positions, however, are less "stage flexible": these jobs should have incumbents with the knowledge, skills, and perspectives relevant to stage 3 and stage 4.

TALENT MANAGEMENT SOFTWARE. The 3×5 card method is a quick and easy one-time event, but it does not set up a sustainable process for managing talent. The right talent management software is a wise investment because it allows you to monitor improvements and changes in your talent pipeline. Unfortunately, the talent management software market has emerged only recently; few robust tools are currently on the market. Instead, most packages are merely sophisticated reporting tools based on data available in a performance management system.

Managing talent requires more than just sophisticated reporting; it requires a comprehensive process that engages the whole organization in identifying, developing, and supporting emerging talent. In considering talent management software intended to support a process based on one-on-one interactions between managers and their direct reports, we have learned to insist on the following critical features:

- Permits employee and manager self-service

- Provides robust security

- Uses a process-based approach linked to the annual people plan

- Includes current and future organizational structure (making it possible to view data by position or incumbent)

- Manages critical personal information, including career and mobility preferences

- Includes markers for potential, promotability, and leadership stage for specific critical jobs

- Provides succession scenarios whose impact can be viewed by role, person, leadership stage, or job pool

- Links to other people systems (such as the performance management system or the learning management system)

Additional features can also be very useful in managing the talent development process:

- Facilitates identifying experience-based development opportunities

- Supports forced ranking

- Tracks external development activities (volunteer work, board service, and so on)

Bridging Individual and Organization Gaps

With the ideal distribution and actual distribution, you have a set of clear leadership development gaps for individuals and at an aggregate. Table 4-2 outlines typical barriers to effective leadership stage transitions.

These barriers to development are particularly useful to understand as you attempt to bridge gaps following assessment through investments in leadership development, which we describe in chapter 5.

Assessment 4-1 is an easy way to determine which of the four stages you are in. Fill this out for yourself and then ask a coworker, coach, or

TABLE 4-2

Barriers to stage development

Stage 1: *Learning the leadership brand*	Stage 2: *Demonstrating brand efficacy*	Stage 3: *Building the leadership brand in others*	Stage 4: *Perpetuating the leadership brand in the organization*
• Impatience • Inability to let go of previous status and build a reputation in the organization • Inability to build relationships • Being competitive in a cooperative team environment • Lack of understanding of the "unwritten rules" • Lack of technical accuracy • Lack of discipline and focus	• Inability to work with others • Refusal to accept independence • Poor technical skills • Lack of self-confidence • Lack of initiative • Inability to focus (for example, starting a lot of things without finishing them) • Failure to see how own work relates to the success of the organization	• Too focused on own work • Lack of understanding of the broader needs of the organization • Failure to see how projects (own and those of others) relate to one another and to the success of the organization • Inability to move with trends or changes • Internal focus: unwillingness to deal with other groups inside or outside the organization • Failure to delegate • Feeling threatened by the success of others	• Unwillingness to spend time outside of own office • Geographic immobility • Inability to cope with ambiguity • Lack of credibility • Misuse of power to further personal interests • Concern with own organization's success at the expense of overall corporate success • Overcommitment • Failure to build and maintain external networks and relationships • Inability to make tough decisions and difficult trade-offs

manager to also fill it out. Then compare to see whether there are any gaps.

There is no right or wrong response. The question is, Does your stage match the expectations you and others have for your role? If it does, you might focus on staying high performing in this role or begin to figure out how to contribute at the next stage. If it does not, then you need to look for a way to develop yourself or find a different job.

Delivering the Right Results in the Right Way

"What's the bottom line?" "What have you done for us lately?" "Cut to the chase!"

ASSESSMENT 4-1

Leadership stage assessment

Respond to each of the five categories to see which description fits your approach best.

1. My approach to work
   a. I can be counted on to do the detail work on a project.
   b. I am an expert in my field.
   c. I coach others in my work group.
   d. I set the direction for a large part of the business.

2. Psychological orientation
   a. Dependent
   b. Independent
   c. Influencer
   d. Power

3. Technical skills
   a. Academic expertise more than proven experience at this point
   b. Expert in my field
   c. Link multiple technical areas together to ensure collaboration and high-quality decisions
   d. Set the direction for how technology should contribute

4. Relationships with others
   a. I am an apprentice to a more experienced person.
   b. Others value me for my expertise.
   c. I manage others.
   d. I sponsor major initiatives and test people for future opportunities.

5. Strategic contribution
   a. Once others tell me what to do, I can contribute.
   b. I provide input to the direction in which we are headed.
   c. I translate the strategic direction for others and ensure they are working in a coordinated way.
   d. I am a major instigator of our strategic direction.

Scoring:

Count the number of a, b, c, and d responses that you have.
   a) A represents stage 1: apprentice.
   b) B represents stage 2: contributor.
   c) C represents stage 3: local leader.
   d) D represents stage 4: global leader.

Your stage is represented by where you have the majority of your responses. Many people find that they are clearly in one stage. Others find that they are partly in one stage and partly in another. This occurs during stage transitions.

Remember that there is not a "right" answer for these stages, except for remaining in stage 1. It's impossible to remain a high performer throughout a career in stage 1. For the other stages, your choice is about how to remain a high performer in that stage or how to effectively move to the next stage. For example, you can remain a high performer in stage 2 by working hard to stay at the cutting edge of your technical skills. In stage 3, you remain a high performer by coaching and managing others. In stage 4, you remain a high performer as you ensure that your firm remains competitive into the future.

Business is full of reminders about the importance of getting *results*—making things happen that keep the company prosperous and its stock value up. But the Enron debacle and the other spectacular disasters of the turn of the twenty-first century provide living proof that results in themselves are not enough to track. If short-term benefits accrue at the expense of the company's legal standing or cultural coherence, its long-term prospects are poor indeed.

Nonetheless, results are important. If someone seems to be doing everything in the right way, but nothing good is happening for the organization, something is still wrong. So what's needed is a system that addresses both results and the way they are produced, backed up by a system that aligns everyone's motivation with the goals of the company.

Performance Management

To make sure that leaders deliver the right results the right way, the organization needs a systematic process for assessing and evaluating performance to ensure that it is creating value for employees, customers, and investors. Many companies attempt to do this mechanically, by focusing on forms and procedures. However, we have found that the best performance management systems—the ones that really contribute to leadership brand building—are much more likely to be concerned with ensuring good dialogue about what's really valued. They have some forms and procedures, but the mechanical stuff is kept in the background. A culture of caring that surrounds and reinforces the performance management process is the most critical element. Another case in point:

Give Us the Numbers

Citigroup had a performance management process that looked only at the financial deliverables its leaders produced. Over time, delivering on the numbers became the only thing that mattered. At first this worked very well in the highly decentralized, high-acquisition environment. However, after a few years, Citigroup began to run into problems created by the way the results were achieved. The Private Bank business was kicked out of Japan for not following banking rules. A few leaders failed to tell customers about problems with the loss of their financial information. The German government sued Citigroup traders in London for alleged unethical behavior. Finally, regulators stopped the company from making further acquisitions until it could fix the way its people delivered results.

Senior leaders, led by then-new CEO Chuck Prince, implemented a Five Point Plan that included major changes to the performance management process. The new process built factors such as responsibility that emphasized not only what results were achieved but how they were achieved. This included attention to customers and to one another in the evaluation and feedback of every leader and ensured that these factors are as important to the final rating as the individual's financial results.

This approach has become a component of Citigroup's leadership brand. It significantly changes the way leaders are expected to operate in the global financial services markets. In fact, Citigroup plans to measure its overall firm and leadership brand as "the most respected financial services company in the world."

The nature of leadership brand is to ensure that leaders achieve the right results the right way. It is critical that both the right results and the right way are integral parts of the performance management process. It is also critical that leaders are willing to spend time having discussions about what high performance looks like and what living the brand means to the success of each individual leader.

Recognition and Rewards

In addition to having strong performance management, you can reinforce your leadership brand by recognizing and rewarding behaviors consistent with it—thus building a culture of effective and productive performance. This is much easier said than done, however.

The difficulty is in the recognition part. Recognizing and rewarding desirable outcomes is far simpler than recognizing and rewarding the right behaviors. For example, it's relatively straightforward to measure outcomes such as increasing profitability, market share, and even employee and customer commitment. These are *lag* measures—things that happen as a result of what has been done. By contrast, *lead* measures—direct assessments of the way results are produced—are more amorphous and therefore much more complex. Just how do you measure how well someone is displaying the sort of savvy that we discussed earlier? Or to what extent someone is displaying collaborative, innovative, or creative behavior? Without some consistent methodology, evaluations of whether behavior has increased, decreased, or stayed the same are bound to show extensive variation.

For an answer, we turn to Steve Kerr, who developed a methodology during his time as chief learning officer at GE and at Goldman Sachs. His methodology allows us to break down abstract ideas into discrete and observable behaviors.

Consider *collaboration* as something a company might desire as a branded competence for its leaders. It's easy to imagine a CEO getting excited about how great it would be if only the firm's leaders were more collaborative. The exercise is designed to turn collaboration into discrete behaviors (see table 4-3). The first question to ask is, What behaviors would we see more of and less of if our leaders were more collaborative?

Once leaders discuss and agree on what collaboration looks like in terms of behaviors that they would see more of and less of, collaboration moves from an unanalyzed abstraction to a set of agreed-upon behaviors. Again, measuring behaviors like these is not intended to

TABLE 4-3

Collaborative behaviors

IF OUR LEADERS WERE COLLABORATIVE, WHAT BEHAVIORS WOULD WE SEE MORE OR LESS OF?	
More	**Less**
1. Taking lunch and other breaks with direct reports and peers from other departments	1. Eating alone or exclusively with other executives
2. Visiting customers often (at least twice a week)	2. Delegating direct customer interaction to others
3. Making unsolicited calls to other departments about how to work together to resolve common problems	3. Staying in a silo and leaving others to get on with their own affairs
4. Initiating cross-functional teams and assignments	4. Using body language or sounds that reflect irritation (frowning, moaning, sighing, cursing, and so on) when asked to be part of cross-organizational projects or teams
5. Talking about the work that other departments are doing and assessing the impact of their work on the leader's own organization	5. Not talking about the work of other organizations and the impact of their work on the leader's own organization

replace measurement of outcomes; the behavioral points serve as lead measures, indicating whether outcome measures are likely to occur.

Kerr's next step is to tie the recognition part of branded leadership behaviors into positive and negative consequences (or rewards and punishments). The simple approach is to ask, If a leader were to exhibit one of these behaviors we want more of, what would happen? A good thing? (+) A bad thing? (–) Or could it go either way? (?) Table 4-4 shows how our example might turn out.

In this particular case, the responses are similar to what we actually get when we talk to people. Much of the time, it's unclear what will happen. Some behaviors might be fairly certain to generate a positive or negative reward—but because the system is not in place to measure behavior, no one can be absolutely sure what would happen.

This is an extremely important point. If people are told that certain behavior is desirable when they can see no certainty about the kind of response it will bring them, they're unlikely to be enthusiastic about it. This exercise also demonstrates why we strongly advocate sticking with a select few branded leadership competencies. Otherwise, you wind up with just too many factors. In our experience, giving leaders just a few critical things to watch for makes it much easier for them to spot and then reward desirable behavior.

It's also important to point out that rewards can be either financial or nonfinancial, or both. Financial rewards like cash incentives and bonuses are always pleasant to receive, but it turns out that nonfinancial rewards

TABLE 4-4

Consequences of collaborative behaviors

IMPACT OF A LEADER EXHIBITING THE SPECIFIED BEHAVIOR	
Behavior	**Response**
1. Taking lunch and other breaks with direct reports and peers from other departments	(?)
2. Visiting customers often (say, twice a week)	(+)
3. Making unsolicited calls to other departments about how to work together to resolve common problems	(+)
4. Initiating cross-functional teams and assignments	(?)
5. Talking about the work that other departments are doing and assessing the impact of their work on the leader's own organization	(+)

are just as powerful for reinforcing behaviors that support the leadership brand. For example, if a more senior leader sees a supervisor actively working with other organizations—even spending time at lunch and during other breaks—to integrate a project, a cash incentive might not be nearly as powerful as a handwritten thank-you note that recognizes the effort.

As leaders live the brand, they must be recognized and rewarded for what they do. It is useful to think of the CEO as the "leadership brand manager"—the one who is ultimately responsible for recognizing talent and ensuring that the right results get produced in the right way. Effective CEOs and senior executives must watch for examples of living the brand and ensure that exemplary leaders know that they are noticed. They should do this with both formal rewards such as bonuses and with nonfinancial rewards such as notes, thanks, unexpected time off, and other powerful acknowledgments.

Conclusion

In our work with executives involved in leadership development, it's not unusual to find out that many leaders have no idea what they should be developing. Without assessment, focused development just isn't possible. Instead, people tend to choose to develop in areas they find most interesting rather than the ones that are most needed.

For example, senior leaders in one global professional services firm recently sent a marketing executive to a two-week program at a prestigious university. The senior leaders believed this executive needed to develop a stronger financial perspective, and they saw the program as including offerings ideal for that purpose. Unfortunately, no one bothered to tell the marketing executive anything about this goal, so the exec naturally lapsed into tourist mode, taking courses in organization behavior, marketing, and globalization and avoiding all discretionary finance courses. The opportunity was squandered.

Strong assessment processes are not only helpful—they are essential to successful leader brand development. When it comes to assessment support, both individual and multirater tools are available, and more information is better than less. It's useful for leaders to have a variety of ways to view themselves—what they know (know), who they are (be), and how their behavior affects others (do). No one should be expected to change just because of one bit of feedback about past behavior. Each leader has choices about what to do and where to focus improvements.

The best use of assessment is to identify which specific things each of the assessed leaders would get the most mileage out of developing— just those few items that will have the most beneficial impact on their own performance and the performance of their organization, not a laundry list. Sometimes this is building on strengths, and other times it involves shoring up flaws or eliminating derailers.

In either case, the feedback recipients should thank those who have provided input to an assessment and tell them what they plan to do as a result. Feedback is a gift. Because it is a gift, people want to know what you think of it and whether you plan to use it. If you violate this principle of thanking people for their gifts, you are less and less likely to get more gifts in the future.

When assessments are a part of a thoughtful development process, there is great likelihood that the leadership brand is realized with leaders who have:

- *The right stuff* (a predisposition to the brand)

- *At the right leadership stage* (the knowledge, skills, and perspectives to do the job at each level of leadership)

- *That delivers the right results in the right way* (clarity about desired results with the declaration of investors, employees, and customers, delivered by way of a course of action consistent with leadership)

5

Investing in Leadership Brand

Public-, private-, and social-sector organizations spend untold amounts to improve the quality of their leadership, yet the results are often disappointing. In our experience, much of the disappointment stems from the typical scattershot approach to development focusing on the individual leader that comes from starting leadership development efforts at step 3 or 4 instead of step 1. When organizations focus on leadership brand and start with a clear case and statement of leadership that connects leader behaviors to customers through the business strategy, the return on development investments improves dramatically.

Firm brands evolve from targeted choices in product design, packaging, and processes. Likewise, leadership brands are not happenstance; they follow a host of decisions about the attributes the firm requires of its leaders, as well as the actions they take and the results they deliver. As a result, instead of spending piecemeal on improving individual leaders, the organization can use its statement of leadership brand to set the criteria for these investments. If a leadership training program or development experience does not support the brand, it is an unwise investment.

Some firms use what our colleague Paul McKinnon calls a *free market model* for leadership. In this approach, individual leaders are left to their own devices and resources to improve. The free market often falters because people lack information to make fully informed decisions. We prefer what McKinnon calls a *chess master model*, where a series of targeted investments focus leaders on experiences they can have to acquire and demonstrate the firm leadership brand. This model is based on a set of assumptions and choices about how to develop leaders through training and development experiences, job experiences, and life experiences. It is often governed by a strong corporate leadership development function who directs the movement of talent.

This chapter outlines our assumptions about developing leadership brand, presents a new formula for developing leadership brand, and describes how to create a unifying process for managing the leadership brand.

Assumptions About Developing Leadership Brand

Investing in a leadership brand has two fundamental differences that complement traditional investments in leaders or leadership. First, leadership brand focuses from the outside in versus the inside out. Most leader training focuses on the inside, either internal beliefs and styles of individual leaders or practices inside the organization that leaders need to master. Leadership brand starts from the outside in, being clear about customer and investor expectations and then orienting leadership brand investments to meet those expectations. Second, leader training often focuses on the individual: how can you improve your personal style or results. Leadership brand development focuses not only on the person but also on the process of creating a cadre of better leaders. These two differences (outside in and leadership versus leaders) rest on a number of assumptions that will guide leadership brand investments to make sure they translate customer expectations into employee and organization behavior through leadership actions:

- Branded leadership investments recognize that not all leaders are equal.

- Branded leadership investments handle the nature-versus-nurture debate.

- Branded leadership investments both build on strengths and moderate any critical weaknesses.

- Branded leadership investments are personalized.

- Branded leadership investments form an integrated system and are not isolated events.

- Branded leadership investments are tied to the business.

- Branded leadership development involves different types of experiences at various levels of the organization.

Remember That Not All Leaders Are Equal

In chapter 2, we argued that even though all leaders add value through their contributions, some leaders work in jobs that are more or less critical for building a firm brand. As a result, leadership brand investments should focus most on those leaders who will most embody the firm brand in either the current or the projected future assignments—or those in critical jobs. In addition to leaders in critical jobs, investments in leaders with potential are more valuable than those with limited or questionable potential. Often, high potentials are defined as individuals who have the possibility of two additional career moves within a relatively short time period (say, five years). We would add to this descriptor that high-potential leaders who deserve increased investment are also those who are most likely to embody the firm brand. Shell, for example, does this by monitoring what it calls the *currently estimated potential* of a leader according to the leader's ability to demonstrate the leadership brand that Shell sees as critical along three dimensions: *capacity* (has the ability to think and make critical decisions, particularly those related to increasing customer and investor value), *achievement* (delivers results, grows, and works in an organized way to serve customers and investors), and *relationships* (communicates well, listens, and nurtures others both inside and outside the organization). Leaders who demonstrate these attributes are considered more worthy of investment than leaders who do not. This runs counter to the traditional leadership investment goal that "all leaders will receive forty hours of training this year." Some should receive more and others less.

Forget Nature Versus Nurture

There has been an ongoing leadership debate as to whether leaders are born (nature) or bred (nurture). Those leaning to the nature side of the equation believe that staffing decisions are the primary predictors of leadership success; those leaning to the nurture side suggest that more investment in training and development experiences will improve leadership. As noted earlier, a number of psychological studies lead to the conclusion that the correct answer is about fifty-fifty.[1] Nature gives leaders predispositions, but with experience those predispositions can generally be adapted to any situation. Predisposition does not imply predestination. Investing in branded leadership means that organizations should recognize the extent to which an individual leader's predispositions are consistent with the brand, and then assess the capacity of a leader to develop the personal requirements consistent with the leadership brand.

Build on Strengths

There are debates in the leadership profession about how much to build on strengths. Some argue that good leaders should identify weaknesses and overcome them; others argue that leaders should focus on strengths and master them.[2] A branded leadership view is that leaders at all levels of an organization need to master those things that align with the firm brand. If a firm is working to be known for exceptional customer service, the leaders need to have strengths in forming relationships, communicating values, and solving problems both inside and outside the company. If a leader cannot align personal behaviors with customer requirements, the leader will not fit and should move on. Intel's firm brand, "advance life through technology," not only encourages leaders to build on strengths, it helps identify which strengths are most critical given the firm brand that they need to emulate. Intel leaders need to demonstrate not only technological savvy but independent thinking and critical judgment skills to continue to sustain their market reputation. We call these the leaders' *signature strengths*—their unique abilities that enable them to succeed. As long as they understand their weaknesses and can compensate for them via their signature strengths, or those of others they recruit to fill the gaps, the development efforts they devote to improving their strengths will usually have a higher payoff than overcoming weaknesses. In addition, at times leaders must focus on moderating their weaknesses when they are career derailers or "fatal flaws." These flaws are issues such as "failure to learn from experience," "unconcerned with the development of others," and other issues related to an inability to help others or continue developing oneself.[3] We extend this work to suggest that fatal flaws are weaknesses that are not consistent with the desired brand.

Personalize Investments

Each leader has a unique learning style. Traditional training programs are too often limited to a take-it-or-leave-it offering of the various instructors' preferred teaching styles. The logic of unique styles also implies that most individuals will be more open to some development assignments than to others and that leadership investments should be tailored to the unique learning styles of the individual leader.[4] Personalized investments matter to the development of leadership brand because firms with a portfolio of product brands will generally outperform firms with a single product brand (think of Disney's strength with operations in theme parks, television, movie production, and products and services versus Knott's Berry Farm amusement park, which focuses exclusively on theme parks). Likewise, leadership brand does best when employees throughout the organization demonstrate a core set of attributes but also have diversity of styles. Organizations that personalize leadership investments model the importance of varied approaches to developing leaders and develop leaders with a consistent brand yet individual styles.

Integrate Leadership Investments into a System

Too often, leadership investments tend to be isolated and piecemeal—a training program this month, a coaching experience next quarter, a temporary assignment the quarter after, a job rotation next year. For an antidote, our colleague Warren Wilhelm calls for a *learning architecture*, where the disparate ways to learn become integrated around a common theme.[5] David Hatch, who helped create the learning architecture at PepsiCo, IBM, and Thomson, also calls for such an integrated system, where the focus of development is not on the individual leader but on the processes that shape the brand the leader represents. A learning architecture or an integrated system is central to the brand metaphor since firm brands require consistency and integration across a host of decisions.

A leadership brand likewise becomes the center point around which a myriad of leadership investments may be made.[6] Research by Executive Development Associates (EDA) found the integration of leadership investments came out on top in their study for building leadership, with 68 percent of their respondents citing it as the number-one priority.[7] So, instead of hiring or promoting a person, sending another to an executive program, and giving another a special assignment, a leadership brand approach requires an integrated talent management system where options for development are mapped against individual leaders' needs, and each leader's development experience aligns with the desired leadership brand, and all related processes reflect and align with the leadership brand.

Tie Branded Leadership Investments to the Business

As we explained in chapter 2, leadership brand development begins with the clear statement of customer and investor expectations as translated through strategy, firm brand, and then leadership brand. These customer expectations define what leaders who embody the brand should know and do. This is the basis for the case for leadership brand and the reason to pay any attention to leadership at all. As an organization looks at how to develop the leaders it needs to deliver business results, knowing what to train on (content) is more important than how to train (delivery). And content needs to be malleable to reflect strategic shifts to meet changing customer needs. As customer needs change, so does strategy, and so must what leaders know and do. As a result, leadership brand investments in training and development constantly balance the overall corporate agenda with the local business agenda. When the corporate brand creates value in the marketplace, it becomes infused into the leadership brand; when the local business unit brand creates more value, it becomes the dominant leadership brand.[8]

Allow Branded Leadership to Expand

As we have discussed in chapter 4, leaders pass through predictable stages as their careers progress. The leadership investments for different career stages should differ. Leadership investments for the apprentice stage should focus on learning how to operate within the existing organization and should reflect a minority percentage of total investments—using highly standardized and low-cost delivery methods. Leadership investments for the individual contributor stage should focus on developing increased autonomy and responsibility for tasks and reflect a slightly larger percentage of investment. Leadership investments for the manager stage should focus on building teams and relationships among individuals and should reflect the majority of the leadership budget. Leadership investments at the strategic stage should emphasize shaping and delivering on goals.

Also, since organizations evolve over time to match the changing expectations of customers, we believe that the individual styles of leadership brand should expand as one moves down the organization. For example, if a new leader generally moves into the senior position every five years, and the organization wants a candidate pool of four leaders from which to select the future leader, then the leadership levels may look something like those in table 5-1:

TABLE 5-1

Characteristics of leadership levels

	Number of individuals	Current place	Age
Level 1	1 person	In top job	55–60
Level 2	4 people	5 years away from top job	50–55
Level 3	16 people	10 years away from top job	45–50
Level 4	64 people	15 years away from top job	40–45
Level 5	256 people	20 years away from top job	35–40

As one goes down the organization, the number of potential candidates for the top job increases as should the variety of the ways the leadership brand is expressed. Since customer expectations fifteen to twenty years out are difficult to predict with confidence, the leaders at levels 4 and 5 should represent a larger array of technical skills and leadership styles than those found at level 2. This spreading out and expanding of the leadership brand is not unlike the way firms work to expand their product or firm brand. Not all products are successful.

Similar to having a product development pipeline, leadership brand investments should be structured to encourage a variety of expressions of the leadership brand. A pipeline of products ensures a multiple-product company where innovation will continually require experimentation. Some colleagues have estimated the following logic for product innovation:[9]

- 3,000 raw ideas

- 300 ideas submitted

- 125 small projects

- 9 early-stage developments

- 4 major developments

- 1.7 launches

- 1 success

Similarly, investing in leadership brand should encourage multiple brands further down the organization, so that the right leadership brand emerges at the right time to help the firm reach its goals.[10]

Alternatively, an individual leader who passes through the career stages we laid out in chapter 4 and is exposed to a variety of organizational, production, and customer challenges is likely to gain a repertoire of experiences and an ability to adapt to changing customer expectations.

A New Formula for Developing Leadership Brand

Over the past fifteen years, a truism about how to develop talent has evolved: 70-20-10. In this logic, 70 percent of learning and development happens in the course of on-the-job experiences, tasks, and problem solving. This makes assignments the most important aspect of any learning and development plan. For example, the real learning of a skill acquired in a training program or of an insight presented in feedback takes place back on the job when the skill or feedback is applied to a real situation. Meanwhile, 20 percent comes from learning from others through sharing feedback, observing, and working with role models, and only 10 percent of learning and development comes from formal training.

The 70-20-10 formula seems to be pervasive in business and beyond. At Google, strategic workers aspire to focus 70 percent on the core business, 20 percent on related businesses, and 10 percent on unrelated businesses.[11] Google leaders argue that this ratio helps them balance winning today with the core against winning tomorrow with the new. At General Electric, Jack Welch maintained that 20 percent of employees were excellent and should be essentially left alone, 70 percent were average and could be developed, and 10 percent were unredeemable and should be forced out. Even in diets, we are encouraged to gain 70 percent of calories from proteins, 20 percent from carbs, and 10 percent from unsaturated fat.

For workplace development, the 70-20-10 formula derives in part from Center for Creative Leadership (CCL) research that asks employees to comment retrospectively on "the most significant experiences" that helped them develop in their careers.[12] In that context, it is no surprise that job experiences come out high. Simple math explains this. If someone is moved into a demanding job, that assignment is likely to take six months, twelve months, or more (a thousand hours and up). In contrast, a training experience is likely to be five days (forty hours) or less. In this light, it is surprising that training gets as much as 10 percent of the perceived impact on leadership investment.

We believe that the three sources of experience (training, work, and life) can each offer unique insights, and that the 10 percent attributed retrospectively to training does not fairly indicate its importance. Effective training offers cognitive models and human relationships that add value to subsequent work experiences by providing a framework for processing them. Similarly, life experiences develop a potential leader's predispositions to be inquisitive, to learn and grow, and to deepen personal values—all of which enhance the impact of both training and work experiences. All three are essential to successful investment in developing leadership brand—it's not a matter of tossing out the least influential 10 percent of development experiences along with the least promising 10 percent of performers on the job.

Further, we believe that once you begin applying the leadership brand concept, the percentages and categories will shift somewhat, say, to 50-20-30. That is, as much as 30 percent of a person's overall development may be derived through training experiences. As leadership brand replaces individual leader development, well-conceived and orchestrated training experiences are likely to be more central to the creation of a leadership brand. In recent years, training programs have shifted from all-purpose events to experiences tailored to the company strategy, firm brand, and leadership brand, and from an emphasis on lecture to action learning as an inherent process. They are designed to offer specific tools and strategies, customized cases, and personalized assessments that make learning specific, relevant, and actionable.

Meanwhile, formal training helps developing leaders filter things that matter from things that do not matter in the face of an onslaught of information and knowledge about the current business environment. Experiences can be like unsifted blogs: lots of information, much of it misleading. So we see investment in innovative and systematic leadership brand training to have ever greater impact in coming years as it helps participants understand, frame, and learn from their formal and informal experiences.

As we see it, work experience continues to be the main factor in developing both leaders and leadership brand—call it 50 percent. This form of development comes from individuals having experiences with new tasks, people, challenges, and opportunities. Learning by doing is still the dominant way that people learn. We also believe that even in an increasingly borderless world, 20 percent of learning will come through life experience. Life experience means that leaders can learn from things that happen to them outside the formal work setting (in volunteer, social, and home environments). As they adapt lessons learned from life experiences into their organization, they are able to learn and grow more quickly. But from the point of view of what a firm can control, it's worth looking first at that crucial 30 percent provided by formal training.

Training: 30 Percent

As noted, much of today's ongoing training investment is haphazard, not built on the assumptions of leadership brand. Such investments result in what we call *tourist training*—that is, participants attend these training programs in much the same spirit as a tourist visits a foreign country. They fly in, see the sights, take some pictures, have some formal and structured experiences, buy some postcards or souvenirs, and then return to the "real world" and resume their former way of life. Their visit is bounded and bundled as an event outside the normal flow of life and recalled from time to time as a pleasant (or not) memory but with little lasting impact beyond memories. A yarn we have shared is, a group of turkeys spent three days learning how to fly by learning the aerodynamics of flying, experimenting, and actually flying; at the end of the three days they all walked home. Tourist training does not last beyond the training event itself.

A guest, on the other hand, engages with locals, may stay in a home or a local B&B where he can meet some real people, troubles to learn the details and concerns of daily life, maybe even enough of the local language to get by, and shares something of his own life. Through the exchange, both guest and local enlarge their perspectives and will doubtless view the strange "other" customs more sympathetically. Neither person is quite the same afterward. Even after going home, the guest might adopt some new habits around food, drink, or dress, and will certainly read the international news with new interest, hoping to learn more. When the guest hears about that place on the evening news, he doesn't say, "I was there!" as the tourist might. He says, "I know that town and those people, and I care what is happening to them." A shift has taken place. Growth has occurred.

Good leadership brand investments in training and development—investments in branded leadership—avoid the tourist trappings and build enduring intellectual, emotional, and behavioral change. This is like product brands that are more than prototypes and actually have a stream of products related to the brand. The development program is less an event than an experience that shapes thinking and action. Ideas are internalized and not just observed. Actions outlined in the program are specific and personal obligations that the participant will do, not abstract things that others could do or have done. Development experiences that install brand build both content and process based on the development assumptions described earlier in this chapter. And these development experiences are not just for an individual leader who randomly visits, but for a cadre of leaders throughout the organization who will learn the right brand from both the content taught and the processes used to teach it.

CONTENT. Sometimes those charged with designing training become enamored with the clever, popular, and creative innovations or gimmicks in training and miss the importance of the content, or what is taught. Since adults learn more when they know the why and not just the what, the content of leadership brand training experiences must be aligned with strategy. This alignment occurs in two ways: horizontal and vertical training. *Horizontal training* focuses on developing attributes that support the leadership brand according to the leader's stage or level. The statement of leadership that we talked about in chapter 3 leads to a series of expectations of what leaders should know. These expectations may be tailored to the specific requirements for leaders at a particular level, as outlined in table 5-2.

TABLE 5-2

Considerations for horizontal training

	ATTRIBUTE		
Level	**Value creator**	**Change disciplinarian**	**Developer**
Officer	Defines shareholder value for the enterprise	Sponsors change initiatives	Reviews talent development processes
Executive	Creates value for the organization unit	Focuses change on the key priorities	Ensures regular talent reviews and progress of key people
Senior manager	Organizes resources to deliver value	Champions change initiatives	Gives opportunities for talented employees to take on assignments
First-time manager	Builds value for the operation or team	Implements change	Seeks to bring in and integrate great talent
Individual contributor	Understands the sources of value creation within the organization	Makes change happen	Learns what is necessary to contribute to the company's success

Participants in horizontal training likely attend as individuals seeking to acquire knowledge and skills to help them succeed at their current level of the organization. The leadership brand is ensured when a large percentage of the organization's leaders share the same training experience. Generally, people moving into a new assignment have a window of opportunity where they are open to learning new skills. It is therefore valuable to get individuals into a level-based training experience within four to six months of taking a new assignment, to help them acquire tools to accomplish the assignment in the right way.

Vertical training focuses less on leadership skills by level and more on using training to implement corporate initiatives. For example, if the senior executives in a firm believe that the organization should improve operating efficiency through applying principles of lean manufacturing (or Six Sigma), they can mandate development experiences whose content turns the principles of the chosen discipline into a set of practices. Teams charged with implementing the initiative attend as groups; during the development experience, they focus on application of the tools to their unique setting. This team-based training helps install the brand to the leader and his teammates.

Both horizontal and vertical training are driven by the strategy and firm brand, and both help embed the firm brand into leadership actions. Both seek to communicate ideas with impact. Both personalize the experience to the learning styles of leaders who attend. Both require preliminary assessments to diagnose what is and what should be. Both communicate the firm brand through what is taught. However, the horizontal program focuses on the knowledge, skills, and values that leaders at different levels of the organization must demonstrate to make the firm brand real; the vertical program focuses on how to implement corporatewide initiatives to execute the strategy. The horizontal experiences generally focus on personal action plans and learning; the vertical experiences focus on teams and how to change organization processes. Both help inculcate the leadership brand among a cross section of employees. This kind of action learning for individuals or teams has been cited as a success factor by 73 percent of companies queried on their prosperity in the current environment.[13]

Many companies have created corporate universities or learning centers to house both horizontal and vertical learning experiences. These centers may be tied to a specific location (IBM has its Armonk facility; Goldman Sachs has one on Pine Street; McDonald's has

Hamburger University in Oak Park, Illinois), or they may be dispersed throughout an organization. These centers sometimes become a short-cut vernacular for mastering the leadership brand: "Have you been to Pine Street?" not only signals an awareness of having attended the training but implies being affected by it. These centers should become exemplars and archetypes of the firm leadership brand. We have used the following questions to diagnose how well the content of training bolsters the leadership brand:

- To what extent would customers or investors be pleased with the outline of the program (learning objectives, participant takeaways)?

- To what extent does the content of the program communicate the firm leadership brand?

- To what extent can someone who sees the content of the program discern the organization's strategy?

- To what extent does the experience reinforce an integrated leadership model that connects to customers or investors?

- To what extent does the program flow from module to module in a consistent way?

- To what extent does the program balance innovative ideas with individual, team, or organization-wide application of ideas?

- To what extent has the program evolved to align with changing customer expectations?

- To what extent will the program content touch a critical mass of leaders so that similar principles are learned throughout the organization?

PROCESS. Content deals with what to train; process deals with how to make sure the training experience delivers what you intend. A number of process choices are required to make sure that the training experience furthers a leadership brand.

Faculty. Faculty should embody the brand they are communicating. One executive dictated that his direct reports all engage others in their organization and share decision making with them—even though that was just one of many arbitrary demands that he made in the absence of any shared decision making on his part. His hypocrisy in demanding that others be participative led to cynicism. Those who address leaders in training sessions should embody and live the message they are communicating. With this generic caveat, four categories of faculty can be enlisted to help make the most of training: inside experts, outside experts, line managers, and external stakeholders (customers or investors, or both).

- *Inside experts.* Training departments often have people who prepare and deliver excellent training modules. These individuals need to be credible both for how they present and for what they have done earlier in their careers. It is especially useful to present internal instructors who have had experience in line management positions where they were successful, and who can focus on technical areas in which they have deep expertise. They may also be certified in the program at hand (such as Six Sigma black belts) and thus able to help others become certified. Often, as internal experts move into an instructional mode, they receive coaching in presentation skills to increase their impact on an audience. They know the company and culture and they can talk with confidence and experience about how to turn ideas into action in the trainees' own environment.

- *Outside experts.* External instructors bring new ideas and knowledge. They transmit practices that have worked in other settings. However, to make knowledge productive, they should also know enough about the immediate business to see how their knowledge will help further the firm leadership brand. They should adapt their ideas to the specific requirements of the organization. They can be paired with internal managers and instructors so that their ideas will have maximum impact.

- *Line managers.* In recent years, line managers have been increasingly used to design and deliver training. One colleague responsible for developing leadership told us that the best thing he could do was to have the senior leaders of the company train other leaders, if only because that forced those doing the training to model the behavior they advocate and teach. EDA found that 75 percent of leading companies used senior executives as presenters for at least part of the training.[14] PepsiCo has been one of the leaders in this area. Its senior leaders do many things to make the training relevant to PepsiCo's situation, including individual coaching of future leaders.[15] This mentoring role goes beyond the confines of the classroom to being accessible to learning leaders once they return to their day-to-day work. They focus their instruction on how to make things happen—for real, at PepsiCo—through leadership action. They have informal conversations over meals or in the evening where they communicate PepsiCo values through stories. They share their own personal journey of leadership at the company and encourage learning leaders to craft their own. They work to be consistent in their day-to-day leadership with what they are teaching future leaders to do. All these ideas help participants in a training experience learn the leadership brand by observing it firsthand. Depending too much on line managers has the limitations of not sourcing ideas from outside the company and becoming insular, training future leaders on what present leaders have done without focusing on what could be, and not having quite as innovative a pedagogy or teaching style (line managers are expected to be gifted teachers).

- *Customers or investors.* For an organization to shift leader training to building leadership brand, it is critical to involve outside stakeholders in the design, delivery, or presentation of the training experience. Customers and investors may participate in each of these steps through their presence (bringing them into the room in person or on video) or their essence (making sure that their concerns are being addressed). Customers can be present at instructional design meetings and voice opinions about what should be taught, or the design team can research customer expectations and make sure that they are infused throughout the design. Customers and investors can help deliver a program as expert faculty, participants in a live case study focused on their own needs, or members of a panel sharing their encounters with the company. Customers can also join a program as participants, working to make sure that their expectations (which are at the heart of firm brand) are understood and translated into action through leadership investments while they also derive the personal benefits of the program itself. Including customers and/or investors in training experiences increases the likelihood that participants will be more than tourists, that they will not only understand what their leadership brand needs to be but find ways to actually do it.

When the four faculty groups form an integrated team, the training will have innovative content (led by outside experts), adapted to the organization (led by internal experts), with relevance to the organization's success (because of customer or investor participation, or both), and with accountability for its application (because of line manager participation).

Boundaries of Training. Training has traditionally been an event or course with a clear beginning and end, held in an off-site location: like tourists, participants fly in, attend the event, and return to work. Increasingly these days, training investments are experiences or processes with malleable boundaries that don't fall so easily into the tourism trap. Before the event, attendees (either as individuals in horizontal training or teams in vertical training) are briefed about why they are attending the course and what is expected from their participation, and follow-up after the event makes sure its effects translate into real-world action.

In some of the university programs where we teach, participants have paid a large fee—in direct program costs, indirect related expenses, and time away from work—to attend a two- or four-week program. When we ask, "How many of you had a meaningful conversation with your boss or other adviser about why you are attending this program and what they hope you will leave with?" often fewer than 20 percent raise their hands. Most economic and personnel investments would require much more scrutiny than the training programs people attend. But the 20 percent who know why they are there are apt to derive the most benefit from their participation. They often have a project or an assignment that they are currently leading or will be charged to lead in the near term. They immediately adapt the ideas presented to their situation, and the training becomes much more relevant to them than it is to others who are simply attending because it seemed like a good idea.

During the modern training course, boundaries are also blurred. Training is less "time away from work" than it is "time to revitalize how to do current work." This means that during the training—which may include cases, lectures, discussions, or small teams—participants continually look at ways to apply ideas to their work setting. In our research on learning, we called this type of training *ideas with impact* and found that it was much more likely to help transfer ideas from a classroom to the work setting.[16] Often called *action learning*, this kind of training constantly encourages attendees to translate the ideas to the challenges they face at work. By so doing, training participants experience the desired leadership brand during the training experience itself. For teams, action learning means applying the principles taught to specific on-the-job applications.

Training as an experience need not end with the course. In fact, the course can be the beginning of a longer-term experience. One company had all participants pair off as partners to coach one another in building a personal action plan that the coach would continue to monitor over time. Another company had individuals send action plans to themselves (in messages delayed three or six months) so they could self-monitor the impact of the training—with copies to the bosses who paid for the event, so they could draw their own conclusions as to its success. One company required that everyone who attended an internal or external training session prepare a short synopsis of key ideas, with two or three specific applications for their work unit that would be shared in the subsequent staff meeting. Another company followed up on training with phone calls from internal training staff to ask participants not only what they learned but how they were able to apply it. And still another company had a three-month reunion, where participants from a two-week training event returned for one day to share how they adapted what they learned. Each of these ideas shifts the logic of training from an event to an experience and thus boosts its success rate and the impact on the organization.

Training Design and Methods. Enormous research has been done on how to train with impact. Here are some specific tips that will increase the impact of your investment in building leadership brand, as opposed to developing leaders:

- *Offer an integrated model for the experience.* We continue to see many training events as parades of stars, with each day or module taught by a thoughtful presenter (either outside faculty, line manager, or customer), then another module from another face, and then another. With little integration, each training module is an isolated event. Branded training requires an integrated message (what our leaders need to know and do to demonstrate a leadership brand consistent with a firm brand) that has distinct modules woven around the brand theme.

- *Use a host of training pedagogies.* Since adults learn differently from one another, different methodologies can and should be used. A mix of lecture, small group discussion, written case studies, live case studies, action learning projects, team presentation, video snippets, technology-based learning, simulations, assessment tools, and so forth can be woven into the training experience to ensure that regardless of each participant's learning style, all will find some methods that work well. Bear in mind that with adult learners, the faculty should be talking about 60 or 70 percent of the time. If faculty allow their participation to fall below 50 percent of the talking time, participants are in a problem-solving session and wonder what the faculty add; if faculty do 85 percent or more of the talking, participants are more likely to be listening than internalizing what is taught.

- *Design modules to follow the concept-illustration-action (C-I-A) rationale.* During a training experience, a host of modules may be woven around the integrated C-I-A theme. Each module should have a clear set of concepts. Concepts represent the research-based theory and principles that frame an issue, or just the commonsense ideas that clearly apply without rich theory and research.[17] These concepts should align specifically with the firm's brand and how it relates to leadership brand. But with content, there must also be illustration, or examples of what others have done with the principles taught. The illustrations may be written case studies of successful (or unsuccessful) firms, live case studies (as when customers attend and share problems), or video cases. Whatever the choice, participants learn by seeing how ideas were actually implemented. Then application follows. Application generally reinforces ideas with personal impact as participants adapt the concepts and illustrations to their personal situation. With the use of C-I-A logic in each module, a personal understanding of the leadership brand begins to emerge that participants can understand, observe, and practice.

- *Build recursive lessons (self-reflective and self-learning) into the training.* The half-life of knowledge is getting increasingly shorter, so all concepts taught in training need to be analyzed and updated consistently. For example, when IBM CEO Lou Gerstner wanted to increase organization capabilities of speed and collaboration, he sponsored a training experience called Accelerating Change Together (ACT). The ACT process was designed to achieve a fast and collaborative approach to leading the business, with a focus on team-based action learning projects. Each team identified eight-, ten-, and twelve-week problems to solve, and then worked collaboratively to identify the right people in the world to solve each problem (and then give them eight, ten, or twelve weeks to solve it). As the teams went through this training experience, they continually unlearned and learned how to improve their projects. Getting an individual leader to understand and adapt a leadership brand may require that the leader be knowledgeable about what the brand requires and reflective about how well he currently lives the brand. Leadership brand is less likely to take hold when forced on individual leaders and more likely to take root when individual leaders experience it through both training and work experiences.

Work Experience: 50 Percent

As we've said, adults learn by doing. At least, they learn when and if they reflect on what they have done and gain insight that allows them to do better in the future. Doing does not lead to learning without reflection—but thoughtful reflection makes work experiences the dominant source for investing in future leaders. Installing a leadership brand among a group of autonomous leaders comes when they experience firsthand the impact of the brand on their behavior and performance.

It is unfortunately easy to get caught in the rut of routines where tomorrow is predicted by today. When this happens, individuals fail to learn and grow—like the retired couple we heard of who moved to a warm climate but spent most of every day watching the same television shows they'd watched from their old home. They moved to a new place but did not move into new experiences, so they were atrophying and not moving forward.

Bob Eichinger and Mike Lombardo discuss the benefits of *hardship assignments*, or job experiences where leaders are stretched by overcoming serious business mistakes, problem subordinates, bad bosses, or challenging business problems.[18] We agree that this type of demanding work experience is an essential part of any leadership development program. Such experiences enhance learning through people, work, and location. These work experiences may also focus attention on the desired leadership brand.

PEOPLE. The human environment of a work experience makes a tremendous difference to each of its participants. Surrounding the new leader with individuals who come from unfamiliar backgrounds and have different cultural priorities—the new boss, peers (team), customers, employees, suppliers, or investors—changes virtually every aspect of the job. Figuring out how to work smoothly with people who are different enables a leader to grow and succeed in a multicultural world. Moving an individual to the organization's leadership brand may come as the individual leader touches and works with people who are different. These experiences will temper biases and nurture learning through exposure to new ideas. Learning generally does not come from spending time with close friends, since the leader already knows what they think and do. But by spending time with new associates, the new leader may be exposed to new ideas and begin to accept new behaviors.

The human environment can also be enhanced through the use of coaches or mentors. Coaches offer personal and professional insights about how a leader's intentions are reflected by actual behavior. Few of us are immune to the tendency to judge ourselves by our intent, even though we judge others (and others judge us) by observed behavior.[19] So coaches make sure that leaders are more self-aware through feedback (highlighting past behavior) and feed-forward (discussing what to do to improve).[20] Coaches can also be guides to the extent to which a leader is demonstrating the desired leadership brand.

Investments in coaches and mentors should be made wisely. There are two types of coaching approaches. *Behavior* coaching occurs when the coach observes and helps shape a leader's actions to be congruent with the desired firm and leadership brand. *Results* coaching occurs when the coach helps the leader identify desired results (often from a customer point of view) and then focus attention on what decisions to make to deliver those results. Both types of coaching have the leader's interest in mind, offer alternatives and ideas outside the current leader's purview, and help the leader get clarity and insight on current goals and style. In addition, the coach offers specific suggestions for how to engage others to help reach the leader's goals and helps make informed *return on time* investments, so that the leader spends time and energy on the right things.[21] Mentors offer insights and guides for navigating the tortuous political and social realities within an organization.

WORK. Demanding work experiences have an element of sink-or-swim; the new leader's unfamiliar duties require swift learning. New tasks may come from working in a different function of the business (say, moving from marketing to manufacturing or from line to staff), a different business unit (moving from a product business to a service business), or a different business challenge (moving from a start-up business to a mature business). In each case, the leadership investment in job experience stretches the learning leader to acquire new insights and skills and expand the comfort zone. Work mobility increases an individual's sense of what the firm brand needs to be that connects with customers. By seeing how different parts of an organization work to serve customers, the leader begins to meld personal skills into a shared leadership brand.

A changing work assignment may be either permanent or temporary. Permanent assignment shifts are important because they take advantage of the S curves people often go through in mastering a new job. That is, they begin a new job with great energy and fresh eyes, and they go through a rapid learning curve to master the new complexities they face. But inevitably, it's not new anymore; people plateau and their energy and passion wane. At this point, many self-rejuvenate by creating a subsequent S curve that continues to challenge and move the individual forward, but others stagnate and end up in routines in their job, at which point it's time for something new.

Don Hambrick found that although time-in-job and productivity vary a great deal, a large percentage of leaders maximized their performance in a job in the three- to five-year range. Some companies move people too soon (every twelve or eighteen months), and so fail to give leaders time to really master the new job and live through the consequences of their choices. Others leave people in place for extended periods (seven to nine years, or more) and may find that the overall level of creativity on the job dwindles over time.[22]

Work experience may also come in the form of special projects or assignments. Dell Computer, for example, works to broaden work experience through a variety of temporary assignments or projects. It often assigns talented leaders to cross-functional projects that attempt to share ideas across organization boundaries, to critical strategic projects for a particular department or function, or to special corporate projects that expand thinking (such as customer segmentation or diversity). In addition, Dell encourages talented leaders to participate in networking, job exchange, coaching, and mentoring assignments.[23]

Teva Pharmaceutical Industries (which has grown dramatically through mergers from a $2 billion company to a $6 billion company) has drafted both a firm identity or brand statement and a subsequent leadership brand statement (see chapter 3). In the process, Teva's top team worked to identify work experiences that would help leaders acquire the knowledge and skills of the leadership brand. They also encouraged leaders to have conversations with their direct reports about ways to expand personal leadership talent. Here is the list of work experiences that Teva leaders could choose as ways to expand their abilities:

• Make a line-to-staff move, or vice versa.

• Coach or mentor someone else.

• Be assigned to profit-and-loss accountability early in a career and then move to successively larger assignments.

• Choose to take international assignments with different culture experience.

• Work in a turnaround situation.

• Be charged with a significant portion of a merger-and-acquisition deal.

• Do a cross-functional rotation.

• Participate in a customer internship.

• Work for a different boss.

• Participate on project teams that are add-ons to the present work assignment.

The add-on projects were all-important in terms of impact and visibility, making it an honor to be selected to be on the team. Some projects involved customer account management; others were start-up businesses, crisis response teams, or innovation teams. When these types of work experiences are open to leaders throughout the organization, and leaders understand how they help them develop the leadership brand, leadership brand roots itself deeper in the organization.

LOCATION. Conditions change as you move away from the environment where you grew up, and in this increasingly global world, few top leaders have the luxury of spending a whole career on home ground. Effectiveness requires learning to perform in multiple geographies.

Despite the leveling effect of technology, countries still have unique cultures and patterns.[24] Learning to live with religious differences and life views in Asia, the Middle East, Europe, Africa, and North America will orient a learning leader to be sensitive and responsive to multiculturalism. It also helps a leader recognize the leadership brand that permeates throughout the global company—not just the variations in their home state. We have a colleague who has worked for a global petrochemical company. He and his family have moved every four or five years and lived around the world, in Asia, Europe, Latin America, the Middle East, and North America. Now in his fifties, he has a strong "feel" for what the company represents in each of these diverse cultures. While the individual assignments were demanding and unique, they taught him some of the underlying and shared assumptions about the company and how it related to customers. As he internalized these lessons into his leadership actions and behavior, he came to embody the firm's leadership brand.

In our Western seminars, we often ask, "How many of you know when Christmas is?" And we get blank stares along with raised hands, as people wonder why we ask such a silly question—one that will obviously have a 100 percent positive response. Then we ask how many know when Hanukkah (or Passover) is. And fewer raise their hands. Then we ask how many know when Ramadan is this year—and we almost never see a hand raised. This makes the point that it is easy to be ethnocentric in life view, opening the way to a discussion about how what you don't know *can* hurt you. Work experiences in global locations broaden leaders' views so they can represent the firm's global leadership brand.

Life Experience: 20 Percent

In a connected, borderless world, learning occurs in multiple settings. Technology has removed boundaries between work and home; likewise, lessons learned from personal experience are increasingly adapted into organization leadership roles, and vice versa.

SOURCES OF USEFUL EXPERIENCE. In seminars, we ask participants, "What have you learned from your life experiences that has shaped how you behave at work?" The answers we get—often remarkably vivid—fall into four categories: service, relationships, challenges, and values.

Service. Service in organizations and areas outside work often helps leaders learn more-effective ways to behave while at work. These external experiences build not only a personal brand but the firm's leadership brand, because the individual leader can compare outside leadership opportunities with inside and can adapt what happens inside the company as a result of outside experiences. Outside service may involve formal and episodic assignments, such as coaching a children's sports team, teaching piano lessons, directing a play, or serving on a volunteer board. In these targeted service assignments, leaders put themselves in the path of learning by doing new things. And being away from work changes the political rules and allows leaders to experience new opportunities or experiment with different styles. Coaching a child's sports team helps leaders learn how to define trade-offs in setting clear goals (winning the league versus playing all players), develop talent (doing practices where people learn skills), and negotiate with demanding stakeholders (parents). These skills become very valuable at work, where managing scarce resources, engaging others, and navigating difficult relationships can go straight to the bottom line. Sometimes by leading a nonwork group, leaders can better recognize the leadership brand in their work setting.

Service also exposes leaders to multiple ways of managing and governing. Being involved in a volunteer organization helps leaders learn how to build an agenda able to capture the hearts and minds of volunteers without economic incentives. These days, the most talented employees are essentially volunteers even though they're getting paid, because they have so much choice about where they can work. Leaders who have learned to enlist volunteers outside work tend to be more effective at doing so at work as well. These leaders may also be more able to articulate what is unique about the leadership brand at work and they may be able to help others engage in it.

Service also connects leaders to a network of individuals who can be helpful in different settings. Joining professional associations (such as Rotary) may help leaders pick up new ideas and gain new information that hasn't been filtered through a company lens.

Relationships. To a great extent, leadership is about relationships and engaging others in a process of change. Leadership brand is translating customer expectations into employee and organization behaviors. To engage employees in new behaviors requires that leaders master the subtleties of change and influence. Often, these lessons come when leaders learn from non-work-related relationships. Raising children has multiple lessons for work. Toilet training a child teaches about setting clear goals, modeling behavior, reinforcing positive outcomes, and being resilient in the face of failure. Working with teenagers teaches most parents about managing differences, encouraging growth, helping others make informed choices and having consequences for those choices, and being patient and resilient in the face of rejection. Staying in relationships for many years (or sometimes even only for months) requires finding common bonds in the face of differing orientations and negotiating win-win solutions. And ending relationships requires learning about when and how to let go.

Relationships outside work can be wonderful forums for experiences at work. Those who treat their children, friends, and associates with respect are likely to treat their employees, customers, and peers with respect. It is difficult to maintain a different relationship orientation at work from the one you use at home, and vice versa. To translate customer expectations to employee behaviors, leaders need to learn to influence with grace, and nonwork experiences can help leaders develop the skills to help make this happen.

Challenges. Most learning occurs from doing hard things. Nonwork experiences are often emotionally, socially, and personally challenging. They encourage learning by having to deal with difficult trials. People we have asked about what nonwork experiences helped them deal with leadership challenges at work have given us many inspiring answers, including these:

- I lost my sister unexpectedly. She was my best friend. It hurt and struck me to the core. I had to reorient myself and my life. I learned at work to be more caring and sensitive to the people issues that I have to deal with as a leader.

- My son was born with a number of physical deformities. He has had to undergo more than forty surgeries in his young life to deal with them. I cringe and struggle with him each time. When I am confronted at work with demanding challenges, I tell myself nothing can be as difficult as what my son is dealing with. And I can move on and get through it.

- I found out that I had cancer. I have been told that it is in remission but that it may return anytime. I realize at work that each day matters, and that I need to be clear about what I am accomplishing, and that I am spending my time and energy on important things. I also found out that relationships at work mean more than just getting a job done. Some people at work become personal friends more than professional colleagues. I feel I have someone to turn to for help.

Illness, loss, and personal challenges are inevitable parts of life. Learning outside work to deal with these tragedies increases resilience at work. When a customer cancels an account, an employee threatens to quit in a huff, or a product has defects, the trouble is less daunting to those who have learned to rise above repeated challenges outside work. External experiences shape internal attitudes and approaches to work. Each of these outside experiences may help in fostering and embedding a leadership brand.

Values. A leadership brand at work should be consistent with the values of the leader outside work. How leaders spend their spare time, how they use their vacation time, how they treat life's innumerable challenges, how they form their moral code, and how they make judgments about what is right or wrong in their lives, all delineate a set of principles for values. Leaders who are self-aware of their values outside work are more likely to be able to bring them inside work as well. This does not mean imposing values on others, but it means acting out of a strong personal code that grounds decisions. Having this personal insight helps the leader know whether the firm's requisite leadership brand is right for him (or not). Ensuring that the firm's leadership brand is congruent with a personal brand helps both endure.

USING OUTSIDE EXPERIENCE. Leaders may learn from their non-work experiences in a number of ways. A challenge is to transfer this learning from outside work into the work. This may be done in a number of ways.

First, leaders hone their predispositions in nonwork settings. A leader's personal predisposition toward learning, relationship building, nurturing others, and accomplishing tasks may show up in off-work activities. Since about 50 percent of leadership traits are inbred, discerning which prospective leaders are more or less predisposed to the attributes required for the leadership brand can save enormous resources. One of the most interesting interview questions for new hires is, "What do you do in your spare time?" This question, if answered honestly, provides insight into a prospective employee's predispositions. Does the person engage in activities that encourage learning and growth? Do they stay intellectually curious by reading, observing others, and trying to improve? Or do they atrophy by repeating the same activities over and over? Investments in targeted selection, leadership brand–based interviews, and other prescreening diagnostics that rely on off-work data to predict on-work actions can be helpful.

Second, organizations can encourage leaders to participate actively in nonwork activities, either informally or by offering time off for life-expanding experiences. When Dave Ulrich asked his dean about taking three years off to do church service, the dean responded, "We as a school are proud of you and completely support you." A formal policy like this one encourages faculty to be involved in community and political affairs, which broadens their horizons and brings fresh, new ideas into the work setting. Work sabbaticals—where valuable employees are encouraged to take a period of time out to have unique and different experiences—are an increasing part of the modern career path. Often, these experiences are service based, such as volunteering for a school, but they may also be task or location based, involving extended visits to a new country.

Encouraging nonwork experiences may be done more or less informally through newsletters, articles in the company paper, luncheons to share experiences, reading clubs at work, or casual conversations where leaders express interest in personal lives and what employees are learning. It can also be formalized by organizing specific sessions where people gather to share what they are learning outside work with one another. For example, Herman Miller has an eclectic board, with members who have great experience in both their professional and their personal interests. At board meetings, members of the board are often invited to spend forty-five minutes to an hour sharing what they are learning about the world. One member shared his work on the evolution of design and how designs have changed in architecture and other settings. Another shared his experience of visiting religious leaders in Africa to work on hunger and overcoming poverty. Another shared his experience of working with hospitals to ensure better health care. Even though none of these experiences were directly related to the work of furniture design and production, they all affected how people on the board and in the company thought about work. By modeling such behavior at a board level, Herman Miller encourages similar behavior on the part of leaders throughout the company. Teams of Herman Miller employees have used personal vacation time to contribute to humanitarian aid causes. When they return, they are encouraged to share their experiences as a way to broaden all employees.

Succession Planning and Leadership Brand

As we see it, an integrated approach to leadership investment would involve 30 percent training experiences, 50 percent work experiences, and 20 percent life experiences. For these three categories to ensure a leadership brand, however, they need to be integrated—and succession planning (or talent management) provides the unifying thread. While the details may differ, generally in succession planning, executives start with the business strategy and then articulate the desired firm leadership brand. With this in mind, they then do quarterly individual talent reviews where they build individual development plans that assess training, work, and life experiences for everyone on the leadership bench. When executives define firm and leadership brand and review the depth of leaders throughout the company against those standards, leadership is more than the person; it is the process, and it is focused not only inside but outside the organization, the essence of brand.

To succeed, succession planning systems need high-level sponsorship—the ongoing interest and support of line managers who spend personal time reviewing individuals for key jobs. This time can be focused on open jobs, where the business leader reviews the slate of candidates for each open position. Or the time can be focused on talent reviews, where the leader reviews the business context and strategy and then considers the next generation of leaders and the extent to which they might respond to these conditions. Reviewing slates focuses on the individual job and the individual; reviewing business conditions and leadership brand focuses on the general cadre or the leadership bench. Regular and periodic review of talent (say, once a quarter or twice a year) ensures continuity of succession planning.

In addition, succession planning systems need to display the following characteristics:[25]

- Work from a shared set of expectations about what makes an effective leadership. This set of standards is drawn from the statement of leadership (see chapter 3) and focuses on specific attributes and results that are linked to customer outcomes.

- Use a systematic process to collect information on potential leaders (see chapter 4). The data process may be supported by computer software (such as PeopleSoft, HRCharter, Lotus Notes, Pilat, or ExecuTRACK) or some other monitoring system.

- Acknowledge flexibility of leadership development based on the needs of the individual. Individual development plans start with individual expectations and opportunities, not some abstract endpoint. This means asking individuals what they want in their personal development. At times leaders may have personal commitments (e.g., children in school, dual-career interests, or other family commitments) that preclude them from taking an assignment. This should not mean that they are forever limited in their opportunities.

- Ensure that individual leaders know how they are doing against a set of leadership brand expectations. This feedback is drawn from observations from multiple sources (boss, peers, subordinates, customers, or clients) and allows the leader to see how to improve for the future.

- Treat individuals differently. Some individuals and some jobs are more critical to the creation of wealth in an organization than others. These positions and these individuals should receive disproportionate management attention.

- Use a variety of experiences to develop leaders. Learning comes from a mix of training, job, and nonwork experiences. These are woven together into a personalized development agenda for each leader, but collectively these investments create the leadership brand as much as the individual leaders.

- Monitor both the quality of candidates who are reviewed through the succession planning system and the impact of the leadership investments.[26]

Succession planning is a time-consuming activity that demands the attention of senior executives. In our experience, the results are worth the investment of time and effort. When succession planning becomes an ongoing process, it continues to improve (and it gets easier when the results begin to show). Without it, leadership brand is a nice concept that may or may not take hold.

Conclusion

Developing leaders who express a shared leadership brand involves a number of novel assumptions about what makes for effective leadership development. Ideally, it involves a substantial amount of specific training, backed up by tailored work experience and non-work-related experience that builds the requisite competencies.

For training, the essence of both the organization's content choices and its process choices is that investments in leadership programs should further the leadership brand. When the content of what is taught is consistent with the brand and when the process by which material is taught is also consistent with the brand, leaders who attend training are more than tourists—they absorb the purposes and premises of the brand and thus become citizens of the new country even if they don't live there full-time.

For work experience, leadership investments pay off especially well when they are couched in terms of carrying out an established leadership brand. It remains true that past work experiences are the single best predictors of future work outcomes. From work experiences, leaders learn firsthand who they are, what they need to do to improve, and how they can improve. The essence of the work experience approach to leadership investment is to encourage leaders to continue to do hard things—to keep dealing with unfamiliar people, tasks, or locations. Leaders who constantly find intellectual, emotional, and social challenges grow and learn, while those who fall prey to routines end up in ruts, doing much the same work over and over again. A firm that deliberately builds its leadership bench makes sure that ten years' experience is really worth ten years—not one year repeated ten times over.

But leadership development doesn't stop with training and focused work experience. Increasingly, it crosses boundaries as people work at home, at work, and in transit. Likewise, lessons learned outside work can increasingly be adapted to improve performance while at work. Ultimately, employees learn and do what leaders model. When leaders are publicly visible in pursuing non-work-related experiences, employees will be willing to do likewise. Even when leaders simply talk about their personal experiences with family, with hobbies, or with community service, it opens doors to enhanced learning and performance throughout the workforce.

Succession planning both unifies leadership development efforts and benefits greatly from them. When the leadership cadre shares a consistent leadership brand, a firm can keep the pipeline full and fill most leadership positions with clear in-house choices that know and do the leadership brand.

6

Measuring Return on
Leadership Brand

EVERYONE KNOWS THE MAXIM that we get what we inspect, not what we expect. But to get the right things requires that we learn how to track and measure what we need to improve. We don't lose weight without weighing; we have never had a student learn much who audited a class without the requirements of grades; and in building a leadership brand, we need to measure what we want to accomplish. We often fall prey to the trap of measuring what is easy, not what is right. Join us now in a case in point:

How Do You Know?

Jordan Pettinger, vice president of leadership development for a rapidly growing global technology company, smiled as she sat down to meet with Bill Zariah, the CEO. She was ready for anything he might throw at her and proud that the first year of the training program she had introduced had received such positive feedback from participants.

After a few minutes of preliminary conversation, Zariah asked, "So how much have we spent on that leadership initiative?"

"Between $21 million and $24 million," Pettinger replied instantly. She had spent a long time coming up with this answer, which was not as easy as she thought it might be. Besides the direct costs of training, she'd needed to count indirect costs, some of which had to be estimated and proportioned, but she felt confident in her estimate.

Zariah paused for a minute and then asked thoughtfully, "And what are the results?"

Pettinger was ready for this as well: "We have put 16,237 supervisors, managers, and executives through forty hours of training, with an average rating of 4.3 on a 5-point scale. And more than 60 percent say they are much better equipped to deal with the competitive challenges we face. We have also gotten great follow-up scores on our competency model. I know you'll also be pleased to hear that we've gotten almost a hundred e-mails from participants thanking us for running this training, including two from your senior vice presidents. It's been very gratifying. Not bad for the first year."

"That's great, but are we *better?*" asked the CEO—with unnecessary force, it seemed to Pettinger.

"What do you mean?" she asked, feeling a little twinge of terror.

"I mean, as a result of spending all this money, do we have better leadership? Are our supervisors, managers, and executives better equipped to deliver the right results next year?"

"I think so, but it's hard to make a direct correlation between next year's results and this year's leadership investments. This is a long-term investment. You have to keep investing until you reach a tipping point with leadership." Pettinger knew she was wandering. "I wish you had told me that these were your expectations up front so I could have prepared differently," she added.

"Why did you think we were investing in leadership?" Zariah asked. He thought the price tag was a lot of money to have poured into something that seemed so amorphous and unlikely to deliver tangible results, but he did not know how to articulate this to Pettinger in a way that would not kill her spirit completely. Instead, he asked her to prepare next year's training budget, already clear in his mind that he should make significant cuts.

Pettinger's dilemma with her boss is far from unique. Senior executives continue to sponsor investments in leadership without any clarity about the impact of their investment. When *BusinessWeek* published its annual survey of executive education, 134 companies from twenty nations reported enrolling more than twenty-one thousand employees in leadership programs, at a cost of $210 million. That's a significant investment in an activity that may or may not produce better leaders or managers.

A recent survey by Bersin & Associates (answered by three thousand leaders and associates in 117 organizations) reported that 63 percent plan to increase spending on leadership development programs despite the fact that 75 percent of HR executives surveyed fail to give such programs a high quality rating.[1] In a subset of the study, twelve hundred respondents from a cross section of company sizes and industries came up with a number of troubling points, as indicated in figure 6-1.

An Accenture study of senior executive views of training a couple of years ago makes the same point and defines the dilemma clearly. As figure 6-1 shows, a vast gulf separates what executives see as the important results of training and the actual results they think training will achieve.

For example, 77 percent believe that training priorities must be aligned with the business, but only 11 percent are satisfied that alignment is current and real. And 72 percent believe workforce productivity improvement is an essential result of training, while only 9 percent believe it has real productivity impact.

No wonder Bill Zariah asked his question: without specific data, he could only conclude that the leadership training he had funded produced good feelings and perhaps renewed confidence. He couldn't say

FIGURE 6-1

Disappointment with training programs

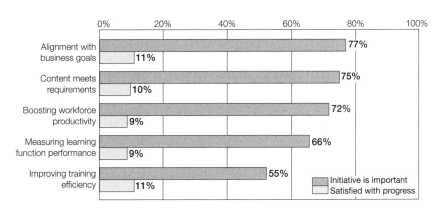

Source: Adapted from Accenture, "The Quest for Exceptional Workforce Performance," white paper, May 2003.

that it would actually drive business performance. Or yield better competitive results on the measures he trusted as a CEO—market valuation, profitability, cash flow, cost to produce, and working capital ratios. Clearly, he had reason to be skeptical. After all, had he just bought each of the participants a good book on leadership and given them a Friday off to read it, would he have gotten the same general reaction?

Two Approaches to Measurement

Over the past fifteen years, the measurement of leadership effectiveness has been characterized by two divergent approaches. One is the competency approach; the other looks for a concrete return on the training investment.

The Competency Approach

According to this school of thought, leadership is defined as a set of attributes or competencies, based on the assumption that good leaders share a particular set of characteristics. "If we build competencies," those who use this approach assume, "results will follow." The intent of this type of leadership development is to increase the quality and frequency of behavior in targeted areas, producing leaders who are better listeners, who engage their employees more effectively, who build stronger teams, and the like. This, in turn, should drive performance.

Competency models are, of course, in broad use in commercial organizations, and they have also been extensively applied in the nonprofit world. For example, in 2002 the State of New York issued a "Report of the Competencies Working Group" that outlined a total of forty-six leadership competencies from which state departments and agencies could choose in developing specific competency models for their organizations. The listed competencies ranged from the very practical "accountability" and "fiscal management" to the more ethereal "emotional intelligence" and "visioning."[2]

What's the problem with competency models? Fundamentally, on their own they are an indirect and therefore problematic approach to the measurement of leadership. To return to the New York State example, visioning may well be a competency many leaders display, but the ability to vision—look out into the future—is not, in itself, evidence of leadership results. How many capable people are able to see the possibilities offered by the future—but not able or willing to take the actions (or the risks) that produce real results? More important, the further out you look, the more difficult it is to speak the same language when it comes to competence. Is visioning the ability to anticipate future trends or to know what to do with them?

In addition, competency models often identify a set of generic traits—vision, direction, energy, and so on—and then they try to find and build next-generation leaders that fit the model. The problem with this practice is that it's a cookie-cutter approach. Consider what happened when we held a workshop for nine name-brand companies. We asked the representatives from each company to send us their leadership competency models, which listed the set of unique characteristics that they sought in their leaders ("has a strong vision," "builds teamwork," "has energy," "demonstrates emotional intelligence," and so on). We then deleted the names of the companies from each model. During the workshop, we asked the representatives to pick out their own. Few of the participants were able to do so; there was little difference between the models of a telecommunications company, a consumer products company, a financial services company, and an aerospace company. The conclusion was obvious: vanilla competency models generate vanilla leadership. And the paradox was clear: by focusing on the desirable traits of individual leaders, the firms ended up creating generic models.

These liabilities of competency models are the essence of Jordan Pettinger's problem. She is unable to respond to her CEO's fundamental question about impact because her training program focuses primarily on competencies that may or may not differentiate performance and that often end up as generic, not branded competencies. As a result, her impact assessment has to focus on activity (how many people received what training), on perceived impact (reports of feeling greater confidence or of being better equipped to handle business challenges), and on the measurement of competencies (testing for abstracts such as business acumen). We often measure what is easy (how many people attended a training program) rather than what is right (how a business met customer expectations as a result of the leadership actions).

Bill Zariah comes from a very different vantage point. He cares about results that can be assessed objectively, and wonders whether this large investment has created "real" value—some measurable difference for his company. For Pettinger, the simple choice was to run the training or not. For Zariah, the more than $20 million taken up by leadership training represented an opportunity cost: money he could not invest in a new incentive compensation program that he believed would drive sales or in additional advertising in his two toughest markets.

Pettinger cannot really answer the question about impact of leadership development, much less leadership brand and her investments in it, unless she more fully understands her choices about measuring impact and their implications. We believe that she—and her real-world cohorts—should be measuring the impact both of leaders and of investments in leadership like her training program. Using the right measures, someone in Pettinger's shoes could have a much better conversation with the CEO paying the bills.

Concrete Return: The Rival Approach

Before she can have a better conversation with her CEO, Pettinger needs to look at measures that constitute a targeted ROI—in the context of this book, call it *return on leadership brand*. One or two well-chosen measures that fit in each of the quadrants in figure 6-2 will demonstrate the value of leadership development investments in terms the CEO will understand.

FIGURE 6-2

Return on leadership brand: Array of measures

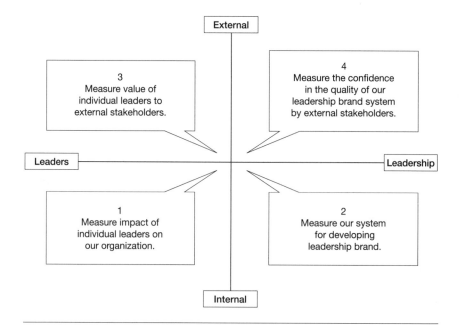

The matrix offered in figure 6-2 (and introduced in chapter 1) looks at leadership brand from the interaction of two dimensions. The first focuses on perspective—that is, who's measuring—and reflects the differing views of internal and external stakeholders. The second focuses on purpose, the more specific goals of developing individual talent (leaders) and of building an organizational system for talent development (leadership). These dimensions form quadrants that create an array of measurement options:

Quadrant 1: Impact of individual leaders on their own organization (called competent leaders)

Quadrant 2: Efficacy of the whole leadership brand system (called leadership capability)

Quadrant 3: Value of individual leaders to external stakeholders (called celebrity leaders)

Quadrant 4: Confidence of external stakeholders in the leadership brand (called leadership brand)

A multitude of other books have focused on how to measure quadrants 1 and 3, so we will focus on measuring leadership capability and leadership brand—quadrants 2 and 4.

Measurement in Practice

Depending on the scope of the leadership initiative (corporatewide, business unit, and geographic region), quadrants 2 and 4 can be measured successfully. What is important is that leadership brand measures are congruent with the firm brand and strategies of the company (see chapter 3).

Measuring Quadrant 2: System for Developing Leadership Brand

In *Evaluating Training Programs*, Donald Kirkpatrick outlines an approach that forms the basis for most of the attempts to measure the overall impact we have observed.[3] He describes four dimensions of impact:

- *Attitude:* Did participants enjoy the leadership development experience?

- *Knowledge:* Did the participants learn something from the leadership development experience?

- *Behavior:* Did participants change behavior as a result of the leadership experience?

- *Results:* Did the participants apply the learning in a way that produced a tangible return on investment?

On its own, this framework can simply look at aspects of quadrant 1—the impact on individual participants. However, it is easily adapted to quadrant 2—measurement of leadership brand, as shown in assessment 6-1.

Of all the measures that could be done in quadrant 2, we recommend focusing on three critical areas:

- Improvements in the case for investing in leadership brand

- Improvements in leadership bench strength

- Impact on key talent retention

IMPROVEMENTS IN THE CASE FOR INVESTING IN LEADERSHIP BRAND. Returning to Jordan Pettinger, it appears unlikely that she was working from a specific, detailed business case before calling for investment in leadership brand in her first year on the job. Had she built a clear case—or if she went back and built one now—she would be far more able to talk to Bill Zariah in terms he understands and cares about: how his leadership investments enhance strategy execution, business profitability, and business value.

In chapter 2, we described two sources for the case for change: one based on achieving strategy and growth objectives and the other built on value drivers. In table 6-1, we add to the charts introduced in chapter 2 and propose some ideas for measurement.

IMPROVEMENTS IN LEADERSHIP BENCH STRENGTH. Quadrant 2 measures the organization's ability to build a leadership pipeline that produces current and future leaders at every level and stage (see chapter 4) who are branded to the company and who can deliver the right results the right way. This is especially important for the critical jobs discussed in chapter 2: the ones that must be accomplished for the business to achieve its strategic intent and often come under pressure during periods of high growth. Senior executive jobs are also typically considered critical.

ASSESSMENT 6-1

Measuring the system for developing leadership brand

	Low	High
1. Attitude—To what extent is there:		
• Agreement on our leadership brand at every level of leadership?	1 2 3 4 5	
• A belief that our leadership brand is a source of advantage?	1 2 3 4 5	
2. Knowledge—To what extent is there:		
• Clarity about what our leadership brand stands for and why it is important?	1 2 3 4 5	
• A clear expectation that each leader should develop toward living the leadership brand?	1 2 3 4 5	
3. Behavior—To what extent do:		
• Leaders know which behaviors are consistent with the leadership brand standards?	1 2 3 4 5	
• Leaders behave according to these brand standards?	1 2 3 4 5	
4. Results—To what extent do:		
• Our leaders deliver on what we promise in the case for change?	1 2 3 4 5	
• Our leaders deliver on our statement of leadership brand?	1 2 3 4 5	
• We have better leaders because of our leadership brand processes?	1 2 3 4 5	
• We retain better talent because of our investments in leadership brand?	1 2 3 4 5	
Total		

Key:

If your score is 45–50: You probably have a strong leadership brand, let your investors know.
If your score is 35–44: You are well on your way to leadership brand; identify where you score lower and focus on that area.
If your score is 25–34: You are struggling in your leadership brand; find one area to improve and start there.
Under 25: Be careful. Your future is in some trouble because your leadership brand is not what it should be. Work on building the case for change.

A simple but important measure is the leadership bench strength index. For the critical leadership jobs in the business, what is the backup confidence ratio? The answer should be at least 1.0—and higher is better. A 1.0 ratio means having one backup in place for each critical job. This includes the job of CEO and the other critical leadership positions.

The fact that so many CEOs come from a few feeder companies is a statement about the size of the improvement opportunity for most companies. However, the backup ratio for the CEO is not enough. Other critical leadership positions can have a huge impact on reinvestable

TABLE 6-1

Measuring case for leadership investments: Strategy and growth

Challenge	Case for leadership because of strategy and growth	Ideas for measurement
1. Workforce planning	We have to develop enough leaders who will help us grow in the future; growth won't happen without high-quality leadership. Leadership matters because having enough leaders ready to grow the business the right way is a business necessity.	• Ratio of start-up successes to failures • Extent to which leaders are in place when needed for growth • Leadership bench strength index: ratio of backups prepared for critical and top jobs
2. Right results the right way	We have to have leaders who demonstrate the values we believe (the firm brand). Leadership matters because leaders' actions demonstrate what really matters most.	• Strategic goals achieved each quarter and each year • Changes in employee commitment scores • Changes in customer loyalty scores • Continuity of investors
3. Strategy shifts	As we move from strategy A to B, we need to evolve leaders who can deliver on the new strategy. Leadership matters because it helps make strategy happen.	• Percentage of outside leaders needed at each level of pipeline during strategic shift over two years • Percentage of achievement of new strategic goals
4. Geography	As we move to new parts of the world, we need leaders who have competencies to adapt to conditions there. Leadership matters because effective leaders can adapt to local conditions and have competencies to transfer knowledge from one area to another.	• Percentage of executive team with experience in geographies that are important to us in next five years • Percentage increase of leaders in targeted geographic areas rather than from traditional internal sources
5. Mix of M&A and organic growth	Future leaders must have the competencies to successfully deliver on both acquisitions and organic growth. Leadership matters because it ensures successful merger integration as well as profitable organic growth.	• Percentage of leaders with solid M&A experience • Percentage of leaders with track record of solid organic growth experience • Length of time to return cost of capital for M&A
6. Critical jobs	Certain critical leadership jobs will be put under tremendous stress during growth. Leadership matters because if the leaders in these jobs are not successful, the strategy cannot be implemented regardless of strengths elsewhere.	• Early, accurate identification of specific critical jobs • Early investments in the development of people to fill these jobs

profits for strategic growth. Recently we worked with a fast-growing company that was an outsource manufacturer to many other large firms. It had focused most of its efforts from a hierarchical perspective on the replacements to the most senior managers and had largely ignored the other critical leadership positions. In this case, its ability to scale geographically and maintain operations excellence was an absolute key to successful growth. After looking at the results from the business case for investment in leadership, the company realized it needed to also focus on the leadership positions related to ensuring operational excellence.

IMPACT ON KEY TALENT RETENTION. One of the outcomes of creating leadership brand is the ability to attract and retain key talent. Great talent attracts great talent. Great talent also delivers better results—both tangible and intangible. This includes higher financial returns as well as higher customer satisfaction, investor confidence, and employee engagement. The talent retention index consists of two parts: *the value of retention of key talent* and *the cost of replacing key talent.*

The strategic and operational value of retaining key talent is obvious—study after study cites the difficulty of replacing exceptionally talented individuals.[4] Of course, General DeGaulle's trenchant observation was correct: "The graveyards are full of irreplaceable people!" Nonetheless, although a managing director of a major investment bank or a top leader of software development may not be genuinely irreplaceable, it takes years to grow one who really fits the organization's needs. Our colleague Jon Younger, formerly the chief learning officer of National City Corporation, uses a talent retention index that looks at the value of talent retention but adds to it the cost of replacement. For example, he quotes a study done some years ago by Bell Northern Research (BNR), the R&D division of Nortel, which estimated the tangible financial costs of replacing a junior software engineer who left after two years on the job. That calculation was as follows:

Time to full functionality (24 months of salary):	$120,000
Benefits (24 months):	$40,000
Training costs:	$20,000
Management time (coaching):	$10,000
Recruiting costs:	$5,000
Total:	$195,000

The BNR calculation was attempting to be as thorough and realistic as possible in assessing the cost of losing a talented engineer. That calculation included both the direct costs—salary, benefits, training—and softer but no less real costs, such as the manager's time. That was a small portion of the cost of replacing this valuable but junior employee, but as individuals increase in responsibility, and particularly as they move into managerial roles that require insight and decision making based on experience in the function and the company, less tangible costs like this become increasingly meaningful—and high. A case in point:

One Moderate Step for an Officer, One Huge Loss for an Organization

When Ray McGuire left Morgan Stanley in 2005 to join Citigroup, the brokerage firm lost much more than "another" senior investment banker. It lost one of its most productive revenue generators, someone who had helped it capture a top ranking in M&A deals and who had been the senior M&A banker for companies such as General Electric and Unilever Group. It also lost its most senior African American executive—an important talent magnet in attracting exceptional young black men and women.

The loss to Morgan Stanley was far more than the developmental costs of training a new managing director: tens and perhaps hundreds of millions of dollars in lost revenue and diminished prestige, plus the increased ability of Citigroup to compete against Morgan Stanley in the future, and the additional future value of young people who would follow McGuire to his new firm instead of joining Morgan Stanley, as they would have had he stayed there.

The nature of investment banks and brokerages, and McGuire's unique position in his industry, make his experience an extreme example of the importance of talent retention. While extreme, it makes the point that is valid even in more mundane circumstances. While individuals are never truly irreplaceable, the cost of replacement can be considerable and severe, particularly in the case of critical jobs and the critical people who fill them.

Measuring Quadrant 4: Confidence of External Stakeholders About the Leadership Brand System

Quadrant 4 is where officers like Jordan Pettinger really capture their CEOs' interest and attention. Quadrant 4 measures are aimed at measuring the value that leadership investments build in the outside world: part of what we call the return on intangibles (the new ROI).

INTANGIBLE VALUE. The meaning of leadership brand within the context of financial performance implies that as an organization develops a distinctive leadership brand, the value will show up in investors' perceived value of that firm's earnings (or stock price). That is, the company's stock price is enhanced by association with a leadership brand regarded as especially valuable. In this context, the company's leadership brand is viewed as having equity or financial value, even though it is an intangible asset, similar to product brands, R&D, and other intangible assets.

Intangibles represent the confidence that internal and external stakeholders have about the future of the business. Companies with strong leadership brands have high intangible value because stakeholders have high confidence in the ability of leaders to deliver future results. We used the Kirkpatrick framework in quadrant 2 to describe four aspects of the impact that training individual leaders can have on the organization's leadership brand. Quadrant 4 adds a fifth level to the Kirkpatrick framework: the impact of intangibles. Table 6-2 expands on this perspective, adding consideration of leadership brand to Kirkpatrick's framework, along with a fifth dimension for intangibles.

Table 6-3 outlines how to measure leadership investments' return on intangible value for key stakeholders.

When contemplating the power of intangibles such as leadership brand, leaders must figure out what they can and should do to create intangible value and to make intangibles tangible. This challenge confronts leaders in publicly traded and privately held firms, at the top and throughout the organization, and in line and staff roles. Wherever they are, leaders have the responsibility to build and protect intangible value. This is an area we've discussed in more detail in earlier work, but a summary is necessary here to put the measurement suggestions in context.[5]

In essence, we see a pattern in how leaders successfully increase their organizations' intangible value: the architecture for intangibles (see table 6-4).[6]

TABLE 6-2

Measuring leaders and leadership

Dimensions of measurement	Individual leaders	Investments in leadership brand
1. Attitude	Perceptions of: • Agreement on leadership brand • Leadership brand as a source of advantage	To what extent have investments in training, job, and life experiences helped build brand?
2. Knowledge	Clarity about what the leadership brand is and expectations for living it	To what extent has the leadership brand been communicated to stakeholders?
3. Behavior	To what extent do leaders behave according to the brand standards?	To what extent are the leadership investments aligned with building the brand? Are leaders' actions consistent with the brand?
4. Results	Do our leaders deliver on what we promised in the case for change and in the declaration of leadership?	To what extent are leadership investments focused on results?
5. Intangibles	To what extent do our investors have confidence in our quality of leadership as demonstrated in higher P/E multiples?	To what extent would investors be pleased with the leadership investments we make. Are they involved? Are the investments focused on the right issues?

Level 1—Trust: Keep Your Promises; Deliver Consistent and Predictable Results. For a publicly traded company, reliable quarterly earnings forecasts are the table stakes for trust in the marketplace; consistency and predictability are what give your company credibility with investors. And for any company, managing expectations and making and keeping promises for service, quality, and delivery ensures credibility with customers, while keeping explicit and implied promises to the workforce builds employee loyalty and morale. Leaders who make and keep promises build credibility, confidence, and conviction.

To address this most basic level of action in quadrant 4, measure the extent to which promises made were kept in the last year. For example, Jordan Pettinger could tell Bill Zariah, "Well, the 2,130 executives who took part in the program have reported completing 67 percent of the goals they established for the year, while those who have yet to take part completed only 40 percent. The program is helping our leaders learn to do what they promise."

TABLE 6-3

Measuring case for leadership investments: The role of leadership quality

Stakeholder	Case for leadership value	Ideas for measurement
Investors	A strong leadership brand increases investor confidence about the future in terms of delivering results and shows up in investor intangibles. Leadership matters because it builds market value.	• Price-to-earnings ratio compared with other companies' in the same industry—over time, not at any one point in time • "Intangibles audit" to measure investor confidence in leadership priorities and capabilities
Customers	As customer needs and tastes change, leadership must adapt to continue to ensure sustainable value propositions that add value. Leadership matters because it increases customer share.	• Increase or decrease in sales, profitability, share of target customers • Measures of customer commitment of target customers (attitude of customers and customer share) • "Intangibles audit" to measure target customer confidence in leadership priorities and capabilities
Employees	Employee attitude is linked to customer retention and satisfaction. Leadership brand ensures ongoing value created for customers by building employee commitment and engagement. Leadership matters because it affects employee competence and commitment.	• Ongoing measurement of employee commitment • Correlating employee commitment and customer retention from survey data

TABLE 6-4

Architecture for intangibles

Level	Area of focus	Leadership brand action potential
4	*Uniqueness*: Improve organization capabilities; build value through people and organization.	Develop shared mind-set, talent, collaboration, speed, accountability, learning, and leadership throughout the organization.
3	*Execution*: Invest in core competencies; put your money where your strategy is.	Provide concrete support for intangibles in R&D, technology, sales and marketing, logistics, and manufacturing.
2	*Clarity*: Articulate a compelling strategy; envision the future.	Encourage belief in and support for customer intimacy, product innovation, and geographic expansion.
1	*Trust*: Keep your promises; deliver consistent and predictable results.	Build and defend a reputation among external and internal stakeholders for doing what you say you will do.

Level 2—Clarity: Articulate a Compelling Strategy; Envision the Future. A compelling vision excites and energizes. Leaders who envision growth build enthusiasm. But they must also define the path the organization will take to achieve that growth, or the vision comes across as empty rhetoric and builds cynicism instead of confidence.

For this level, Pettinger could report along these lines: "As always, this year our employee attitude survey asked about the extent to which people felt confidence in the company's direction. And our score went from 4.0 to 4.4 out of 5, a 10 percent increase. This kind of high and climbing confidence among our employees will help build trust among our investors when you share the information with them."

Level 3—Execution: Invest in Core Competencies; Put Your Money Where Your Strategy Is. Any gap between the proclaimed direction of future growth and the allocation of money, time, and attention generates skepticism about the intent to deliver on the promised growth. For example, if a leader articulates a platform of growth through product innovation, then investors and employees expect to see higher-than-industry-average levels of investment in R&D and marketing. Leaders invest in core competencies to increase the probability of strategic success. These core competencies represent both knowledge and performance in the "guts" of the business and knowing how the business creates value.

What could Pettinger do with this? Her report on how the company invests in core competency areas compared with the rest of the industry is good. What she needs to add is something about the results of those investments; for example, an R&D investment should lead to new products introduced, new patents, or revenues from new products, and marketing could be tracked by customer share or market share. By the same token, leadership development investments should lead to higher quality of leadership as perceived by internal and external stakeholders.

Level 4—Uniqueness: Improve Organization Capabilities; Build Value Through People and Organization. Organization capabilities are the ways an organization applies people and processes to the tasks of competition. These capabilities essentially become the organization's identity. They define what it is good at doing and, in the end, what it is. Here are six of the most basic capabilities an organization needs to emphasize:

- *Talent:* We are good at attracting, motivating, and retaining competent and committed people.

- *Speed:* We are good at making important changes happen fast.

- *Shared mind-set:* We are good at ensuring that customers and employees have positive images of and experiences with our organization.

- *Accountability:* We are good at the disciplines that result in high performance.

- *Collaboration:* We are good at working across boundaries to ensure both efficiency and leverage.

- *Learning:* We are good at generating and generalizing ideas with impact.

Of the four levels of intangible value, organization capabilities are the most difficult for a competitor to duplicate. They delight customers, they engage employees, they establish reputations among investors, and they provide long-term sustainable value.

Pettinger needs to sit down with Zariah and ask him to choose the two capabilities that would most enable his business strategy over the next year to eighteen months, use the intangibles audit with the firm's executive team, or derive the critical organization capabilities from the firm's strategy statement. Zariah will probably start out wanting all of them, but Pettinger must hold the line, explaining that world-class performance in two capabilities would be both a tremendous achievement and a tremendous amount of work—something to be achieved only with real focus. Then she can establish baseline measures for the critical capabilities, focus training around those capabilities, and measure the contribution of the leadership investments as they improve measures of the critical capabilities.

THE INTANGIBLES AUDIT. Pettinger can help Zariah choose the winning capabilities by taking an independent route to measure each level of the architecture for intangibles—or she could do what we call an *intangibles audit.*[7] An intangibles audit allows leaders to identify which factors in the architecture for intangibles will have the greatest impact on future success, just as a financial audit allows them to monitor cash flow—and it's just as important. By assessing which intangibles are most important given the organization's strategy, measuring how well important intangibles are being defined and delivered, and offering an action plan for improving intangibles, an intangibles audit serves leaders at all levels of the organization: it helps the board of directors assess over-all firm capability, and it helps senior leadership create strategy, mid-level managers execute strategy, and frontline leaders make things happen.

No two audits will look exactly the same, but our experience has shown us that there are some right ways to approach the process and some wrong ways. Following are a few points that people in Pettinger's shoes can recommend to the CEO.

Get Focused. It's better to excel at a few targeted areas than to diffuse leadership energy over many. We always ask executive teams what they think the audit will tell them before they see the results. In many cases, they tell us that they are confident they will have positive scores in the first three levels (keeping promises, articulating clear strategy, and en-abling core competencies). Sometimes they are right, but more often than not, we find that customers or investors tell them they are not clear about the strategy or how they are investing for superior technical competencies.

Leaders should choose no more than two or three issues that will re-quire their time and attention; they should aim to make at least two world class. This means prioritizing and identifying which areas will have the most impact and will be easiest to implement. One company may choose to focus on capabilities of talent, leadership, and speed; an-other on ensuring that its strategy is well understood by all stakeholders.

The remaining issues identified in the audit should aim for perfor-mance at levels comparable to those of other organizations in the same industry. Investors seldom want to know whether an organization is av-erage or slightly above average in everything; they want the organiza-tion to have a unique and distinct identity that aligns with its strategy.

Recognize Interdependence of Intangibles. While you need to be fo-cused, it's important to understand that each level of the architecture for intangibles depends on the others. While you should target no more than one or two for primary attention, the most important areas often need to be combined. For example, the capability of speed won't be enough on its own; you will probably need fast product innovation or fast customer intimacy. As improvements are made in any area, they tend to improve the others. We assume that none of these areas are built without leaders, so working on any one of them builds leadership capability. As quality of leadership improves, talent and collaboration issues often surface—and in the process of resolving collaboration and talent issues, accountability and learning are usually strengthened.

Learn from the Best. Compare your organization with companies with world-class performance in your target strategy and capabilities. It's likely that these companies won't be in the same industry as you are; it's often helpful to look for analogous industries where a company may have developed extraordinary strength in the areas you desire. For example, lodging and airlines have many differences, but they're comparable when it comes to several driving forces: stretching capital assets, pleasing travelers, employing direct service workers, and so on. The advantage of looking outside your own industry for models is that you can emulate them without competing with them, and they're far likelier than your top competitors to share their insights with you.

Create a Virtuous Cycle of Assessment and Investment. A rigorous assessment helps company executives figure out what factors will be required for success, which helps them determine where to invest. Over time, repetitions of the assess-invest cycle result in a baseline for benchmarking.

Compare Stakeholder Perceptions. Like 360-degree feedback for leadership assessments, organization audits may result in differing views of the organization. It's instructive, for example, when top leaders perceive a shared mind-set, but employees or customers do not. Involve stakeholders in improvement plans. If investors rank the firm low on capability, for example, the CEO or CFO may meet with the investors to talk about specific action plans for moving forward.

Match Capability with Delivery. Leaders not only need to talk about capability, they need to demonstrate it in results; rhetoric about capabilities shouldn't exceed action. Expectations for delivery should be outlined in a detailed action plan. One approach is to bring together leaders for a half-day session to cover the questions that the plan should address: What do we want to accomplish with this capability (including a measurable outcome)? Who is responsible for delivering the capability? What are the decisions we can make immediately to foster this capability? How will we monitor our progress in attaining this capability? What actions can leaders take to deliver this capability? Actions may include developing education or training programs, designing new performance management systems, and implementing structural changes to house the needed capabilities. The best capability plans have a ninety-day window, specifying actions and results that will occur during that time frame. Managers own and are responsible for these plans, while HR professionals may be their architects.

Avoid Underinvestment in Organization Intangibles. Often, leaders fall prey to the trap of focusing on what is easy to measure, not what is useful to measure. They read balance sheets that report earnings, economic value added (EVA), or other economic data, but miss the underlying organizational factors that may add value. At times the capabilities can be very concrete.

Don't Confuse Results with Activities. An organization capability is a bundle of activities, not any single activity. A management activity such as leadership development needs to be conceived in terms of the capability it creates, not just the activity that takes place. Instead of asking what percentage of leaders received forty hours of training, leaders should be asking, "What capabilities did our leadership development process create for our organization?" Breaking these activities into desired results (see table 6-5) is a useful exercise for each component of leadership brand building.

TABLE 6-5

Desired results of leadership brand–building activities

Activity	Desired results
Building case for investment	Clear linkage of leadership brand–building to strategy execution and leadership reputation building
Statement of leadership brand	Unique logic for what leaders stand for in this organization; allows decentralized leadership development activities that add up to overall intent
Assessment of leaders	Identifies leadership gaps in pipeline; provides focus for individual and organization development
Development of leaders	Ensures that leaders have the requisite "know, be, do" for their current position and are building on these levels to support further progress
Measurement of leaders	Gauges effectiveness and efficiency of leadership efforts
Reputation of leaders	Ensures awareness of all stakeholders so they will continue to buy into investments

TABLE 6-6

Menu of options for return on leadership brand:
Individual leaders and leadership brand measures

Quadrant	Possible measures
Quadrant 1: Impact of individual leaders on their own organization	• Percentage of leaders with individual development plans based on 360-degree feedback that draws on our leadership code and declaration of leadership • Percentage of leaders who have received 360-degree feedback that is based on building branded leadership competencies in the last twelve months • Percentage of leaders whose individual development plans track individual stage progression: to what extent do I want to be a high performer in my current stage or to move to the next development stage in the pipeline? • Percentage of critical jobs congruent with stage development: to what extent do we have leaders with the right skills and perspective for the expectations of their job? • Number of development jobs consistent with experiences defined as critical in the case for investment: to what extent are we providing development experiences that are consistent with enabling our strategy (turnaround, M&A, staff and line work, geographic and cross-cultural experiences, and so on)?
Quadrant 2: Efficacy of the whole leadership brand system	• Improvements in the case for investing in leadership brand • Improvements in leadership bench strength index • Impact on key talent retention index
Quadrant 3: Value of individual leaders to external stakeholders	• Number of speeches to targeted industry groups • Number of headhunter calls at senior levels (whether leader leaves or not) • Impact of the departure of individual leaders on your market valuation and other company valuation • Number of media articles about your people • Amount of increase in industry association visibility (people in officer positions and the like)
Quadrant 4: Confidence of external stakeholders in the leadership brand	• P/E multiple compared with others in your industry • Increase in intangibles audit scores for different stakeholder groups (especially in targeted areas) • Number of favorable media articles about your leadership brand • Increase in confidence about your unit of corporate senior executives (survey) or of your company as a whole • Increase in your budget year over year (business unit, geography, division, team) • Favorable allocation of resources to your area

Conclusion

As so often happens, the CEO review session presented in this chapter went off the rails because the leadership development officer's view of leadership overemphasized leadership competencies and focused solely on the role of individual leaders as the rationale for leadership investment. By contrast, a conversation based on an array of measures of return on leadership brand will lead to sustained investments in leadership and high confidence in the department's accountability for its sizable budget.

It's easy to imagine Jordan Pettinger going to Bill Zariah with the options presented in table 6-6 and reviewing what he is most interested in measuring the following year. To the extent to which Pettinger can demonstrate how branded leaders bridge external customer identity with internal employee behavior, she is on track.

7

Building Awareness for Leadership Brand

THE MOVIE *Field of Dreams* contains a great promise, "If we build it, they will come." We often do things that don't have such clear outcomes or chances of success. One of the reasons leaders may not have full impact is that sometimes people are not aware of what the leaders are doing. Even great leaders, if their ideas or actions are not seen or understood by others, will not have much impact. The line should be, "When they know we have built it, they will come." Let's consider a case:

Hiding Your Light

Ashley McKenna, CEO of a rapidly growing high-tech firm in Ireland, is an exemplar of most of the ideas in this book, but she's not getting nearly as much mileage out of them as she should. She believes in leadership as a source of value and in the critical role of leaders in strategy execution. Her executive team has worked together to create a declaration of leadership that successfully connects employee behavior and customer expectations. She and her team have assessed their leadership pipeline, and they're working on addressing the remaining gaps through a variety of investments. Internal measures demonstrate that these investments are paying off.

However, McKenna does not view these investments in leadership as something to brag about. She believes that customers, analysts, investors, potential employees, and the community at large should see the fruits of her leadership brand in the business results her company is getting, and that should be enough to help her firm grow into global markets. It frustrates her to read media speculation about her company's ability to keep pace with its growth opportunities and to see that it has only an industry average price-to-earnings ratio.

She can change the media speculation and average P/E ratios if she hangs in there. External and public awareness can come in bold or quiet ways. Quiet, consistent behaviors can eventually create awareness, as they have for Alan Lafley and Doug Conant.

Sometimes It's What's Inside

Alan Lafley, CEO of Procter & Gamble, has delivered what he calls a "quiet revolution." Although few of P&G's initiatives have been written up in magazines, he has quietly done what needed to be done to reenergize the company, and outsiders are taking notice.

There's a similar story at Campbell's. CEO Doug Conant came in six years ago to a broken company. Without a lot of hoopla, he quietly began to fix things—starting with simple hygiene factors (improving the physical setting, dropping the idea of making the company store a profit center, and the like), and then working to express appreciation and build a community so as to enhance collaborative ties within the workforce, followed by building a company university to emphasize learning, and finally developing the legacy he wished to leave, a company-wide sense of high morale and individual value. He argues that it was necessary to go quietly through the four steps to fully engage employees. Awareness on the outside may eventually follow from quiet actions that culminate in a discernible story or message. And he has been successful with strong metrics in financial, market share, innovation pipeline, and workforce. For example, some of Campbell's most recent Gallup employee engagement scores are in the top quartile, and Gallup considers the engagement for the top 370 managers to be world-class.

There are many ways to build reputation. Tony La Russa, manager of the St. Louis Cardinals, was quoted in *Sports Illustrated* on the cumulative effect of little things: five stolen bases equal a run; three runs equal a victory. As George Will, in describing baseball managers, phrases it: "The result of little things is not little."[1] When George Pataki beat Mario Cuomo in the race for governor of New York, it was a bit of a shock. Cuomo was better known and more eloquent. But

Pataki said over and over and over again, "Too liberal too long." By the time of the election, voters had finally recognized his message and acted on it.

It isn't necessary to manage by headline or slogans, but you do need to manage the awareness process. In our leadership development experience, we run into senior executives who, like Ashley McKenna, avoid talking with stakeholders about what they are doing to develop leaders. They say things like "We don't brag about this work" and "We don't toot our own horn" to describe how they feel about creating awareness about investments in quality of leadership. In a high-tech firm like Ashley McKenna's, however, more than half of the market value comes from confidence in the future. Such a firm has more need of an activist approach than a household name like P&G or Campbell's does.

McKinsey & Company is a privately owned management consulting company and focuses on solving issues of concern to senior management in large corporations and organizations. Known as "The Firm" to employees and customers, it was founded in Chicago in 1926 by James McKinsey, a professor at the University of Chicago. McKinsey was succeeded by Marvin Bower in 1933. Bower oversaw the firm's rise to global prominence. For many years, McKinsey was the unchallenged leader in consulting, and its alumni went on to head leading companies, often former clients, leading to additional business for The Firm. To this day, McKinsey continues to build its leadership brand reputation by honoring those who leave rather than fighting them. It does this by tracking and publicizing its successful alumni. On McKinsey's Web site, there is a featured section called "Alumni in the News," with three sections: Features, Late Breaking News, and Who's News. On a recent day there were three features, thirteen Late Breaking News items, and a page and a half of Who's News.

Three recent features on this Web site include: [2]

- *"Two Alums Expand Tourism in China"*: "It's not news that China is big news lately. Our alumni population is growing there along with the economy, and we are thriving in a number of industries. Two alumni are making an impact in tourism. Click here to read more about them."

- *"Stephan Pauly Brings Mozart to the 21st Century"*: "Stephan brings his McKinsey skills to bear as CEO and Artistic Director of the Mozarteum Foundation Salzburg."

- *"Bill Drayton Paints a Vision of Changemaking"*: "The founder and CEO of Ashoka: Innovators for the Public, Bill Drayton argues that the emergence of a large scale entrepreneurial citizen sector can help solve society's most pressing problems."

In Late Breaking News, we learn that McKinsey alums are doing important work:

- "Ted Hall Joins Board of Dolby Laboratories"

- "Shawn Weidmann New President at Teleflora"

- "Alison Watkins Joins Board of Woolworths"

Finally, in Who's News, we can learn more about the following:

- "Catching up with Fred Hilmer, the new Vice-Chancellor and President of Australia's University of New South Wales"

- "Manoj Jain creates innovation in the online research field"

- "Georgia Lee makes a splash in the film community with 'Red Doors'"

These constantly updated news flashes are pretty impressive. McKinsey has turned a potential negative—people who did not make partner and got booted out or people who did not enjoy the lifestyle of pressure and travel—into a huge positive. McKinsey's current and future employees feel confident that they are a part of a strong alumni association, even if they leave the company. Ideally, others can find such creative ways to boost their leadership brand reputations.

Quality of leadership is a key intangible, and letting external stakeholders know what you are doing and why you are doing it—without overpromising, of course—ensures that your company is accurately valued in the marketplace. As long as you don't go overboard, it's an error to hold back; if you don't help stakeholders recognize the leadership capacity your company is building, you are likely to find that the market undervalues your capabilities. Assessments 7-1 and 7-2 provide instruments that will help you see how you stand on promoting your internal and external reputation for leadership.

Using the Brand Strength Matrix

We have used the term *leadership brand* to underscore the point that a company's approach to leadership and its development is a real asset. It

Internal leadership reputation indicators

To what extent do we . . .

	Low	High
1. Invest until we reach a tipping point: We know that it takes time, money, and energy to build a track record for knowing how to select, develop, and retain top-notch leaders.	1 2 3 4 5	
2. Build and not just buy: We are always very selective about who we choose and then develop.	1 2 3 4 5	
3. Make everyone a recruiter: We keep every employee on the lookout for talent.	1 2 3 4 5	
4. See talent as a corporate property: We see talent as a corporate asset, not a business unit asset. It doesn't work to hoard people in a business unit, so we insist on moving them around so they gain broad experience and we can see how good they are.	1 2 3 4 5	
5. Have a point of view about great leadership: We have a method for developing great talent.	1 2 3 4 5	
6. Stay tough-minded: We have clear expectations and apply rigorous assessment with lots of feedback.	1 2 3 4 5	
7. Have a visible agenda: Our executives are out beating the drum and talking about the importance of leadership.	1 2 3 4 5	
8. Find a home for a good guy: We never pass up a great talent, and will find a place for someone who can perform the right way. The converse is also true—we won't keep a dud.	1 2 3 4 5	
9. Spend time: Our senior leaders see leadership development as a critical priority.	1 2 3 4 5	
10. Give it away: We track the careers of people who have left us and succeeded elsewhere.	1 2 3 4 5	
11. Conduct employee attitude surveys that tell us what employees think about our leaders: We listen, so we don't need to count *Dilbert* strips on the walls to deduce what people think of us.	1 2 3 4 5	
12. Have a clear, positive leadership brand: We know and value what our leaders are "known for."	1 2 3 4 5	
13. Tell stories and myths about our leaders—past and present: Our culture thrives at the corporate campfire.	1 2 3 4 5	
14. Have a sense of leadership goodwill: People follow what leaders say, and give leaders their vote by their actions.	1 2 3 4 5	

(continued)

ASSESSMENT 7-1 (continued)

Internal leadership reputation indicators

To what extent do we . . .

	Low High
15. Retain loyalty among key players: Our leaders have the loyalty of those who know them best.	1 2 3 4 5
16. Ensure rapport: Our leaders have an easy rapport with employees; they get along, share ideas, and are approachable.	1 2 3 4 5
17. Have leaders who instill confidence: Employees have confidence in their leaders and believe that leaders are on their side and making the right decisions.	1 2 3 4 5
18. Have leaders who are accessible: Employees can reach our leaders if they have something to say.	1 2 3 4 5
19. Have the confidence of the board of directors: Our board knows and trusts our senior leadership.	1 2 3 4 5
20. Willingly act on leaders' decisions: Most employees trust a new direction our leaders propose, whether it's a program, product, or other action.	1 2 3 4 5
Total	

Key:

90–100: You already have high awareness. If you can back it up, you should keep doing what you're doing.
70–90: You have moderate awareness. Start applying some ideas about communication with each stakeholder.
Under 70: Get busy.

would be unthinkable to have a product brand and not create awareness about it. The same is true for a leadership brand. While the organization will reap important indirect and direct benefits whether the brand is well known or not, the benefits to having a recognized (and rewarded) leadership brand are too significant to pass up.

To help think about harvesting the strength of your leadership brand, consider this simple formula for the product branding process:

$$\text{Efficacy} \times \text{Awareness} = \text{Strength of brand}$$

These two factors—*efficacy* (Does the product do what you say it will do?) and *awareness* (How many know about it?)—create the 2×2 brand strength matrix shown in figure 7-1.

One side of the matrix reflects efficacy. High efficacy means the brand has the ability to deliver completely on its promise, whether it concerns a product or a person or a whole system. Low efficacy is the inability to

ASSESSMENT 7-2

External leadership reputation indicators

	Weakness (1)	Average (2)	Strength (3)
Investors			
1. P/E for last period of time			
2. Investor reports about the company and about leadership			
3. Stock movement days after investor meetings			
4. Honesty in reporting good news and bad			
5. Industry reports by analysts about your leaders			
6. Exposure of a broad number of executives to analysts			
7. Discussion of your leadership brand in your annual report			
Customers			
8. Knowledge of why customers buy from you rather than your competitors			
9. Content analysis of the business press (*BusinessWeek*, *Wall Street Journal*, *Forbes*, *Fortune*, and so on) reveals stories that address your leadership style favorably compared with that of your competition			
10. Willingness to admit mistakes and act decisively when things go wrong			
11. Frequency with which your leaders are tapped by search firms as a source of talent			
12. Frequency with which your leaders are asked to be on boards and speak at conferences			
13. Willingness of your leaders to deliver on promises or be honest about misses and make corrections			
14. Extent to which your leaders know key customers by first name, and customers know them			
15. Extent to which your leadership brand process is a source of attracting customers			

Key:

40–45: You have remarkable investor and customer awareness. Keep doing what you are doing.
35–39: You have moderate success. There is some room for improvement.
Under 35: Get working on it.

FIGURE 7-1

Brand strength

Stakeholder awareness

		Low	High
Efficacy	High	2. Untapped advantage	4. Sustained advantage
	Low	1. No one cares	3. Shooting star

deliver on the brand promise: this brand is not able to do what it is supposed to do. The other side of the matrix reflects awareness. High awareness means that the brand has a far-reaching reputation—lots of people know of it. Low awareness means that the brand is relatively unknown. Here's how the four quadrants apply to leadership brand.

1. No One Cares

If you have both low efficacy and low awareness, ignore publicity until you have more to work with. If we—Dave and Norm—formed a singing or dancing duo, we would fall into this category. In leadership branding terms, this might apply to start-up entrepreneurs who can't raise venture capital because they don't yet have enough experience to build confidence in what they could do.

2. Untapped Advantage

Norm's cousin, Craig Carmichael, is a very creative inventor who lives in Victoria, British Columbia. Periodically, Carmichael will get in touch to see whether we have contacts with companies that might be interested in marketing one of his inventions—a device to optimize the costs of heating and air-conditioning machinery for commercial buildings, for example. Carmichael's inventions always work—that is, they are always high in efficacy. Because he is so independent, however—he wants to live in his house on the beach in Victoria and not travel around talking up his ideas—he lacks awareness or public visibility. He makes a good living, but unless he finally lands a sponsor who will market one of his inventions and start building real awareness, he's unlikely to get rich.

In leadership brand terms, Ashley McKenna, the Irish CEO, is in this "untapped advantage" category. McKenna has created high efficacy with her investments in leadership but low stakeholder awareness. Companies with untapped advantage are the superb firms no one has yet discovered. In today's world, they are becoming hard to find—with the transparency imposed by the legal climate, most are quickly discovered. But leaders here do what they say without fanfare and hoopla. Knowingly or unknowingly, they emulate Northwestern Mutual's slogan: "The Quiet Company." Their goal is to deliver excellence rather than talk about delivering excellence—but they can find themselves in the position of having less opportunity to deliver it because of their unwillingness to stand out.

3. Shooting Star

This category, low efficacy but high awareness, has many examples in virtually every field and from any country. Think of the losing candidates in the last national election—how many names can you remember? At one time, these candidates seemed extremely important, but a year or so after the election, most voters have trouble remembering their names—much less their platforms. Another illustration is found in Milli Vanilli, a pop and dance music duo formed by Frank Farian in Germany in 1988 and fronted by Fab Morvan and Rob Pilatus. The group's debut album achieved high sales internationally and won a Grammy Award for Best New Artist in 1990. However, success turned to infamy when the award was revoked after it was revealed that the purported singers did not actually sing on the record.[3]

From a leadership brand perspective, Al Dunlap is a notorious example. "Chainsaw Al," as he was known, became famous for a few years as he racked up billions of dollars in the 1980s and early '90s by taking over companies such as Scott Paper, selling off their assets, and then selling the company. Dunlap was feared, hated, or respected, depending on whether you were an employee who was laid off or an investor who enjoyed the run-up in the stock value. His failure at turning around Sunbeam ended his career.

4. Sustained Advantage

This is the branding dream—high efficacy and high awareness. For example, U2—founded in 1976 and among the most popular acts in the world since the mid-1980s—has sold approximately 50.5 million albums in the United States and upward of 170 million worldwide. It has had six number-one U.S. albums and nine number-one U.K. albums. Since the release of the album *The Joshua Tree*, U2 has often been referred to as the biggest rock band in the world by fans and critics alike. The band has won twenty-two Grammy Awards, the most for any recording artists. Lead singer Bono has taken this fame and used it as a platform to prod world leaders to eliminate debt and raise money for third world countries.[4]

In leadership brand, General Electric is the undisputed heavyweight champion for efficacy and awareness. Jack Welch began using Crotonville, GE's university, to build confidence in current and future leaders. Today, led by Jeff Immelt, GE targets leaders in customer businesses in emerging markets like China and invites them to go through GE's vaunted leadership development process. Few, if any, refuse, and those who attend become GE fans—and customers. As the ultimate feeder firm, GE has developed a succession of highly successful leaders for itself and a host of other companies, building exceptional intangible value for shareholders.

To see how important building reputation for leadership brand is to GE, we looked at several years of its annual report and read the first section: "Letter to the Stakeholders." This section communicates to external stakeholders what's on the mind of the senior officers of the company and is typically about growth and financial concerns. GE's is different. Following are the section titles of the year 2000 report:

- Integrity
- Relishing Change
- The Customer (a tirade against bureaucracy)
- Using Size
- Annihilating Bureaucracy (more)
- Leadership
- Training
- People
- Informality[5]

It's not accidental that most of these issues relate to what leaders can do to build value to the customer through leadership.

In 2003, Jack Welch had left and Jeff Immelt was now CEO. His letter to shareholders in the 2003 annual report contained the following sections:

- Technical Leadership
- Services
- Customer Focus
- Globalization
- Growth Platforms
- The GE (Leadership) Team (two pages, the longest section)[6]

The tradition continues with a focus on how GE leaders build value by focusing employee behavior on customer concerns and then communicating these investments to customers, employees, and investors. GE continues to communicate to customers and investors that quality of leadership brand is a key factor in GE's future success.

There may be another company that communicates its reputation to external stakeholders for leadership brand more than GE does, but we didn't find it.

Interpreting the Quadrants

For sustained prosperity, any brand needs both efficacy and awareness—there's no point in publicizing something that doesn't work, or in hiding something that does and hoping people will somehow divine its presence. When it comes to a leadership brand, building efficacy is more complex than building awareness; chapters 1 through 7 focus on efficacy, and this chapter turns to the simpler process of increasing stakeholder awareness more quickly and efficiently than by simply letting the results speak for themselves.

The areas of most interest for companies working seriously on leadership brand are the untapped and sustained advantage quadrants. The shooting star does not need more awareness—companies in this class need to focus on learning how to sing and play the guitar. And those in the no one cares quadrant don't really matter; quite simply, no one cares if no one cares.

Building Awareness

The first step is to understand your stakeholders. Our colleague Mike Panowyk has done some compelling work about how values differ, pointing out that each stakeholder group has its own interests—specific things its members want to know about your leadership brand. These differences are captured in table 7-1, along with some preliminary ideas about how to build awareness based on what each stakeholder group values.

Building stakeholder awareness about your leadership brand involves three steps:

1. Invite the stakeholders in.

2. Develop a communications plan.

3. Take action.

Invite Stakeholders In

Reach out to your stakeholders—especially those that influence other stakeholders—and actively solicit information about their view of your leadership brand. This includes the media reps and analysts who write about your company and its leaders. This information should be systematically collected and then analyzed to find patterns of perceptions about your leaders and your leadership. Only when you understand what people think can you begin to formulate ways to influence their perceptions.

Beyond just serving as a source of data, asking stakeholders for their perceptions about your company allows you to create an extremely valuable forum for dialogue and exchange. In chapter 6, we described an intangibles audit, a process that assembles internal and external stakeholder feedback about intangible issues such as leadership brand. This information is extremely helpful for creating a baseline from which to measure the impact of investments in leadership. It works much like a 360-degree feedback process that includes provision for the subjects to meet with the sources of feedback to talk about the results of the survey and describe intended action—an interaction that is much more effective than just getting feedback privately and hoping that the actions you take will have the effect you desire.

The story of Chuck Prince and Citigroup, told in chapter 2, illustrates the importance of stakeholder relations. In addition to taking action that fixed the problem that had led to Citigroup's being barred from further M&A activity (efficacy), Prince initiated a series of meetings with internal and external stakeholders to communicate progress (awareness). Among other things, this involved writing cases about the

TABLE 7-1

Stakeholder interests

Stakeholder	Leadership brand value proposition: *This company builds leaders at every level who . . .*	What to communicate	Action to build awareness
Employees	Care about and know how to deliver employee motivation and opportunities for growth and development.	We have a clear leadership brand process that builds high-quality leaders I am proud of. It's clear how I can and should develop myself to be a part of this winning team.	• Conduct employee surveys. • Take action on results. • Tie back to the employee survey so employees connect survey with action. • Publicize results. • Listen to employees. • Spend time with employees (town hall meetings). • Solicit employee input (via suggestion systems or other means).
Customers	Ensure customer satisfaction and commitment so I will get the service and experience I desire when I interact with this firm.	This organization has leaders, people, and capabilities that appeal to me.	• Include questions about leaders when appropriate on customer satisfaction surveys. • Invite customers to leadership development events as designers, participants, or presenters. • Invite them to be on panels at leadership and employee events. • Actively communicate. • Ask employees to behave as if they are customers.
Investors	Deliver investor understanding and future confidence about strategy and results.	This organization has invested to deliver sustainable value in ways that matter to its customers and investors.	• Describe case for change, investments, and measurements in annual report. • Link results back to investments. • Actively communicate. • Involve investors in internal events.

(continued)

TABLE 7-1 *(continued)*

Stakeholder interests

Stakeholder	Leadership brand value proposition: *This company builds leaders at every level who . . .*	What to communicate	Action to build awareness
Executive team	Are proud to be a part of this company. Demonstrate awareness of leadership brand and follow through on it.	Leaders build, model, and reinforce all aspects of the leadership brand process.	• Talk about the ways in which leadership inside reflects customers outside. • Ensure visibility to others so they can become better leaders.
Suppliers	Ensure supplier dedication and commitment.	This organization differentiates what it does best from what we can do better for it.	• Include key suppliers in leadership development. • Actively communicate with them. • Ask for their perception about your leaders in surveys.
Analysts	Ensure confidence in future prosperity.	This organization has leaders, people, and capabilities that differentiate it from other investment alternatives.	• Introduce your leadership bench to analysts as appropriate. • CEO should explain how and why company is investing in leadership. • Ask for their perception about your leaders and your results.
Regulators	Embed confidence in compliance with prescribed rules and regulations.	Leaders in this organization establish effective governance processes, roles, and accountability.	• Review how your leadership system considers compliance and ethical leadership. • Ask for regulators' perceptions in survey about your leadership system.
Peer CEO	Have earned my admiration as a benchmark for best practices in developing branded leaders.	This organization will sustain a competitive lead because of its investments in a leadership brand system.	• Initiate best practice visits. • Write articles and give speeches—display openness to media opportunities. • Ask for peers' perceptions as appropriate about your leadership system.

ethics issues for use in leadership education, a step that was initially seen as problematic because of concerns that these cases could be used against the company in court by defendants who had been fired as a result of the problems. To Prince's credit, he vetoed the concerns and demanded that the cases be written realistically so that all leaders and employees involved would understand the potential for missteps.

Whether through surveys like the intangibles audit or just by inviting stakeholders to help solve a problem, the combination of taking the right actions and regularly communicating the real issues with regulators, members of the board of directors, analysts, customers, and employees leads to better and more positive perceptions of a company. At Citigroup, Prince was able to build his own leadership brand around the importance of customers, employees, and the company while involving multiple stakeholders in the solution of a difficult problem.

Develop a Communications Plan

Any good communications plan should consider several important factors:

- What we want to communicate (the message)

- Who should share the message (the sender)

- Who should receive the message (the receiver)

- When the message should be shared (the timing)

- How the message should be shared (the process)

THE MESSAGE. As depicted in table 7-1, stakeholders are all interested in different aspects of the leadership brand value proposition. We have found that the various types of stakeholders don't change what they are interested in over time. Instead, when changes or problems arise, it is the intensity and frequency of the message that shifts.

For example, assume your CEO has done a great job over the years and then retires. This retirement creates an opportunity and a threat for a variety of your stakeholders. However, what to communicate to each stakeholder group remains consistent with table 7-1. Employees need to be assured that the new CEO is still interested in the process of building leadership brand and that these leaders will retain the kinds of values about leadership brand that have existed in the past. The new CEO may change aspects of the leadership-brand-building process, but the case for investment and the mechanisms for how to assess, develop, and measure leaders are likely to remain relatively consistent. And above all, the point that the value of leadership brand building itself remains an important aspect of what the company continues to do must be communicated from the perspective of how leadership brand enables employees to continue to learn and grow and have committed relationships with their leaders. Stories about how the new CEO has delivered financial results but has also cared about people and created opportunities are relevant.

Investors have different interests from employees and so need communication that reinforces their interests about the new CEO. Again, the primary communication to investors should focus on the ongoing commitment to the leadership-brand-building process, but the descriptions of the value of the process in these communications should focus on the ability of the system to deliver promised results today and in the future. Investors need to be reassured that the company will continue to deliver high-caliber leaders who can achieve desired results. Communicating stories about leaders the new CEO has mentored or coached who have gone on to deliver stellar financial results will help reassure investors that the intangible value associated with leadership brand will be retained.

If the full value of the leadership brand is to be protected, customers, the executive team, suppliers, regulators, analysts, peer CEOs, and any other interested stakeholders will each need reassurance that the organization remains committed to leadership brand building in terms that relate to their interests and concerns.

THE SENDER. Most communications about leadership quality need to come from the CEO. The CEO is the brand manager of leadership and so has ultimate responsibility for all communications about it. Communications about the case for investment in leadership and the general approach as well as messages about key results should come from the CEO to analysts, investors, employees, and customers. It's especially useful for the CEO to write about leadership development issues in the annual report.

In addition, the CEO can augment these efforts by inviting a variety of other company players to collaborate. In chapter 8 we discuss the roles a variety of players have in shaping and building the brand. Here's how they take part in publicizing it:

- *Head of HR.* HR's job is to coordinate the leadership branding process inside the firm and help get the message out to internal and external stakeholders. Specifically, messages about the development process should come from the head of HR. This includes messages about the logic for new assignments in the company as well as about training and development content and process.

- *Line executives.* As line executives communicate to internal employee groups, they should continually communicate and reinforce the importance of the leadership brand. They do this by tying successful business results to the leadership brand process and by making it a part of what they talk about. They also do it by modeling the leadership brand and actively coaching leaders in their organization in developing their styles of the leadership brand.

- *Public relations.* As PR professionals communicate newsworthy stories about the firm, it's important that they integrate the leadership brand story into other events. From launching successful new products to delivering on earnings, to overcoming a disaster, it's important to tie the leadership brand into the story as it is communicated.

THE RECEIVER. Communication research tells us that receivers of information need to hear a message ten times for every unit of understanding. Consistent and redundant messages have more impact than loud, bold, but infrequent blasts. Leaders must find every opportunity to share messages that are consistent with each stakeholder's interests.

THE TIMING. We like former IBM CEO Tom Watson's statement: "We never reorganize except for a good business reason—and if we haven't reorganized in a while, that's a good business reason."[7] In the current context, we adapt it to say, "We never communicate to stakeholders unless we have a good business reason—and if we haven't communicated in the last three months, that's a good business reason." It makes a great deal of sense to have at least some kind of quarterly communication with all stakeholders about what your company is doing, and at least one of these communications every year should focus on the quality of your leadership and your leadership brand.

If a business problem has an impact on all stakeholders, communication frequency could be increased to once a month, once a week, or even once a day, depending on the severity of the problem. For example, if your company has some kind of accident that harms people, communication should be frequent (probably at least daily), straightforward, and transparent until the problem is resolved and interest wanes. The way your leaders handle emergency situations communicates a great deal to your stakeholders about your leadership brand.

As we keep saying, your leaders are the bridge between the outside and the inside. Emergency situations usually bring awareness with them. The efficacy of your leadership brand is either verified or disproved during times when you most need leaders to step up and do the right thing. When leaders do step up and live the brand in times of crisis, the media and other stakeholders witness it—and wonder whether their own leaders would have stepped up as admirably. When leaders don't step up, the glare of publicity shines harshly on your shortfalls.

THE PROCESS. Some hints about sharing messages to build credibility:

- *Share frequently.* Stakeholders don't want to be surprised with large dumps of information; they want to know what to expect through frequent contact.

- *Present the logic behind the guidance.* Sharing anticipated results is not enough; stakeholders want to know the logic behind the projections. People understand the what if they understand the why.

- *Tell people quickly if circumstances change.* Unexpected events change how business is run, and good communications frequently share problems and concerns as well as solutions.

- *Build in feedback loops.* One-way communication happens when leaders talk and everyone else listens. The danger of this is that leaders may be answering questions no one really cares about. Two-way communication happens when leaders encourage dialogue and deal with questions directly, and it's far more effective than just talking and hoping.

- *Offer honest answers.* It's tempting to bluff when you're asked questions that you can't answer on the spot, but candidly acknowledging the lack of information and then making a commitment to find the answer and get back with it is much likelier to make a lasting good impression.

Taking Action

One of the problems with gathering stakeholder perceptions about your leaders is that you won't always like what you hear. Another is that you definitely won't like all of your stakeholders' ideas about what you should do in the future. Again, this is similar to asking for and receiving 360-degree feedback that turns out to be conflicting. Anyone who has received feedback from boss, peers, and direct reports knows that different people can perceive the same situation and interpret what it means and what should be done to improve in dramatically different ways.

The same is true when leaders of an organization solicit feedback about the quality of overall leadership and what direction it might take. Another case in point:

Stakeholders Pursue Their Own Perceived Interests

A couple of years ago, we worked with a global hospitality company that had gone through tremendous changes in the past year, including a demerger, a hostile takeover, and major restructuring around a new strategy. During the year, analysts regularly took shots at the incompetence of the company and its leadership. As part of the restructuring, significant infrastructure costs had been eliminated, bringing the company back to industry parity with its competitors. The CEO and the executive team felt that a major milestone had been achieved with this sustained reduction in costs and wanted to focus on other factors more consistent with their new strategy, such as building the brand and achieving greater customer intimacy. Given all the changes of the previous year and the leaders' ability to surmount each obstacle, it seemed like a good time to get some stakeholder feedback.

The expectation was that stakeholders would support this new direction. After all, the CEO had navigated the pitfalls of the preceding year with great success, and he now clearly set forth his intention to focus on brand building—what could go wrong? However, the results of the audit proved that this belief was misplaced.

Franchise owners, target customers, employees, suppliers, investors, and the executive team were in agreement that the company should pursue the customer intimacy direction, but analysts uniformly proposed more cost reduction. The exasperated CEO wanted to please the analysts but strongly believed that continued cost reduction would undermine the intended strategy. However, rather than just move ahead with his own plans, he decided to sit down with the analysts and share the data from the audit with them.

This simple gesture made all the difference. He thanked the analysts for their input and showed them the data about how the other stakeholders were in agreement about the future direction, and how this input was different from their input. As a result, most of the analysts left the meeting both impressed and inclined to support the company. In fact, one of the analysts who'd been most negative now wrote a report about the quality of the new leadership and how they had succeeded in doing what he had thought was impossible.

The principles in this example are timeless. Action should be taken only after stakeholder information is gathered and decisions are made about what to do with the information. It is not necessary to do what every stakeholder suggests, but it is important to thank them all for their input and to tell them what you have decided to do and why. When you repeat this cycle, others are more willing to give you feedback again in the future. What is more important, the value of the information is ensured with your follow-up about what you are doing.

Conclusion

Think back to Ashley McKenna. What would you advise her to do? Basically, we believe McKenna has done the right things first, but now she needs to build greater stakeholder confidence in the future of her company by creating awareness of what her leadership brand is and why it will make a difference. She can do this by understanding what each group of stakeholders cares about and then launching a communications process that regularly informs those stakeholders about what they want to know.

McKenna needs to make sure that talk and action about leadership branding are the same. Our friends at Herman Miller understand this, so they waited to introduce their new systems product at the national meetings until it was done and ready to ship. At the time, the common practice in their industry was to introduce design products and ideas at the meeting while the products were still concepts. When the Herman Miller leaders waited until the products were available, they did much better. Customers liked the concepts, but they liked even more being able to order them. The same principles hold true for leadership brand: it's important to have built a system that works before talking much about it. But when the leadership system is working, it's just as important to make sure it's understood and appreciated.

8

Preserving Leadership Brand

"**O**NE, TWO, THREE—point!"

This isn't a kids' game, it's a serious leadership exercise. Working with companies on improving their decision-making practices, we often specify a decision and then ask everyone around a table—usually a leadership team or committee—to point to the person who is primarily responsible for making this decision. After we work through the almost inevitable resistance—this can seem like a childish and silly thing to do—we find that the exercise often clarifies who is publicly accountable for a decision.

Unfortunately, when the discussion involves building a leadership brand, "One, two, three—point!" doesn't work. No one has enough fingers to point in all the required directions. Building a leadership brand requires consistent attention of those throughout an organization. At Hewlett-Packard, the *everything is possible* brand identity affects R&D professionals who invent new ideas, manufacturing employees who continuously improve production processes, marketing professionals who seek new ways to go to market, and administrative staff who find creative ways to shape and design the organization. In this chapter, we suggest the specific ways in which different groups share the responsibility to build leadership brand, including members of the board of directors, the CEO, line leaders at all levels, the head of HR, and the head of learning.

Board of Directors

Members of the board of directors have a fiduciary duty to the firm's investors and owners. They ensure that leaders operate with appropriate financial discipline and governance processes. In the aftermath of the recent highly publicized instances of corporate malfeasance, where senior leaders acted outside appropriate financial and ethical standards, boards have come under increased scrutiny. While new board members are nominated by the existing members, often with senior management guidance, increasingly boards are being challenged to be both transparent and independent.

Transparency means that board recommendations and decisions must adhere to a high ethical standard and be made public. Sarbanes-Oxley, legislation that requires boards to be more forthcoming with decisions and to rigorously audit financial and organizational processes, has forced boards to be more directive in their governance. *Independence* means that while board members may be recommended and vetted by management, they are elected to serve investors and need to make decisions without undue management influence. Increasingly, boards have fewer "inside directors"—people who are also senior executives of the company—and more members who come from other organizations.

Boards are involved in influencing the organization's leadership brand in several ways. A primary task of a board is to select the company's next CEO. The CEO sets the managerial tone for the entire company. With increasing scrutiny of CEOs (and shorter tenures in that office), boards need to constantly monitor current CEO and executive team behavior and plan for CEO turnover.

In addition to managing CEO succession, boards are expected to fulfill their stewardship duties to shareholders by building confidence in the future of the firm's strategy, financial and capital structure, product design and distribution, and leadership brand. They generally use a committee structure to monitor the details of these responsibilities. This means that boards have subcommittees, each targeted with oversight of a particular aspect of the organization. Financial or audit committees supervise the financial processes and auditing functions. Governance committees manage the nomination of board candidates and ensure a process of ethical governance within the company.

Leadership brand is increasingly gaining the attention of boards, often through compensation committees. Traditionally, these subcommittees have focused on CEO and officer-level compensation, but increasingly they are expanding their scope to include a focus on leadership brand as part of their charter. A couple of subcommittee and board charters illustrate the attention boards are giving to reviewing leadership brand capabilities and practices:

The purpose of the Leadership Development and Compensation Committee of the Board of Directors of Sun Microsystems shall be to discharge the Board's responsibilities relating to compensation of the company's Section 16b officers (The Executive Officers) and to administer the company's stock plans and U.S. Non-qualified Deferred Compensation plan. The committee has overall responsibility for approving and evaluating the Executive Officer's compensation plans, policies, and programs of the company. The Committee will also review and provide input to the executive and leadership development policies, plans, and practices that support Sun's ability to develop and retain the superior executive and leadership talent required to deliver against our short and long term business strategies *[emphasis added].*[1]

The purpose of the HR and Compensation Committee of the Board of Directors of the Hewlett-Packard Company is:

- *To discharge the responsibilities of the Board relating to compensation of HP's executives and directors . . .*

- *To review and provide guidance on HP's HR programs such as its global workforce programs, talent review and leadership development and best place to work initiatives . . .*[2]

These corporate governance guidelines established by the Board of Directors of Google Inc. provide a structure within which our directors and management can effectively pursue Google's objectives for the benefit of its stockholders . . . Principal Duties of the Board of Directors . . .

- To Evaluate Management Performance and Compensation. *At least annually, the Leadership Development and Compensation Committee will evaluate the performance of the chief executive officer and the other officers. On an annual basis it will determine the compensation of the chief executive officer and the other officers. It will also evaluate the compensation plans, policies and programs for officers and employees to ensure they are appropriate, competitive and properly reflect Google's objectives and performance.*

- To Review Management Succession Planning. *The Leadership Development and Compensation Committee will review and recommend to the Board plans for the development, retention and replacement of executive officers of Google.*[3]

Each of these innovative companies has added to board oversight the responsibility not only to pick the next CEO but to invest in building the next generation of leadership, or what we call the leadership brand. To ensure a leadership brand, boards—as a whole or via targeted committees—should do the following.

OPERATE AS A BOARD CONSISTENTLY WITH THE ESPOUSED FIRM AND LEADERSHIP BRAND. Board governance should reflect the leadership brand that the company wants to create. That is, board members and the board overall as a body should reflect the leadership code outlined in chapter 1. Board members should have personal proficiency with a commitment to learning, integrity, and passion. Board members should have a point of view about the future and spend time envisioning what can be and should be for the organization to position itself to win in the future. Boards should be focused on execution, monitoring the extent to which promises made are kept and the extent to which the organization's functions work efficiently and effectively. Boards should ensure a flow of talent by monitoring current employee morale and attitude. And boards should be nurturing the next generation of talent by discussing and meeting with future leaders. But in addition to the leadership code, the board should reflect the statement of leadership brand crafted through the work in chapter 3. If the company chooses to build a customer identity based on innovation, the board should also act with creativity and innovation. If the company espouses a firm brand focused on efficiency and reliability, the board should focus its attention on similar issues. The board and its members should embody the firm brand. Customer expectations should be a part of board discussion so that board members recognize the behaviors they should demonstrate as a board that reflect these external expectations. This does not mean that board members do not have individual differences and voice alternative and independent points of view, but they need to recognize and encourage their organization's leadership brand.

EMPLOY GOVERNANCE THAT SETS THE PATTERN FOR THE FIRM. Traditionally, boards are judged by external groups (such as Institutional Shareholder Services) on visible, public matters (for example, how many of the board members are from inside the company rather than outside, what experience board members have, how many attend meetings). Increasingly, if the board is to reflect the firm's leadership brand, the board should be accountable for how it operates. This means that boards might do reviews of board members by other board members according to the statement of leadership brand for the company; that boards should discuss how they process information, make decisions, and allocate time, to ensure that it is consistent with the firm and leadership brand; and that boards should govern themselves with the same standards to which they hold leaders throughout the company.

REVIEW THE CEO FOR EMBODIMENT OF LEADERSHIP BRAND. When boards set CEO (and officer) compensation, the standards applied should not just be "at the 75 percent level of industry average." This kind of numerical benchmarking has been partly responsible for the escalation of CEO salaries—almost everyone wants to be above midpoint on the salary surveys. Instead, the board should be clear with the CEO about the leadership brand that the company should embody, and then evaluate the CEO and other officers on the extent to which they live that brand. This evaluation can be done by information collected from the CEO's team, employees, board members, and external customers and investors. This data can and should be collected annually before setting CEO compensation. In other words, pay-for-performance for the CEO should reflect not just how well she led the firm to get results, but how those results were achieved. It is the board's responsibility to gather a wide range of data to make informed and accurate assessments of performance, not just rely on whether financial guidance was met or exceeded, whether media reports highlight the firm's practices, or whether the CEO's direct reports are satisfied and engaged.

FOCUS ON NEXT-GENERATION LEADERSHIP. Boards should be aware of depth of leadership and how successfully measures are implemented to identify and develop future leaders who can create results. While management governs the firm and makes recommendations, board members should be able to make informed decisions about the quality and depth of leadership. This means that board members should spend time with a wide array of leaders inside the company, not just the CEO or president. This can come from formal presentations to the board, site visits by the board to locations within the company, or informal conversations between board members and managers about company affairs. Board members should be able to make informed judgments about the quality of leadership at least a couple of levels down the organization.

REVIEW SUCCESSION PLANNING. Most firms today have succession planning processes (called talent management, leadership succession, high-potential reviews, or the like, as discussed in chapter 5). Every year, boards should look over a synthesis of the next-generation leadership work. This effort would include a review of the leadership brand, the quality of leaders at each level, distribution of leaders at each stage, efficacy of investments made in leadership development, and plans for key leaders. Board members who see deep into the leadership talent pool can recognize the next generation of leaders as they develop within the company, and have confidence that investors' and owners' interests will be protected.

We have provided a board leadership brand audit in assessment 8-1 that can be used as a diagnostic to review the extent to which the board works to ensure a leadership brand.

CEO, President, and Senior Leaders

In a world of increasing transparency, the CEO has become the public face of most companies. In traditional job satisfaction research, a large portion of the employees' satisfaction was tied to "leadership." This generally meant the immediate supervisor, who represented the firm's interests to the employee. Today, commitment surveys have generally replaced satisfaction surveys, but leadership still scores as a significant predictor of commitment. Increasingly, however, it refers to the confidence an employee has in the senior leaders of the company, not just the immediate supervisor. With information ubiquity, employees (and customers and investors) develop a sense of the executives of the firm through media interviews, Web sites, and other communication vehicles. Senior leaders live in glass houses; their lifestyles, for good or ill, are made visible, magnified, and watched by many.

As a result, the CEO, president, and other senior executives must not only manage the leadership brand but live it. Unless they exemplify and personify the brand they espouse, they will be a source of cynicism and skepticism. Employees watch what leaders do, how they treat others, what they talk about, where they spend their time, how they deal with both good news and bad, and how they make decisions. Leaders

Board assessment

- Does your board foster your leadership brand?
- Does the board spend time on the right issues?
- Does the board make decisions in a timely way?
- Do members of the board reflect the desired brand?
- Is there a mix on the board to get different points of view?
- How well does the board deal with dissent?
- How well does the board counsel the CEO and senior leaders?
- How well does the board perform the technical duties it must perform (such as ensuring fiscal accountability and setting compensation)?
- How well does the agenda of the board meeting reflect what customers and investors would want to see?
- How well does the board know industry trends and competitor analysis and provide honest views of how the firm is doing?
- How well does the board deal with fundamental value issues?
- How much oversight does the board give on creating the next generation of leadership?
- How thorough and regular are the board's reviews of the CEO?
- How well does the board build compensation policies that communicate and support the brand?
- How well does the board audit organization capabilities?
- How well does the board hold people accountable for decisions?

who want to establish a leadership brand that will outlive them need to start by looking in the mirror. Ask yourself, What is my leadership brand? What am I communicating about organization strategy and execution, talent management and development, and personal proficiencies in our company? How would others characterize my leadership brand—and is it consistent with what I want and with what I want customers to know us for? If leaders are not congruent with the desired direction, their demands for leadership unity, or brand, will fall on deaf ears.

CEOs who embody the leadership brand are transparent and visible to employees inside and customers and investors outside the organization. This transparency often shows up in how leaders spend time. A simple way for leaders to diagnose their current brand is to do a time log.

We have used leader time logs in a variety of ways to explore how leaders' behavior reflects what employees see in leaders' work. In one company, for example, we identified the expectations of leaders through speeches, policy manuals, and other directives from corporate headquarters. We listed these expectations and then asked leaders to estimate how much time they would need to spend to fulfill them. We then asked a sample of leaders to keep a time log of what they did for a week: who they met with, what issues they discussed, where they met, and so on. When we compared these two lists, we found that leaders felt it would take them about seventy hours a week to fulfill the corporate expectations, but that they were only spending about 40 percent of their actual time on the things directed by headquarters as they focused on the day-to-day activities that drove the business. This created enormous frustration among leaders who were trying to be responsive to both corporate expectations and local requirements. As a result of this study, corporate leaders dramatically changed the way they communicated with leaders and became much more willing to listen than to direct.

We have also used time logs to ask leaders to calculate what we call *return on time invested*. This simple calculation implies that leaders should invest their time as carefully as they invest their money. When the strategy or firm brand directs that they become more innovative, for example, we ask leaders to look at their last week or month through the eyes of a time log and then consider how they might have spent their time if they had been more prone to innovation. This exercise generally results in leaders' identifying specific actions that they could take to personally reflect the brand they need to project—a matter of putting your brand where your time is. Usually this is not a dramatic time shift, but subtle shifts in who leaders meet with, what issues they focus on, where they meet, and how they work.

CEOs, by virtue of their position, have enormous potential for impact on others and the organization. Meeting with employees in focus groups, lunches, problem-solving teams, or by wandering through work spaces enables senior leaders to communicate their brand to employees. One leader we know takes out his monogrammed letterhead and writes five to seven personal notes per week to employees who contribute to the company's success. Another has found that writing a personal thank-you letter to the employee's mother has enormous impact on the employee, even more than a note to the employee would have had. Still another CEO has a monthly online chat room session, open to any employee in the company who wishes to converse with him. In each of these cases, the personal touch from the CEO communicates and embeds the CEO's brand in ways that inspire employees to improve their own work.

But even when leaders personally live the desired leadership brand, that is not enough to embed the brand. They need to ensure that it is not just their example that matters but the work that they do. In the Hewitt study of the top twenty leadership companies, leading companies had 35 percent more CEO involvement in leadership activities than comparison companies, as well as 34 percent more board involvement. This involvement comes from paying attention to the following leadership issues.

COMMUNICATING THE IMPORTANCE OF LEADERSHIP. Leaders communicate that leadership matters in a variety of formal and informal ways. They can talk about quality of leadership brand in their public forums—the CEO letter in the annual report, shareholder calls, and speeches. They can regularly raise leadership issues in staff meetings, new employee orientations, employee focus groups, and interviews inside and outside the company. They can monitor the quality of leadership through a number of tracking devices, including the ones we suggest in chapter 7. In one large global firm, the CEO performance dashboard for the company includes the number of leaders moving from one area to another within the company—an index of which senior leaders are consumers or creators of leadership talent. This metric communicates to employees the importance of creating leadership. In another, anytime a high potential gives notice, the CEO receives e-mail notification, and a counteroffer is presented within twenty-four hours.

SPENDING TIME ON LEADERSHIP ISSUES. One successful CEO said that he spent 40 percent of his time on leadership issues. When pushed to verify this large amount of time, he said that he personally reviewed the promotion slates of over fifteen hundred job positions (in a company of 140,000 people). This meant that he would personally get to know the candidates who might take these key positions, then review the candidate slates, and modify them as he felt appropriate. He felt that "strategy follows people" and that getting the right people in the right place ensured that strategy would take care of itself. By personally spending time on leadership issues, he protected and furthered the leadership brand—and future results.

CRAFTING AND PERSONALLY OWNING THE STATEMENT OF LEADERSHIP BRAND. This takes direct attention. It is not enough to— as one company did when it encountered the leadership brand concept—send the head of HR off-site with a team to craft the brand and return and present it to the senior leadership team in a subsequent meeting. It was no surprise that leadership brand never became a business priority for that company or that it never had a significant impact; from the get-go it was merely a business issue that could be delegated to others and then reviewed by the senior team. Leadership brand needs to be crafted, touched, and owned by the senior leadership team. They need to spend time debating and claiming the statement of leadership. When the senior leaders have their fingerprints and voiceprints on the leadership brand, it becomes more credible. The CEO must be personally involved in leading this effort for it to have legitimacy and impact.

HOLDING OTHERS ACCOUNTABLE IN PUBLIC AND PRIVATE FOR ACTIONS CONGRUENT WITH THE LEADERSHIP BRAND. One of the ultimate tests of a statement of leadership is the extent to which it guides action. Leaders who act consistently with the brand should have good things happen to them; those who don't should have bad things happen. CEOs must establish a discipline pattern to make the leadership brand real. This might mean removing a leader who does not embody the leadership brand, no matter how talented that leader may seem in other ways. When someone gets replaced, it sends a loud message throughout the company about the things that matter most—and the things that will not be tolerated.

The first quarter in a new assignment is critical for any new leader. In this ninety-day period, the leader often has to make calls to create or update the full leadership team. This means articulating the leadership brand, assessing current personnel against it, and making required changes. When we ask leaders what they would have done differently early in their leadership tenure, almost all say that they should have moved faster and been more bold. And when pushed about where they should have moved more boldly, almost all point to the movement of people. They say that they held off because they were friends with those who needed to be moved or they wanted to be sure to give individuals multiple opportunities to learn and grow. Almost universally, they later felt that this delay had been an error; the people their managerial intuition identified as unable to live the leadership brand should have been moved sooner rather than later—for their own sake as well as for the sake of others in the company.

While public actions communicate the brand and its importance, private conversations often have even more impact. In speaking quietly with other leaders, senior leaders communicate what they really feel and what matters most to them. These private conversations can occur in the office, in transit, or off work. It is often in the most casual settings that senior leaders share their heartfelt and candid desires for and assessments of the company. If in these more personal moments the importance of leadership continues to be discussed, the word spreads that the leader is serious about building leadership.

MONITORING LEADERSHIP INVESTMENTS. As we have discussed, the amount of economic and human capital spent on leadership is increasing. The adage "What gets inspected is expected" is correct—when CEOs spend time monitoring leadership brand investments and their results, they communicate the importance of leadership and of building better leaders. The leadership brand monitoring can focus on people: Who should attend a particular learning experience? Who should help design or deliver an in-company learning experience? Who should be assigned to a permanent or temporary job assignment? When leaders know that the senior team is personally involved in monitoring their development, they are likely to take the development experiences seriously.

The monitoring can also include a review of the impact of the experience. One leader would periodically do a development review of the officers of the company, asking what experiences the officers had that enabled them to be successful. He found that some training experiences had more developmental impact than others. He also found that some job assignments, especially assignments outside their home country, were critical to the development of these officers. Over time, the company developed a rule of thumb that to become an officer, one needed an extensive work assignment outside one's home country. This directive came from the CEO, recognizing the importance of broad experience in the development of the officer cadre. In another company, a leader personally encouraged off-work development assignments. Future leaders in the company were encouraged to be active in political and social affairs outside of work. This led to a leave-of-absence policy that encouraged leaders to participate in outside assignments that fostered their development.

BEING PERSONALLY INVOLVED IN BUILDING THE NEXT GENER-ATION OF LEADERS. One study showed that, compared with ineffective leaders, effective leaders know the names of more potential leaders in their company. The personal connection is not just a matter of knowing the names—effective leaders also know the predispositions, aspirations, strengths, and weaknesses of potential leaders. Companies building next-generation leaders often start early to build a dossier on a potential leader. In one company, the head of leadership development prepared a one- to two-page synthesis of each potential leader's strengths and weaknesses every year that was circulated to senior leaders. These synopses read more like magazine articles than like performance appraisals, but they captured the essence of the next generation of leaders. CEOs read and devour précis like these to get to know the future leaders.

Senior leaders also become exemplars of the leadership brand. At PepsiCo, Dell, P&G, GE, and other companies renowned for their leadership, senior executives teach the leadership brand to other leaders in leadership training settings. By teaching the leadership brand, these leaders publicly commit to living it. And because the leaders are both teaching and living it, other leaders grasp the criticality of the brand, and their own commitment to living it improves as well. PepsiCo has also found that when leaders teach leadership, it results in greater teamwork, stronger personal relationships between the senior leader and other leaders, greater loyalty, and more alignment with the vision and key strategic issues.

CEOs embody both the firm and leadership brands. They are the ultimate brand managers not only of products and services but of the leadership bridge between customer expectations and employee behavior.

Leaders Throughout

In practice, the leadership brand must be infused into every leader within the organization. Since the leadership brand is the bridge between employees inside and customers outside, and since customer expectations are bound to evolve, the leadership brand at the top must also evolve. This means that leaders throughout an organization need to demonstrate both consistency with the present brand (by being aligned with today's customers) and the capacity to adapt to changing customer expectations. This often makes it desirable to encourage leaders early in their careers to explore a variety of experiences so they build broad skills as conditions change. When they do so, the organization can pick future leaders who are different from the present leaders but still fully integrated into the company culture and leadership brand.

While leadership brand differences can exist among leaders throughout an organization, leaders throughout the organization must also demonstrate similar levels of commitment to building the leadership brand. Some leaders—the less effective ones—are consumers of leadership; others are producers. Consuming leaders minimize and drive out talent; producing leaders magnify and engage talent. Consuming leaders operate black holes from which few other leaders emerge; producing leaders create the next generation of leaders for their organization and often an entire industry. Consuming leaders make themselves feel important; producing leaders share credit and make others feel important. Consuming leaders make decisions alone; producing leaders involve others in decision making. Consuming leaders hoard information; producing leaders share information. Consuming leaders revel in the perks of their position; producing leaders distribute financial and nonfinancial perks. Consuming leaders thwart the development of future leaders; producing leaders generate future leaders.

Just as a leader is responsible for generating cash for the corporation, so too should a leader be responsible to help generate the next set of leaders. A measure of leaders' producing leaders is the extent to which leaders develop and emerge from a particular leader's organization. Executives often track the number of leaders who emerged from a given organization and who moved on to succeed elsewhere. This leadership genealogy can be seen in sports. In professional football, for example, Bill Parcells (former coach of the Dallas Cowboys) has produced a host of other successful coaches:

- Bill Belichick, New England Patriots

- Tom Coughlin, New York Giants

- Romeo Crennel, Cleveland Browns

- Al Groh, University of Virginia

- Sean Payton, New Orleans Saints

- Charlie Weis, University of Notre Dame

Parcells's coaching brand has transferred to multiple generations, thus ensuring his legacy as coach not only of his team but of the entire professional football league. In college basketball, other producing coaches (John Wooden, Mike Krzyzewski, and Dean Smith) earn their reputation through the work of rival coaches they have led and inspired.

Producing leaders exist at any level of an organization. They may be more visible at senior levels, where they have amassed a cadre of disciples who have learned and implemented some of their ideas. But they also exist in middle management, where they encourage others to be engaged and creative, and in frontline management positions, where they build empowered employees. At any level, producing leaders build a leadership brand by cultivating competence, sharing decision making and authority, imparting information, and distributing rewards.

Cultivating Competence

Competence has to be more than skin deep. Here's a case in point:

The Would-Be Big Frog

We once worked with a leader who seemed competent. He had a vision, made decisions consistent with the vision, and had employees who liked him and felt personally dedicated to him. But he had one problem: he surrounded himself with people not quite as talented or effective as he was, who relied on him and depended on him to take the lead in most decisions. He willingly did so, measuring his success by the esteem his subordinates felt for him and by his ability to get things done himself.

Despite his influence, he was not a producing leader—few, if any, of his employees ever moved to other positions in the company, and when he left, the company had no real backup for him in place. His absence created a leadership vacuum that took years to fill.

Producing leaders have the confidence to surround themselves with competent subordinates, frequently with those whose talents exceed their own. They enjoy the challenge of working with people who have good ideas and who push them to greater heights, and they do not get defensive when people who work with them express an alternative point of view.

In her thoughtful biography of Abraham Lincoln, Doris Kearns Goodwin points out that one of Lincoln's rarest and most endearing leadership qualities was his willingness and ability to surround himself with those who differed from him.[4] She titled her work *Team of Rivals* because four individuals who lost to Lincoln in the 1860 Republican primary were graciously invited to join his cabinet. In their cabinet roles, they often disagreed with each other and with the president. But from these disparate points of view emerged more thoughtful actions that enabled Lincoln to lead the United States through the greatest crisis in its history. Likewise, producing leaders surround themselves with subordinates who are not like them. These leaders demonstrate their personal confidence and competence by inviting those who are confident and competent to join them. Then they listen to the ideas and opinions of these individuals. They encourage dialogue and debate, delegate real authority and power, and allow their people to develop and grow.

Producing leaders cultivate competence by investing in the next generation of leaders through helping install the leadership brand. They personally prepare and review individual development plans that give future leaders a sense of what they can aspire to become and how to go about reaching these aspirations. They appoint these leaders to demanding assignments where they will learn and grow by doing hard and demanding things. They help these leaders learn from mistakes. Rather than hoarding or hiding these leaders from others, they give them visible assignments and then support their requests to move to other positions in the organization. All these actions culminate in the establishment of the leadership brand.

Producing leaders demonstrate their competence by encouraging others to establish their own competence.

Sharing Decision Making and Authority

Producing leaders understand how to make decisions themselves, but even more they know how to share both decision making and authority with others. They give their subordinates decision rights and opportunities to be responsible and accountable for completion of projects. They delegate authority with accountability and consequences to others so that others can learn and grow.

Sometimes this delegation of authority comes from building reporting relationships and organizational structures that give junior leaders opportunities to be accountable and responsible for a line of business early in their career. As organizations get more complex, often this complexity leads to matrix organizations where some are responsible for functional excellence, others for product design, and still others for geographic sensitivities. These individuals then form teams to collaborate to make sure that the matrix organization brings specialist knowledge to all decisions. Unfortunately, the complex matrix organization, with specialists collaborating through teams, often does not give any individual the opportunity to be fully responsible for managing all the dimensions of a business. In other organizations, leaders are given smaller, then increasingly larger responsibilities where they can demonstrate their ability to accomplish tasks, projects, or division- or business-wide goals. Leaders who produce future branded leaders structure organizations in ways that enable people to control the processes that will let them be accountable for outcomes.

Leaders who produce leaders also help future leaders observe and learn about decision processes. Consuming leaders often make decisions and move on. Producing leaders will review how they thought about the decision process and share the logic and rationale they used in coming to a decision. In debriefings, they will reveal why they did what they did and help developing leaders see not only what was decided but the thought process behind the decision. In addition, they develop future leaders by reviewing not just the decisions they make but the steps and thought processes they use to come to a decision. One leader frequently used the nonthreatening phrase "help me understand" to explore future leaders' thought processes: *Help me understand* why you chose option A over B . . . *Help me understand* the information you collected in coming to your conclusion . . . *Help me understand* how you thought about involving people in this decision . . . *Help me understand* what you learned from your experience . . . These queries pushed future leaders to reflect on the decisions they made—and also on why and how they made them, which led to insights that were valuable for future decisions.

Producing leaders often engage future leaders by asking them, "What do you think?" "What are the options?" or "What would you suggest?" These questions push the onus of decision making back to the future leader. In one organization, when employees came to the leader with a problem or challenge, she would repeatedly respond in this fashion. Over time, employees learned to approach her with a problem only when they could also come up with a recommendation. This leader realized that in most cases the employee raising a problem had thought about it longer and had more experience with it than she did. When encouraged to be reflective and solution oriented, employees assumed responsibility for decisions and learned to be better leaders in the process. Where the leader had unique experiences with a particular problem, she would give guidance while explaining why she chose as she did, and future leaders grew from this experience as well.

Producing leaders make decisions about allocating resources to create the leadership brand. These decisions can be made about money (how to determine what to spend), people (who should be assigned to what task), and time (how leaders apportion their time to specific projects). By thinking carefully—and explicitly communicating trade-offs to those in their organization—about spending money, people, and time, leaders produce future leaders. Some leaders make the mistake of thinking that any one of these three types of resource is sufficient for building a leadership brand. It requires all three. Spending money but not allocating people or time is likely to result in project budgets that start with high energy but fizzle because of lack of competence or attention. Assigning people but not giving them the money or attention they require will frustrate employees who are unable to make things happen. Putting personal time into a project but not people or budget will create cynicism and lack of sustainability.

Imparting Information

Producing leaders do not hoard information; they share it. Since access to information is often a source of power, producing leaders who share information are also sharing power. Sometimes they share by disseminating information that is given to them. At other times, they create information sharing by asking leaders to collect the information firsthand.

By sharing information, producing leaders help future leaders learn how to go from data to decision making. In a world of information ubiquity, the challenge is often turning information and data into insights and decisions. Producing leaders help others see that information should be used to reach a decision, not just to have information. When employees come up with ideas or recommendations, producing leaders often ask, "What is the decision you want me to make?" This question shifts the focus from the information to the decision.

Producing leaders also share candid information. One company we worked in had what we call a *cultural virus*—in this case, always being nice and never sharing bad news. This "nice-itis" meant that when things went wrong, people always made excuses and offered plausible reasons. No one wanted direct and honest confrontation about what should or could have happened. In this organization, leaders were not growing, because they were not willing to look honestly at anything that went wrong. Without the candid conversations that could have generated corrections, errors continued and mistakes were repeated and not learned from.

Candid conversations need not be unkind. With reasonable privacy and an atmosphere of support, people can be led to explain what happened and why, and also to learn and improve for the next iteration. Candid conversations are not personal attacks, and they do not focus solely on what went wrong; they are an opportunity to observe and report patterns of behavior that will help the future leader turn information into insight and eventually into action. By sharing information, leaders build the leadership brand in others.

Distributing Rewards

Another leadership team we worked with moved toward becoming producing leaders by cultivating competence through training and other experiences, sharing decision making and authority by involving others, and sharing information by letting everyone know what was happening and why. Unfortunately, this team then took a disproportionate percentage of the financial and nonfinancial rewards for themselves.

Their efforts to produce future leaders fell short as individuals developed skills and looked elsewhere for better rewards—and the team wondered why. The reason: they had lost track of the need to distribute rewards equitably so that future leaders would have an incentive to move forward.

We often use a simple illustration to capture the concept of equitable reward distribution. Assume that four levels of leadership are involved in a project. The project succeeds and the business reaps 100 units of benefit. How would you as a leader distribute these 100 units across the four levels, with you, the leader, being level 1:

Level 1:

Level 2:

Level 3:

Level 4:

Total: 100 units of gain

Generally, leaders will find some reasonable way to share the 100 units of benefit: 40-30-20-10 or sometimes 25-25-25-25. We then ask them to look at total compensation (base salary, bonus, and deferred compensation such as stock or stock appreciation units) and see how the distribution actually occurs. What we generally find is that leaders will project a distribution of the 100 units far more equitable than what actually exists. In some companies the actual appropriation looks more like 60-20-10-10. Senior leaders often get a very high percentage of the rewards. The rationale for granting senior leaders greater rewards may be market comparison (leaders in other companies are getting comparable rewards), but it creates inequity. The ratio of total CEO compensation to average worker compensation has risen dramatically in recent years, as indicated in figure 8-1.[5]

This disparity can be an incentive for aspiring leaders to get to the top leadership position—so as to get their leadership goodies at last—but it ultimately disheartens more people than it encourages.

Nonfinancial rewards also send signals about leadership. Traditionally, rising leaders tied their status to office size and privacy. To combat this, one company created an open office among the executive team. Each executive had a personal desk area in an open office where they

FIGURE 8-1

Ratio of CEO to average worker pay, 1965–2005

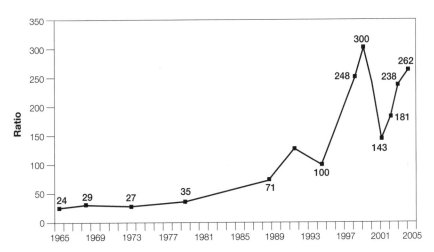

Source: Lawrence Mishel, Jared Bernstein, and Sylvia Allegratto, *The State of Working America, 2006/2007*, 2006, Figure 3Z, www.epinet.org.

could see one another, converse easily, and share information. There were plenty of conference rooms where private conversations could be held, but the open office enabled leaders to encourage the next generation of future leaders by allowing them to observe what leaders actually did. Other nonfinancial rewards may be used, such as public recognition, prize assignments, personal notes, unexpected time off, sabbaticals, and simple praise.

Leaders at all levels of an organization can become producing leaders. They invest in the next generation by helping them build competence, authority, and information, and by giving them suitable rewards. These producing leaders create a leadership legacy and brand that endures beyond any individual leader. Assessment 8-2 offers a self-audit you can use to determine the extent to which you are now a producing leader who builds leadership brand.

HR Leaders or HR Generalists

In recent years, human resource leaders have moved to positions of influence in articulating and executing company strategy and direction.[6] Senior HR leaders who work as generalists either for the entire company or for a major division of a company play a key role in shaping, delivering, and sustaining a leadership brand. As discussed earlier, the CEO is the ultimate owner of the leadership brand, and leaders throughout the organization demonstrate the brand by what they know, do, and deliver. But HR leaders foster a leadership brand in many ways.

FIRST, THEY EMBODY THE BRAND IN THEIR PERSONAL BE-HAVIOR. HR leaders are very visible throughout most organizations because they directly and indirectly touch everyone in the company, set the standards and norms for behavior within the company, and coach other leaders to demonstrate the leadership brand. We worked in a company where the head of HR was accused of sexual misconduct. Though he was not convicted, evidence of inappropriate behavior did come to light. Because of his role in the company, his behavior was magnified many times over, and the company struggled to establish a clear and definitive standard on leader misconduct. HR leaders live in the limelight; employees throughout a company observe what they do and how they do it.

ASSESSMENT 8-2

Consuming or producing the leadership brand

Leaders as consumers of leadership	Circle the appropriate number:	Leaders as producers of leadership
Competence		
Hiring people not quite as good as you	− 3 − 2 − 1 0 +1 +2 +3	Appointing people to report to you who are more talented than you
Surrounding yourself with sycophants	− 3 − 2 − 1 0 +1 +2 +3	Surrounding yourself with those who will disagree
Impeding the development of the next generation	− 3 − 2 − 1 0 +1 +2 +3	Investing in the development of the next generation
Punishing others when they fail	− 3 − 2 − 1 0 +1 +2 +3	Encouraging and coaching others to learn from failures as well as successes
Decision making and authority		
Spending time haphazardly or randomly; not managing your calendar aggressively	− 3 − 2 − 1 0 +1 +2 +3	Investing time as carefully as money or other resources
Making most decisions alone	− 3 − 2 − 1 0 +1 +2 +3	Delegating authority and re-sponsibility to others
Delaying difficult people decisions	− 3 − 2 − 1 0 +1 +2 +3	Making difficult decisions, particularly around talent
Information		
Hoarding information	− 3 − 2 − 1 0 +1 +2 +3	Sharing information with others
Explaining what should be done	− 3 − 2 − 1 0 +1 +2 +3	Explaining why things should be done
Unwilling to confront or share bad news	− 3 − 2 − 1 0 +1 +2 +3	Willing to coach others by feedback and feed-forward
Rewards		
Taking a disproportionate share of the financial rewards	− 3 − 2 − 1 0 +1 +2 +3	Appropriately sharing financial rewards with others
Accumulating the nonfinancial rewards of leadership	− 3 − 2 − 1 0 +1 +2 +3	Distributing the nonfinancial rewards to others

Interpretation:

20–36: You are a producer of leaders; people will want to work for you.
0–20: You are moving in the right direction; keep moving in this direction.
Below 0: Watch out—you're likely to be lonely in your old age.

SECOND, THEY SHAPE THE HR POLICIES THAT TOUCH EVERY EMPLOYEE FROM ENTRY TO RETIREMENT. These policies guide all the decisions about hiring, pay, training, promotion, appraisal, and transfer that are made in between. HR policies need to reflect the leadership brand. If, say, Apple's leadership brand centers on innovation, then the sustaining practices for innovation come from the way Apple hires, trains, pays, and promotes people who innovate, and the way it communicates about innovation. When these HR practices align and integrate with the desired leadership brand, it becomes sustained.

Unfortunately, in many companies, employees are hired for skills ABC, then trained to do DEF, paid for GHI, and often communicated to about JKL. This lack of congruence among HR practices creates confusion. The critical elements of the firm's leadership brand should show up consistently in all HR practices and policies. Senior HR leaders institutionalize a leadership brand, separating it from the personality of the CEO and integrating it into the fabric of the organization.

One of the trends in HR is to link internal HR practices to external customer and investor expectations, and this is consistent with the leadership brand representing the firm brand. If leadership brand is the bridge between the external customer and internal employee behavior, then HR practices represent the traffic on this bridge. Organizations have moved from wanting to be the universal employer of choice to being the employer of choice for employees that their best customers would choose. In many organizations, customers are directly involved in hiring by helping define requirements for future employees and interviewing potential candidates; customers are involved in compensation by ensuring that the appraisal process focuses on behaviors and outcomes that the customers perceive as valuable; customers can participate via 720-degree feedback (feedback that reaches outside the company, as compared to 360-degree feedback, which focuses only inside it), and by occasionally helping to distribute financial and nonfinancial rewards to employees.[7] HR leaders ensure that HR practices reflect the desired leadership brand and connect customer expectations with employee actions.

THIRD, HR LEADERS COACH, ARCHITECT, AND FACILITATE THE PROCESS OF ESTABLISHING THE LEADERSHIP BRAND. As *coaches*, HR leaders work directly with individual business leaders to align their behavior with their desired outcomes.[8] One of the desired outcomes for any leader should be to demonstrate the right leadership brand, so HR professionals can *coach* to help build this brand. They do so by building trust, making behavioral observations, offering candid and supportive feedback, and doing feed-forward by suggesting new behavior consistent with the desired leadership brand. As *architects*, HR professionals turn the desired leadership brand into a blueprint for action that shows up in HR practices and policies. As *facilitators*, HR professionals manage the process of change to ensure that what is wanted actually happens.

In our research, we have found that to coach, architect, and facilitate, HR professionals must become credible activists (having personal credibility but also having a point of view, or what we call *HR with an attitude*); culture and change stewards (being able to turn events into patterns and turning what is known into what is done); talent managers and organization designers (aligning and integrating HR practices); and strategy architects (ensuring that the right people are involved in shaping strategy and that strategic clarity emerges from it).[9] Here's another case in point:

Living Leadership

Jeff Childs, senior vice president of HR at U.S. Cellular, is a good example of an HR leader who helps build the leadership brand by word and deed. He believes that HR is not just aligned with strategy, it is an inherent part of the strategy. At U.S. Cellular, the business model starts with effective (branded) leadership that drives associate (the company's term for employee) satisfaction, leads to customer satisfaction, and generates business results. This leadership-to-results linkage is called the dynamic organization (D.O.), and serves as a model for decisions made by the leadership team. The D.O. model says the company will achieve profitable growth through a customer satisfaction strategy, and will deliver on customer satisfaction by leveraging the power of human capital as driven by leadership.

U.S. Cellular leaders teach the D.O. to associates both by modeling the way and by classroom instruction. They lead by inspiration, not regulation, and ensure that others do likewise. While these concepts sound easy, they also place greater accountability on leaders. Decisions must be explained in terms of the whys, as opposed to the whats. Discussions must be open and honest at every level. As an executive officer, Childs demonstrates this communication style in every interaction with associates, including a series of "straight talk" visits he conducts in the field. He embodies the style he encourages others to live.

He also drives the leadership philosophy through HR practices. Whenever possible, leaders are promoted from within to fill leadership roles because they are already well adapted to the D.O. When going outside, U.S. Cellular assesses candidates for more than simple job skills, seeking people who fit with the company's values and desired behaviors. Recently, the U.S. Cellular talent acquisition team developed an advertising strategy that emphasized the company's culture rather than the technical requirements of the position. Using this strategy, HR drew candidates to the company culture or brand, rather than just to a specific role.

Current leaders are expected to demonstrate the right leadership brand. One example is through a week-long pipeline class called the "Leadership Development Workshop" that gives frontline associates a chance to determine whether they have the basic skills to be a leader in the D.O. and provides the fundamentals of how to use the company's vision and the D.O. to grow as leaders. A follow-up to that course is "Servant Leadership" training, which builds on the company's belief that leadership is a privilege, not a right. Each member of the executive team, including Childs, teaches a portion of this program, further demonstrating the importance of leaders teaching leadership.

By modeling the leadership brand and by weaving it into these HR practices, Childs has helped his organization achieve its goals. The company's churn in the industry is among the lowest, at 1.5 percent—meaning that once customers join, they want to stay. Its customer survey scores are high, and its business continues to outperform industry standards and expectations.

U.S. Cellular's leadership brand has been successful because Childs has translated customer needs into leadership expectations, and he understands the business and the strategy well enough to know where to invest for maximum impact (in his case, frontline associates and leadership brand applicant screening).

HR Specialists

While HR generalists work directly with business leaders in ensuring the leadership brand, HR specialists in training and development also play a key role in establishing the leadership brand. In chapter 5, we discussed ways to invest in leadership brand through training, job, and life experiences. While CEOs and other business leaders are the owners of these investments, the individual generally charged with setting them up has come to be called the *chief learning officer*. This title shifts the focus away from leadership investments as events to learning through training, job, and life experiences.

Chief learning officers, or others responsible for investing in leadership development, have the challenge of creating what our colleague Warren Wilhelm calls a "Total Learning Architecture."[10] Linking leadership brand into a learning architecture ensures that learning investments further the business strategy and help build a leadership brand, that multiple learning methodologies are used and tailored to the needs of the individual, and that learning occurs at individual, team, and organization levels. The leadership brand metaphor ensures that learning specialists focus learning investments on connecting leader behaviors and actions to the desired firm brand. In assessment 8-3, we offer an assessment to diagnose the extent to which your organization's learning specialists are building a total learning architecture suited to a leadership brand.

An effective learning specialist builds leadership brand by paying attention to the following:

- *Ensuring accountability to the senior line managers.* The CEO is the ultimate owner of the leadership brand, and business leaders throughout the organization must be responsible and accountable for leadership. If senior leaders do not spend time, energy, and attention on the firm's leadership brand, they communicate that leadership is not a priority. And their diverse personal brands become the icons that others will follow—leaving consistent, predictable results up to chance. Learning specialists must continually reinforce line executives as the owners of the leadership brand by keeping leadership on their agendas (board meetings, staff meetings), having leaders speak out in public for the brand, and ensuring that leaders take personal ownership of building the brand.

Measuring the effectiveness of learning specialists

To what extent does your organization's learning architecture include the following:

	Low High
1. Accountability by line managers for overseeing and directing the learning investments	1 2 3 4 5
2. A clear line of sight and link between learning investments for leaders and firm brand	1 2 3 4 5
3. An assessment of the leadership brand that can be administered for the organization and for each individual	1 2 3 4 5
4. A personalized approach to learning tailored to the needs of each leader	1 2 3 4 5
5. Education and training experiences that focus on application	1 2 3 4 5
6. Systematic task assignments that give leaders opportunity to learn from doing	1 2 3 4 5
7. Opportunities to adapt life experiences to improving leadership at work	1 2 3 4 5
8. Involvement of customers in design or delivery of the learning experiences	1 2 3 4 5
9. Participants' awareness of why they are involved and what they need to learn	1 2 3 4 5
10. Measurement of learning results in terms of how they support the leadership brand	1 2 3 4 5
Total	

Key:

43–50: Your company's learning specialists are outstanding. Hold on to them—others will try to take them.
36–42: You have good learning specialists.
28–35: Your learning specialists are average.
20–27: You might need new learning specialists.
Less than 20: Move your learning specialists to a competitor, and hope they stay.

- *Linking the leadership brand to the firm brand.* The bridge between customers and employees must become clear through the way learning specialists invest in future leaders. Learning specialists should make sure that all company-promoted training, work, and life experiences reflect the desired leadership brand. To make this happen, learning specialists should translate customer identity and expectations into programs and learning investments.

- *Assessing leadership brand.* Competency models should be based on the leadership brand. Assessments of overall leadership within the company (for example, extent of backup talent) and assessments of individual leaders should then be based on these leadership brand models. Learning specialists draft and craft both the competency model and its use for assessment.

- *Tailoring the development of individual leaders into a leadership brand.* Leaders bring predispositions to their work as well as personal learning styles. Learning specialists can build individual development plans that help leaders recognize their own strengths and weaknesses and improve their personal leadership brand. Learning specialists have the knack of balancing the overall organization leadership brand and the individual's personal leadership brand.

- *Creating leadership investments in training, work, and life that shape and develop the leadership brand.* Learning specialists should be experts and innovators in investing in leadership development. This means using and integrating the principles and practices we review in chapter 5 into a total learning architecture.

- *Involving customer ideas and actions into internal leadership practice.* Learning specialists succeed when customers would be delighted with the way leaders are developed. This means that customer ideas and expectations show up in training experiences and work assignments. It means that customers personally participate in leadership development. Learning specialists know key customers and involve them in appropriate ways to help the organization respond to their needs.

- *Helping leaders be accountable for their own development.* Learning specialists become one-to-one coaches for budding and producing leaders by helping them learn and grow from their experiences. In organizations with talented learning specialists, leaders throughout the organization know what is expected of them, how they are doing against those expectations, and how they can develop to meet future expectations.

- *Monitoring leadership brand.* Assessing leadership brand comes from ensuring that the right things are done the right way, and also from showing a return on leadership intangibles (see chapter 6). Learning specialists have a leadership brand scorecard that helps business leaders know how the brand is evolving. Thus they are central to talent management.

When learning specialists do these activities, their organizations are more likely to have a total learning architecture dedicated to the leadership brand. To make this architecture happen, learning specialists must not only master learning theory and practice, they must also be able to adapt this knowledge to the business. When this adaptation occurs through the brand metaphor, learning specialists can speak many languages: the language of the customers and what they expect, the language of the business and what investors require, the language of employees and what they value. Speaking these languages enables learning specialists to work in all the domains that can make or break the leadership brand.

Conclusion

Leadership brand is a team sport. It requires that people throughout the organization have individual talents and accountabilities but work together as a team to make the leadership brand happen. Boards of directors oversee and govern the creation of the brand. CEOs and senior executives embody and manage the brand. Line managers throughout the organization live the brand in day-to-day interactions and become producing leaders by investing in the next generation of leaders for the business. HR generalists coach, facilitate, and architect the development of leadership brand. HR specialists offer specific learning insights that turn customer expectations into leadership attributes and results. This collective team is unified around a shared commitment to bridging customer expectations and employee behaviors through leadership brand.

9

Implications for
Personal Brand

THE PREVIOUS CHAPTERS have demonstrated the value of and how to build an organization's leadership brand. This brand becomes a key capability of successful organizations because it turns customer expectations into employee behaviors. This chapter shifts gears and focuses on your personal leadership brand. Without a personal and authentic commitment from individual leaders, even the best organization leadership brand becomes a fad and a farce, creating more cynicism than value. Leaders who try out for and play a leadership role they don't believe in quickly lose credibility. When someone's personal brand doesn't match the desired firm brand, employees notice and become skeptical. By contrast, they can sense authentic leadership. Ultimately, followers define leaders—and followers admire those who are grounded in word and in deed; they come to trust and have confidence in genuine leaders.

A personal leadership brand is an individual's identity, reputation, or distinctiveness as a leader; it identifies strengths and predispositions and includes provisions to mitigate the effects of weaknesses. Top management and other visible leaders often become known by their personal brand. In our teaching, we often put up pictures of famous leaders (Winston Churchill, Bill Clinton, Margaret Thatcher, Desmond Tutu, Nelson Mandela, Tony Blair, Charles de Gaulle, Golda Meir, Abraham Lincoln, and others) and ask participants to write down their impressions of these leaders' personal brands. Despite some variety based on politics and country of origin, inevitably the resulting descriptions of these leaders' personal brands display high congruence. Each of these leaders has a personal brand, one that is shared with the world and well known, and that draws on the brand holder's signature strengths.

Your own personal brand reflects who you are more than who you say you are. This personal identity becomes a reputation that others respond to and reinforce. Mature leaders realize that over time people will tend to forget some of the things leaders do (meetings attended, speeches given, goals set and accomplished), but they will remember the results of these acts and the personal style that leaders demonstrated. Who we are speaks louder and longer than what we do and may even overpower real character flaws. But what we do is what creates our enduring brand. Winston Churchill's enduring brand highlights his ability to rally citizens to fight in major world conflicts; it largely ignores his personal difficulties. Jack Welch will be remembered for his ability to create enormous wealth through strategic clarity and organization disciplines; his early "Neutron Jack" image is largely forgotten.

Personal brand and signature strengths are not just for senior leaders—every employee has a personal brand. Tom Peters argues that everyone must become a brand and not just an employee.[1] Another case in point:

One Person's Brand

Kalpana Mistry, senior vice president of human resources for VITAS Healthcare Corporation, is of Indian descent. Born in Uganda, where she lived until the age of thirteen, when she and her family had to flee Idi Amin's dictatorship, they went to England as refugees. She completed her education in England, worked in a national soft drinks manufacturing company, and then moved to Miami, Florida, to enter a marriage arranged in the Indian tradition.

In her personal life, she was forced to adjust to a very traditional environment where women were seen as subservient to men. She had two children, but the abuse and fear led her to leave with her children, who were three and four years of age at the time.

At that point, Mistry started her career in an entry-level job. After seven years, she had worked her way up to vice president of HR for a banking institution in south Florida. She was then recruited as vice president of HR function for a national health-care company in south Florida, which grew from seven hundred to over eight thousand employees within eighteen months of her appointment. She helped the company grow and expand nationally; then, when it had to declare bankruptcy, she worked with the downsizing. She changed careers to work with the fifth-largest school district in the United States (Broward County, Florida), with over 260,000 students and 28,000 employees. Mistry was responsible for all HR functions, including eight collective bargaining agreements, as well as safety policies and risk management. During her time in this role, she also initiated school planning, quality performance management programs, and guidelines on discipline and hiring.

In 2002, Mistry was recruited to head HR for VITAS Health-care Corporation, the largest U.S. provider of hospice care. She has consistently been the bridge between those using the hospice services and employees. To develop employee attitude and behavior, she has implemented employee suggestion systems, surveys, performance management programs, training, and introduction to new technologies. VITAS has grown from four thousand to more than ten thousand employees since she joined it, and is now focusing on compassionate end of life care and the needs of pa-tients and their families. For example, when the organization was impacted by the critical shortage of nurses, Mistry initiated a partnership with her former employer, Broward County School District, to develop and launch a new nursing program in its vocational and technical schools, with a focus on an end-of-life curriculum, making this the first of its kind in the nation. She has consistently been involved in community service projects with her association with the Himalayan International Institute of Yoga Science and Philosophy, a not-for-profit organization head-quartered in Honesdale, Pennsylvania, and is now a certified instructor and teacher in yoga. She is working on global humani-tarian projects to address issues of illiteracy, inequality, poverty, hunger, disease, and HIV/AIDS and visits Uganda and south central India to work on these projects. As a result of her per-sonal efforts, VITAS Healthcare Corporation has expanded her role in HR to represent the company in this endeavor and contributes toward this effort. Through all these activities, Mistry has acquired a personal leadership brand of respect,

professionalism, creativity, and humanitarian aid. She has lived
that brand throughout her career and in her personal life. Her
life demonstrates that a personal leadership brand may occur at
any level in an organization.

When a leader's personal brand aligns with the organization's leadership brand, leaders are both congruent and credible. Jeffrey Immelt
shifted the GE brand from Jack Welch's focus on organization disciplines like Six Sigma and strategy planning to top-line growth through
innovation and invention. To do so, he made sure that his calendar
(time), passion (enthusiasm), attention (resources and support), and
rhetoric (private and public speech) were focused on invention.[2] He
personally sponsored a number of initiatives (at the customer for the
customer, customer dreaming sessions, growth traits and assessments,
imagination breakthroughs, innovation labs, and so forth) that helped
foster growth through innovation.

In this chapter, we provide a set of personal analytics to help you discern and demonstrate your own personal leadership brand and create
signature strengths. These analytics follow the same dimensions we
used in characterizing an organization's leadership brand. They can be
applied within the context of an organization's leadership brand, or
they can be used to create your personal leadership brand independent
of any organization (at work, in your community, or in your personal
relationships) you are a part of. If you find that your personal brand is
at odds with the organization's leadership brand, you should consider
finding ways to narrow the gap through shifting the brand, if appropriate, or finding a better fit somewhere else.

Create the Case for Change

In chapter 2, we talked about building the case for leadership. An organization's leadership brand exists because it helps the organization
reach its goals for growth and it helps the organization deliver value to
key stakeholders. At a personal level, brand or identity exists and persists because it helps people reach personal goals. The best argument
for building and sustaining your personal brand is the help it will give
you in reaching your own goals.

Another Personal Brand

Our colleague and friend Marshall Goldsmith has a personal and
public desire to help successful leaders get even better—by
changing behavior for the better, for themselves, their people,
and their teams.[3] To deliver on this desire, he has successfully
mastered his personal leadership brand as executive coach. He
believes that through coaching, he is able to help good people
become better and realize their full potential. He has worked to
create and master a coaching philosophy and identity. He writes
articles, gives talks, and does magazine columns about his coaching philosophy. As a result of his focused work, he has established
the Marshall Goldsmith School of Management (Alliant International University's business school is named for him) and has
created a coaching brand and philosophy. He has found a link
between his desired outcome (helping others) and his desired
personal leadership brand (world's premier coach).

At the personal level, the case for change also requires that leaders
analyze their willingness and commitment to be leaders. Leadership
comes with a personal price. The benefits of being a leader must outweigh the price of leadership.

Leaders live under a microscope—others observe and watch their
behavior carefully. As a result, leadership means losing personal space
and paying the price of visibility and scrutiny. Dave recently spent three
years leading missionaries for his church. During this time, he wore a
suit and tie every day, as that is the expected attire in his group. Taking
the advice of a colleague, he experimented for about six weeks with
buttoning his suit jacket every day. Within this short time, most of the
missionaries were buttoning their suit jackets. Then for a couple of
months, he never buttoned his jacket, and the missionaries soon did the
same. This relatively trivial example highlighted the extent to which
others observed and modeled his behavior. In organizations, leaders'
behaviors are observed, magnified, and exemplified. When a new CEO
of a car company drives a competitor's car, employees notice. When a
senior executive flies coach instead of first class to save money, the
leader's actions are noticed, mimicked, and magnified, for good and ill.

Leaders pay a personal price of exposure to public scrutiny. At times this scrutiny exposes malfeasance, but at all times it puts leaders on alert. One leader who became a CEO lived in a neighborhood surrounded by company employees, who were all interested and observant neighbors. He said that he could never feel as if he got away from the office until he moved into another area with relatively few employees from the company.

Leadership also means increased accountability. Individual contributors are accountable and responsible for their personal actions; leaders take responsibility for how their actions affect others. Accountability for others means that leaders may often do things they don't want to do personally but that benefit others. When we asked Gary Hamel, a business thought leader, about what he saw as essential to good leaders, he said:

> *We live in a cynical world. People are assumed to be "in it" for themselves. Yet selfishness limits impact, in that a lack of genuine empathy makes it difficult to enroll others in your cause. True leaders don't ask, "What can you do for me?" but rather, "What can I do for you?" In a sense, while great leaders are politically astute, they are also apolitical, in that they rise above personal and/or sectarian interests. An example would be Nelson Mandela. A great leader is a populist who nevertheless avoids pandering to sectarian interests. Great leaders are empathetic and ennobling. In our over-hyped, over-marketed-to world, people can tell when they're being manipulated. Authenticity is a huge multiplier of individual impact. And, at its core, authenticity is not about being "true to oneself" (whatever that means), it is about being true to the interests of those whose lives you want to improve and change. Mercenaries, careerists, and egomaniacs are me-centered. Great leaders are you-centered.*[4]

Leadership inevitably involves conflict. One of the realities of any situation is what we call the 20-60-20 rule. That is, about 20 percent of the people will immediately agree with your leadership decisions, about 20 percent will never agree, and about 60 percent will be open to being convinced. Accepting that a sizable segment of your audience is unlikely ever to agree is a part of the leadership reality. Leaders who make bold and courageous decisions often have naysayers. We believe that leaders often have to make 55-45 decisions—decisions that are tough and could go either way. (Do we locate a facility in location A or location B? Do we invest in project A or project B? Do we hire person A or person B?) If the answer is clear (80 percent chance of being right), it's probably best to let others make the decision. The leader's job is making the close calls. But once made, a 55-45 decision requires a 95-5 personal commitment to action and implementation or the choice will fail. This means that some percentage of people would have made the other decision and may not be on board.

Leadership requires risk taking and change. Leaders who focus on the past are likely to end up with an identity for the past and not for the present or the future. Leaders must evolve and adapt to changing conditions. For example:

Leading Furniture

Mike Volkema became president and CEO of Herman Miller in the mid-1990s. He had a personal passion for innovation, trying to help shape Herman Miller as the innovation leader in the office furniture business. He encouraged new products for the changing workplaces of the future (seating, tables, storage, personal space, and so on). Herman Miller was known as the innovative company. Then the economy took a nosedive, and the industry and Herman Miller's revenues dropped slightly more than 40 percent in a two-year period. Volkema's predispositions and personal brand had to shift from decisions to innovate to decisions to rationalize work. This meant closing sites, making cutbacks, and focusing innovation investments. While all this was risky and not what he was predisposed to do, he made this leadership shift. As a result, when the economy recovered, Herman Miller was well positioned to recover along with it.[5]

Leadership is not for everyone. It comes with a price of visibility, accountability, conflict, and pressure for adaptability. People who are not willing to pay these prices for leadership would be better off not becoming leaders. Having a personal brand requires that leaders perceive that the benefits of the brand outweigh the liabilities. Clearly understanding the value of the personal benefits to you and the personal price of the costs you might incur before you begin to shape your leadership brand helps develop resolve to endure the difficulties that await you on the road to achieving it.

Master the Leadership Code

In chapter 1, we briefly introduced what we called the leadership code, the basics of leadership that all leaders must master to succeed. Leaders must do the basics well. If they don't do the basics, the brand is not sustained. These basics of leadership explain 60–70 percent of a leader's success. The leadership code also applies at the personal leadership brand level. Leaders must reach a minimum threshold in each of the five dimensions of leadership code from which to build their personal leadership brand.

In organizational roles, leaders build *personal proficiency* through their ability to learn, work with energy, and show character, courage, intellectual prowess, wisdom, and moderation. This array of personal attributes is also central to personal leadership brand.

Leaders also need to be *strategists* by having a moral compass, guiding principles, an agenda, or a sense of purpose. In organizations, successful leaders have a strategic point of view. Leaders are *executors* when they make sure that promises are met and things are delivered. As individuals, leaders need to do what they say they will do, be accountable for results, and meet expectations. Leaders are *talent managers* when they engage, motivate, inform, persuade, and direct others. By definition, leadership is not a solo act. From an individual view, personal brand comes only as individuals are able to see themselves through the eyes of others. Leaders are *human capital developers* when they develop the next generation of talent so that the company will outlive them. Leaders with a personal brand also invest in others. Centering on others allows leaders to expand their impact. This means sharing credit when things go well and taking blame when things go poorly. It means asking, "What do you think?" when people ask questions, to help the questioner become more thoughtful and reflective.

Leaders must have at least minimal competence in all five of these leadership code factors. But then they should excel in one or two. The leadership code suggests the foundations of a personal brand. Individuals with a personal brand know where they are headed; they are likely to get there, with others, and also to help others get where they need to go. Just as a good firm or product brand instills confidence, a strong personal brand built on the leadership code gives a person the opportunity to influence others.

Create a Personal Leadership Brand Statement

The leadership code defines the fundamentals, but a personal brand needs to be distinct and unique. As we noted in chapter 3, the statement of leadership is what defines a branded leader and provides the other 30–40 percent of effectiveness not supplied by the leadership code.

As you shape your personal leadership brand, pay attention to the initial impression you make. First impressions are not necessarily sound, but they can create indelible imprints that bias future interactions.[6] Physical demeanor (dress, grooming, and language), emotional demeanor (attitude and resilience), and social attitude (ability to interact and collaborate)—all these send signals to others that shape and reinforce your brand.

Sometimes personal brands or identities emerge from a series of incidental and seemingly discrete actions. How an individual spends time often communicates priorities and interests. Discovering and shaping a brand comes from asking, Who do I spend time with? What issues do I tend to address? Where do I spend time? How do I make decisions and process information? Imagine a past and future time log. When you look back at the last four to six weeks, how did you invest your time? What brand did that communicate? In the next four to six weeks, how could you invest time to shape your desired brand?

First impressions or emerging personal brands can be adapted through a disciplined process. We have identified six steps a leader can take to craft an intentional leadership brand. While we apply these steps to an organization context, they can also be applied to other settings. They adapt the logic developed in chapter 3 for an organization's leadership brand. Assessment 9-1 lays out the basic considerations for each step in the process.

Step 1: Strategy

What are the major results you want to achieve in the next twelve months at work?

Personal leadership brand begins with clarity about the results you want to accomplish as a leader. Whether in a business or other context (community or social), these results may be tangible or intangible, and they should reflect the interests of four stakeholder groups: customers, investors, employees, and the organization as a whole.

ASSESSMENT 9-1

Creating a personal brand

Step	Question	Worksheet for actions
1	What major results do I want to achieve in the next twelve months in my professional life?	Investors: Customers: Employees: Organization: (Flag the two stakeholder groups most important to your brand development.)
2	What major results do I want to achieve in the next twelve months in my personal life?	Emotional well-being: Social well-being: Physical well-being: Intellectual well-being: Spiritual well-being: (Flag the two types of results most important to your brand development.)
3	What are six words that characterize what I would personally want to be known for as a leader (see assessment 9-2)?	_____ _____ _____ _____ _____ _____
4	What are three phrases that combine the chosen six words that capture my desired identity?	_____ _____ _____
5	What is my statement of personal brand, combining results and identity?	I want to be known for _____, _____, _____, so that I can deliver _____ and _____ at work and _____ and _____ outside work.
6	How can I make my brand identity real to those inside and outside the workplace?	Key stakeholders . . . . Touch points Boss Peers Subordinates Customers Family Friends Neighbors Casual acquaintances (List the types of encounters—the touch points—where brand development is likely to be most effective for stakeholders in each group.)

First and foremost, identify how you can add value for customers. As we have discussed, a leadership brand is the bridge between customer expectations and employee behavior. Each leader should identify targeted customers who directly or indirectly receive value from goods or services the leader produces. Defining the customer-desired results helps you figure out what to deliver.

Investor results can be defined by focusing on investors you must serve. These investors' interests may show up in the stock price as defined by shareholders of the corporation or in budgets set by a company headquarters. Knowing what investors expect will help you be clearer about the leadership brand required to meet those financial expectations.

Employees also have expectations and desired results. When you define employee outcomes in terms of commitment, productivity, retention, or competence, you can be clearer about your required leadership brand.

Finally, we have talked a great deal about organizational outcomes in terms of the capabilities an organization must demonstrate to deliver strategy. When you set out to shape or evolve your personal brand, it can also help to highlight the organization capabilities required by your unit.

As you think about possible outcomes from customers, investors, employees, and the organization, you will begin to identify patterns and themes that materialize from these stakeholders. In this regard, the personal brand comes by answering the question What do others require of me?

Step 2: Outside Application

What are the results you want to achieve in the next twelve months outside work?

We have observed a shrinking gap between what happens at work and what happens outside work. Boundaries between the two areas of life are blurred as technology integrates personal and professional lives. Personal leadership brand should apply equally to the results required at work and results desired in a personal life.

So in addition to specifying desired results from professional stakeholders, you can articulate desired results from personal stakeholders. These results may include emotional well-being (self-awareness, mood management, self-motivation, empathy), social well-being (relationships with friends, families, casual acquaintances), intellectual well-being (learning, personal growth, hobbies), physical well-being (health, grooming, appearance, hobbies), and spiritual well-being (sense of purpose and peace). When you develop a perspective and set of desired results in these states in your personal life, you will find you have a sense of purpose and direction.

Step 3: Outcomes

Given these professional and personal results, what do you want to be known for?

To begin the process, look over the list of possible attributes in assessment 9-2 and pick the six that appeal to you most.[7] Picking the top six descriptors from the list may be difficult—they're all positive. However, part of creating an identity means focusing on desired images and not attempting to be all things to all people.

Sometimes we have found it helpful for those working to craft a personal leadership brand to ask those who know them best to identify the top six attributes that they are (or could be) known for. The tip we give people when they do this for someone else is to think about what their subject is really good at doing. What are this person's greatest attributes as a human being?

ASSESSMENT 9-2

Possible attributes

Flag the six words that best reflect what you want to be known for.

Accepting	Creative	Independent	Pragmatic
Accountable	Curious	Innovative	Prepared
Action-oriented	Decisive	Insightful	Proactive
Adaptable	Dedicated	Inspired	Productive
Agile	Deliberate	Integrative	Quality-oriented
Agreeable	Dependable	Intelligent	Reality-based
Analytical	Determined	Intimate	Religious
Approachable	Diplomatic	Inventive	Respectful
Assertive	Disciplined	Kind	Responsible
Attentive	Driven	Knowledgeable	Responsive
Benevolent	Easygoing	Lively	Results-oriented
Bold	Efficient	Logical	Satisfied
Bright	Emotional	Loving	Savvy
Calm	Energetic	Loyal	Self-confident
Carefree	Enthusiastic	Nurturing	Selfless
Caring	Even-tempered	Optimistic	Sensitive
Charismatic	Fast	Organized	Service-oriented
Clever	Flexible	Outgoing	Sincere
Collaborative	Focused	Passionate	Sociable
Committed	Forgiving	Patient	Straightforward
Compassionate	Friendly	Peaceful	Thoughtful
Competent	Fun-loving	Pensive	Thorough
Concerned	Good listener	Persistent	Tireless
Confident	Happy	Personal	Tolerant
Confrontive	Helpful	Playful	Trusting
Conscientious	Honest	Pleasant	Trustworthy
Considerate	Hopeful	Polite	Unyielding
Consistent	Humble	Positive	Values-driven

Whether the selection depends mainly on personal choice, the observations of others, or alignment with desired results, focusing on the top attributes helps define an identity at the core of personal brand.

Step 4: Definition of Your Identity

Combine these six words into three two-word phrases that reflect your desired identity.

The combination of six words into three phrases allows you to build a deeper description: not only what you want to be known for, but how you will probably have to act to get there. For example, *calmly driven* differs from *inventively driven*, *tirelessly driven*, or *productively driven*. Experimenting with the many combinations that you can make from your six chosen words helps you reflect on which descriptor most captures your personal leadership brand.

Step 5: Your Leadership Brand Statement

Make a "so that" connection between what you want to be known for and your desired results.

Your declaration of personal leadership brand captures both the identity you want (from step 4) and the outcomes of this identity (step 1 and step 2). To create this declaration, you can complete the following sentence:

I want to be known for _____, _____, _____, so that I can deliver _____ and _____ at work and _____ and _____ outside work.

Notice how this statement transfers personal identity into deliverable results. This "so that" combination is what makes the personal brand more than merely a personal value statement and aligns it with results. Product and firm brands succeed and endure because they lead to customer loyalty to these brands. Winning product brands are not just inherently interesting to the consumers, they lead to consumer action. Likewise, linking the personal leadership brand to a desired result ensures that the leadership brand is likely to endure. It is not the end in itself; it is a means to other important ends.

This declaration of personal leadership brand can be validated with the following diagnostic questions:

- *Is this the brand identity that best represents who I am?* Do I have passion for this statement? This question tests the personal validity of the leadership declaration statement. Would you like those who know you best to know you for what you describe as your declaration of leadership? Is it consistent with your self-image? Would you be willing to claim it as your identity? If you lived this declaration of leadership, would you see yourself as successful? Are you willing to tell others that this is your personal leadership brand?

- *Is this brand identity something that creates value in the eyes of my organization and key stakeholders?* Is this something that is needed? Does the personal brand you declare align with the firm's leadership brand? If not, can you see yourself fitting into the firm over time? Will individuals who start demonstrating your personal leadership brand be more or less likely to succeed in your organization?

- *What risks am I taking by exhibiting this brand?* What will it keep you from understanding and doing? This is an important question— it can be tempting to choose a brand identity that supports organization values but not your own personal values and strengths. For example, in most strong technology-oriented firms, technical know-how and acumen is usually valued over salesmanship or an interpersonal orientation. It would be a mistake, however, even in such an organization, to disguise yourself as a technical leader if what really drives you is something else. Acknowledging the things your personal brand keeps you from understanding and doing helps you build a team that can compensate for areas that are not your strengths and actually increases your leadership efficacy.

- *Is this brand identity something I have a predisposition toward?* Can I live it? Do you have the ability to translate the images you articulate in your brand into day-to-day behavior? If you look at your calendar for the last few weeks, does it reflect your brand? Can you make specific time commitments to live the leadership brand you espouse? Can you translate it into decisions and choices you make?

The declaration of leadership brand forms the heart of a leader's identity and reputation. It defines who the leader is, what the leader does, and how the leader wants to be treated by others.

Step 6: Expectations

How can I make my brand identity real to my key stakeholders at work and outside work?

As noted, espoused but unlived brands create cynicism because they promise what they do not deliver. At work your personal leadership brand should be communicated to all those you come in contact with. With your boss or a trusted coach, you might say what you are trying to be known for and find out whether your desired brand is congruent with the organization's goals. You might ask your boss or coach to help define behaviors that would be consistent with this brand. And you might imply that if and when you live this brand, good things should happen to you, such as salary increases and work opportunities.

With peers, you might see how your brand allows you to complement their work. Teams can be stronger than all their individual members because individuals bring unique talents to the team. You might notice how your brand matches and complements those of your peers. If you are too much like them, you add little value. If you are too little like them, they will not accept or connect with you.

With direct reports, you can communicate what you expect not only in terms of outcomes but also in terms of how people should work to deliver those outcomes. You can help your employees recognize the pros and cons of your leadership brand as they try to forge their own.

With customers and those who use your services, you can regularly check to make sure that your personal brand reflects what they want and expect. As a leader, you are the bridge between the customer expectations and employee actions. Being attuned to key customers will help you validate and verify the accuracy and sustainability of your brand.

At work, with bosses, peers, subordinates, and customer stakeholders, you can begin to monitor your behavior at each touch point. A *touch point* is simply an interaction with someone, be it a meeting, a presentation, a casual conversation, a reporting session, or any other time you get together. As you monitor yourself in each of these exchanges, you can check the extent to which you are living your leadership brand.

Outside of work, your personal brand also has great impact. How you behave with family, friends, neighbors, and casual acquaintances allows you to be congruent and learn. Sometimes, leaders learn about the impact of their personal brand from working with people off the job. For example, we have worked with senior executives who want to discover the essence of engaging and committing employees. When we talk with these executives about how they deal with their teenage children, we can often learn how their personal brand at home will affect how they accomplish their employee engagement goals at work.[8] Your brand should be a positive statement of what you desire for your real self. Living it might be difficult sometimes, but it should be natural.

Nelson Mandela has a clear declaration of personal brand. He wants to be known for his character, integrity, and values. He has applied these personal attributes to the liberation of his people. Like other great leaders who used their personal brand for public change (Gandhi, Martin Luther, Martin Luther King Jr.), he realized the powerful impact of his personal demeanor on his public goals. His brand is powerful enough that it has perpetuated an Internet myth; words have been attributed to him that he could have, or should have, said—but in fact did not. He has been widely (but inaccurately) quoted as saying, in his 1994 inaugural speech,

> *Our deepest fear is not that we are inadequate . . . Our deepest fear is that we are powerful beyond measure. It is our light, not our darkness that most frightens us. We ask ourselves, who am I to be brilliant, to be gorgeous, talented and fabulous. Actually who are you not to be? You are a child of God. Your playing small doesn't serve the world. There is nothing enlightened about shrinking so that others won't feel insecure around you.*
>
> *We are born to make manifest the glory of God within us. And as we let our light shine, we consciously give others permission to do the same, as we are liberated from our fear, our presence automatically liberates others.*[9]

Periodically Assess Yourself

Assessment deals with the simple question, How am I doing? Keep asking yourself this question—leaders improve by learning and they learn by assessing. Failure to learn means failure to grow and evolve. Failure to assess leads to failure in learning. Unfortunately, assessment has its own risks; it can be underdone or overdone. Underdone assessment results in action without feedback or ideas from others and is apt to make you arrogant and ignorant of the need for correction. Overdone assessment results in leading primarily in response to opinion polls or requests—subject to the whims of others and out of touch with your personal core.

Personal brand assessment begins by having the right attitude about assessment. Assessment—accepting input about your leadership brand—starts by realizing that you have personal ownership of and accountability for your brand. Others can give you feedback and suggestions on what to change, but you are ultimately accountable for your brand. As the receiver, you own feedback you receive. It is as important to refrain from overreacting and immediately doing everything you are told as to avoid underreacting by ignoring it. As you listen to what people tell you, watch for patterns. Over time patterns emerge and corrective action can be taken to adjust those patterns. Assessment begins with an open and inquisitive mind, but also with an awareness that the information received should be collated with other input and that the outcome should fit your personal brand, not someone else's.

Beyond willingness to learn, assessment requires looking in the mirror and honestly evaluating your strengths and weaknesses, your successes and failures. All leaders have both strengths and weaknesses. Generally, people overestimate their strengths and underestimate their weaknesses.[10] To figure your strengths and weaknesses, once again look for patterns. When given a choice, what activities do you generally prefer to do (strengths)? Avoid doing until the last minute (weaknesses)? When you ask others about what worked or did not work in a given situation, what are the consistent patterns that emerge?

Getting input from others is trickier than it seems. Sometimes people have limited exposure to your leadership behavior, so they cannot provide a complete picture. Someone who sees you in one setting may interpret your leadership brand by the setting, not your overall pattern of behavior. People also may have a bias in their observations of your leadership brand. They may see in you what they see in themselves—it's a common human tendency to react to others by way of our own filters and biases. People may also have political or personal agendas in providing feedback. So for honest assessment of strengths and weaknesses, it helps to call on a variety of people, the more the better. It also helps to find a few trusted advisers who have your interests in mind and who will offer suggestions you can trust. Sometimes the easiest way to identify true professional friends is by the honest and helpful feedback they are willing to offer. They disagree without being disagreeable; they can have tension without contention; they focus on behaviors and not personalities;

they don't let mistakes linger; they care and demonstrate long-term loyalty not tied to any one incident; they are direct but not directive.

Assessment also includes monitoring what career stage you are in, how well you operate in that stage, and what career stage you would like to attain. As discussed in chapter 4:

- Apprentices (at stage 1) should be assessing the extent to which they are able to follow directions and perform assigned tasks at the requisite level of quality.

- Individual contributors (at stage 2) should be assessing the extent to which they are independently able to define tasks that need to be done.

- Managers (at stage 3) should assess the extent to which they focus others on accomplishing tasks as a coach, an idea leader, or a super-visor or manager.

- Leaders (at stage 4) should assess themselves for how well they position tasks for the future growth of the company by providing direction, sponsoring key people, and representing the entire organization to outside stakeholders.

As you recognize your present stage, you can begin to assess how well you perform what is expected of you. This allows you to be a high performer in your current stage, and to move on to the next stage if you choose.

Ultimately, personal assessment helps you know how well you are doing, what you should be doing more and less of, and where to invest your energies to improve. Lacking accurate assessment, leaders may be duped into mistaken thinking and erroneous actions.

Invest in Yourself

More people aspire to greatness than become great, and it is easier to espouse a relevant personal brand than to live it. Nonetheless, it can be done, with the proper investment in training, work experience, and life experience. A few basic principles underlie the process.

- *Be honest: do the mirror test.* People who are overweight generally don't like to climb on a scale or look in a mirror. But avoiding the facts does not make them go away. Investment begins with honest assessment, as discussed in the preceding section. Honest assess-ment leads to frank investment. Of all the skills you have and might choose to develop, some are signature strengths where you can predict that with proper work, you can be in the top 10–15 percent of performers, while some, even with great investment, seem likely to peak in the 50 percent range. Using assessment to tailor investment allows you to develop signature strengths in a few areas rather than average strengths in many areas.

- *Start small: set realistic expectations.* To invest in yourself requires the ability to change and to learn. At rare times, change is dramatic and enduring. More often, you see cumulative effects where little things add up to big things. Investing in any change works best when you start small, with realistic expectations. Small and simple successes build confidence and encourage future successes.

- *Experiment: put yourself in the path of something new.* Investing in your brand probably means moving out of your comfort zone and experimenting with something new. While all of us have predispositions, we also have the capacity to try new things. For example, Michael grew up in manufacturing. He had a knack for how to build products with high quality on time. As he gained increased success, he became seen as a high-potential employee who had qualities that would lead him into senior management. But to make this move, he had to learn how to succeed outside manufacturing. This meant a stint in marketing, sales, and corporate finance. While none of these assignments were easy, each of them taught him about working with people, systems, and numbers. In each assignment, he dedicated himself to learning not only the technical aspects of the job but the culture and behaviors of the job. He became a very successful general manager.

  Experimentation that invests in your leadership brand might mean attending a class that stretches you by offering you new ideas, giving a public presentation when public speaking is difficult, holding a follow-up performance review on an employee when you have a high desire to be liked, meeting with a group of difficult customers to try to meet their needs, or taking a permanent or temporary assignment that is outside your comfort zone. Leaders invest in themselves by trying new things.

- *Keep learning and focus on the future.* Experimentation without learning leads to accepting failure as a pattern. Learning requires reflection on what worked and what did not work. If something did not work, then learners ask why not and how the lessons from this experience could transfer to another setting. If something did work, then learners ask why and once again try to move the new insight to another setting. Leaders who invest in their brand constantly learn by asking what worked and what did not, synthesizing lessons into patterns, and adapting insights to the next setting. Learning requires excellent skills in observation of the setting, of other people in the setting, and of oneself. We have often advised leaders who want to improve their personal brand to "put their head on a swivel" and notice what is going on around them, how they are responding to those signals, and how they feel inside.

- *Be resilient and rejoice in rejection.* One of the earmarks of branded leaders is their capacity to cope with disappointment, to be resilient, and to rejoice in rejection. Disappointment is inevitable for any leader who aspires to become better. Rejection means that you are doing hard things. Never being rejected means never having tried. While the disappointment from rejection often creates personal pain, public embarrassment, and private angst, it can also be a source of strength. If rejection and disappointment can lead to clarity about what matters most and about your will to pursue a desired brand, you will find yourself a much more humble (by the rejection) and resolute (by the resilience) leader. You will also find friends who support you for who you are rather than for what you do. Resilience helps as you invest in new jobs, tasks, and life experiences.

- *Take advantage of unplanned opportunities.* Planned opportunism exists when you have worked hard to create your brand. You have planned where you are going and why, how to get there, and who to ask for help along the way. You have done your homework. Then, more often than not, an unexpected opportunity arises. Something that was outside the scope of your original plan but is clearly a good thing to do. And having done the planning, you can seize the opportunity, integrate it into your plan, and move forward quickly.

With these principles in mind and in practice, you will be more likely to select and attend training as a visitor, not as a tourist. The most useful training is not something separate from work, it is an experience that helps you do your work better. You will enroll in training programs that push you to learn new things. You will become an active participant in the training and take risks to learn. You will move ideas from the classroom to the workplace.

New work assignments are also opportunities to develop your brand. Instead of falling into a rut and doing the same job in the same old ways, you will look for work that challenges what you know and gives you new experiences, or you will find new and different ways to do your existing work. New challenges may come in the form of the task (moving from marketing to manufacturing), the people (working with people of different backgrounds), the business setting (moving from a short- to a long-cycle business), or the role (moving from stage 2 to stage 3). As you take on new assignments, they become opportunities to try new things, to challenge yourself, and to let yourself morph into something else.

Experiencing and learning from life also clarifies your personal leadership brand. How you spend your personal time communicates your signature strengths to others and to yourself. Spending personal time in activities that expand your understanding will help you at work. Intellectual curiosity can be built by new hobbies, activities, or studies. Social expansion can come from finding new friends. Emotional maturity can come from doing things that have been hard for you to do. Physical stamina can come from exercise and nutrition. Spiritual well-being can come from being sensitive to the transcendent. Experience and development in each of these personal states will shape your personal brand as well as your professional brand.

Measure Your Progress

Measurement refers to how well you are doing at developing your leadership brand. Progress as a leader often comes from honest inquiry about yourself. Some of this measurement may come from others. Another case:

Who Am I Really?

We worked with a leader who had a tendency to offend his subordinates and peers by being overbearing and domineering. He would tell subordinates what to do in minute detail, and then observe and criticize their work constantly. His subordinates quickly became disgruntled with him—and thus less inclined to do what he required. This created a vicious circle, since he then tried even harder to control them. When some of his subordinates revolted and refused to follow his edicts, we were asked to coach him. It took a while to get his attention and to get him to own up to the consequences of his behavior. He was judging himself by his intent, which was to help subordinates learn how to do work in a more disciplined way, but his subordinates were judging him by his behavior, which they found domineering and intrusive. He had inadvertently created a personal brand as a slave driver and naysayer.

For him to measure his brand, we encouraged him to contact former subordinates—by e-mail, on the phone, or in a letter—and tell them that he was honestly working to learn more about his leadership style, and that he would welcome feedback from them. He asked them to share some of his signature leadership strengths, or things he was good at; some of his weaknesses, or things he struggled with; and three or four adjectives that came to mind when they thought of his leadership brand. He encouraged people to respond, and a number of them did so. When he found patterns in these responses, he was able to measure how he was doing as a leader more accurately. He thanked those who replied and then began to create some specific action plans for improvement.

In this case, we were hired to coach and help a leader measure and improve his brand. We have seen other leaders who do periodic reviews on their own. One leader takes time every six months to review his progress. He blocks out about three hours to reflect honestly on how he is doing on the leadership brand that he wants to demonstrate. He considers what he planned and accomplished in the past six months, then anticipates the next six months and how he hopes his brand will evolve. He generally does this work privately and monitors it on his own, but it allows him to personally measure his success.

In chapter 6 we reviewed four measurement quadrants. In quadrant 1 leaders measured their impact on the organization. At a personal level, you can measure the extent to which you are fulfilling the desired outcomes of your personal leadership brand in both professional and personal settings. In quadrant 2 leaders measure the impact of their investments or development efforts. At a personal level, you can assess how much you have learned in the past and which training, work, or life experiences most helped you learn. When you learn how you learn, you can begin to make progress in evolving your leadership brand. In quadrant 3 leaders measure the extent to which their brand influences key stakeholders. At a personal level, you can measure the extent to which those who matter most in your life are helped or hindered by your brand. To what extent do your signature strengths support and encourage others? To what extent do your inevitable weaknesses keep you from relating to others? In quadrant 4 leaders assess the impact of their firm's leadership brand on building confidence in others. At a personal level, you can examine how your leadership brand builds confidence in you among those you serve.

Also in chapter 6, we proposed what we call an intangibles audit, whereby leaders evaluate the intangible value they create for others. A personal intangibles audit can be performed as well on the four dimensions of intangible value. Level 1 suggests that leaders keep promises. At a personal level, you can look at how well you keep promises you make by keeping expectations reasonable and by insisting on meeting commitments. Level 2 suggests that leaders articulate a clear strategy. For a personal audit, ask how clear you are about your goals and objectives. How well have you articulated what you want to become and shared that with others? Level 3 proposes that leaders succeed by demonstrating technical competencies. At a personal level, ask to what extent you have obtained and mastered the technical competencies necessary to reach your goals. Level 4 suggests building organization capabilities to deliver on the promises made on its behalf. At a personal level, capabilities represent what you are good at and how you get things done. When you do a personal intangibles audit, you can begin to measure your leadership brand progress.

This measurement allows you to develop your brand and adapt it to what you want to be known for. You can observe how other people evolve their leadership brand by measuring what they do and how they are doing. For example, Jimmy Carter left the presidency after one term with a somewhat tainted image. The economy was in a shambles, rescue efforts for kidnapped hostages had failed, and confidence in his judgment was very low. However, over subsequent years, with dedicated work through Habitat for Humanity, peacemaking, and service, he was able to resuscitate his image and create a new brand as a Good Samaritan, peacemaker, and diplomat. In another shift, Bill Gates founded Microsoft and became known for his aggressiveness and business competitiveness. But when he donated a great deal of his personal fortune and his time to philanthropy, he began to change his cutthroat image to one of concern and compassion.

Personal brands evolve. When they evolve through regular and rigorous measurement, they can be shaped in ways that communicate desired outcomes. Without measurement, your personal brand is apt to meander without direction. You become known for lack of direction, stability, and character.

Build Awareness of Your Brand

Ultimately, your personal leadership brand has impact when it has both efficacy, in being the right brand, and awareness, in that others see and act on it. Making others aware of your personal brand comes by both word and deed. Being able to articulate your signature strengths to yourself and to others allows you to put words on your brand. Acting consistently and predictably according to your personal brand allows others to begin to define and identify you through your brand. When others relate to you and talk about you in a way consistent with your brand, it is more likely to endure. Another case in point:

Holding the Line

While Dave was serving as president of the church mission, he and his wife worked with more than five hundred young men and women who had volunteered for eighteen or twenty-four months as full-time missionaries. In this assignment, they devoted themselves to good works and living by a strict set of rules. In the process most of these missionaries developed an identity of who they were and who they wanted to become. At the end of their missions, they returned home to pursue personal and professional goals.

One young man talked to Dave toward the end of his stint and expressed great concern. A few weeks after returning home, he was going to enter the military. He said that he was afraid that some of the habits and routines he had developed as a missionary might not go over well among his prospective comrades. He wanted to know how to retain the values he had developed in his mission in this new and different environment. Dave suggested the "four threes" to embed his desired brand in those he associated with:

- *Three hours.* In your first three hours with the new recruits, everyone will be nervous, acting out, and trying to see how they fit in with the group. Live your values for three hours in what you say, how you talk, and how to carry yourself.

- *Three days.* In the first three days, people will try to take on roles in the newly formed group. They will try to become accepted by others by what they say and do. Again, quietly but consistently live your values. This may affect what you read, your language, your personal demeanor, and the way you relate to others.

- *Three weeks.* In the first three weeks, some group norms will begin to emerge. Continue to live your values when the recruits have their first leave, when they have weekend passes, and when they go into public places. This does not mean you exclude yourself from others when they do things you don't agree with, nor do you judge them, but *you* live *your* values.

- *Three months.* After about three months, if you continue to quietly and persistently live your values, you will find that those in your group will have assigned you an identity, and they will treat you accordingly. When someone from outside the group invites you to do something that is not aligned with your values, your comrades will probably tell others that you do not do these things, before you have to say anything.

At first, Dave said, it will be somewhat difficult to live your values because they may be different from the norm. But after three months, it will be easy to live your values because your friends will expect it of you, and they will communicate to others what you believe and why.

Some time later, the young man told Dave that indeed the first few hours, days, and weeks had been difficult, but that over time, he began to assume an identity in his platoon. After a few months, his squad mates buffered him from doing things against the brand he wanted to portray.

Everyone who wants to sustain a personal brand does so through small, simple, and consistent actions. When others see these actions and when they begin to believe them, they respond in kind and reinforce them. Public awareness of a personal brand reinforces the brand.

Public expectation also at times makes it difficult to change a brand if you want to. But brands can and do evolve when new behaviors replace old ones and when those around you realize that you are serious about the new brand you are creating.

Conclusion

This book reframes how to think about and reframe leadership. First, focus on the outside in instead of the inside out. Outside in means that customer (and investor) expectations should frame, focus, and influence leader behaviors. When leaders know and do things that add value to customers, they are more likely to be doing the right thing. Second, focus not only on the personal attributes of a noble or successful leader but on leadership, or the cadre of leaders within your company. Based on these two principles, a leadership brand bridges the firm's identity in the mind of those outside (customers and investors) with the behavior of its employees. When an organization has a leadership brand, customers have positive images of the firm, investors perceive the firm as possessing intangible value, employees feel more committed, and leaders are creating enormous value.

Yet leadership brand for the company begins with leadership brand for the person. Until every individual leader is able to demonstrate and live a personal brand that is congruent with the desired company brand, the company brand is unreliable. The journey to leadership brand begins with the self.

Appendix A

Criteria for a Firm Brand

A FIRM'S BRAND may be translated to a leadership brand. To help you make this transition, we have identified criteria for an effective firm brand that will lead to the right criteria for a leadership brand. Table A-1 summarizes these criteria and how they apply to leadership. It also offers examples of firms that have met these criteria. By showing the connection between the criteria for firm brand and leadership brand, this appendix fleshes out the brand metaphor and shows how it informs leadership thinking.

When leaders respond to these criteria of a brand, they shift attention from the individual as a leader to the institutional quality of leadership within their organization and from the inside to the outside.

Do the Basics Well

Brands work only if they do the basics well. Brands that promise what they cannot deliver create cynicism and erode confidence. It is better for a brand to promise less and deliver more than to overpromise and underdeliver. Likewise, leadership brand requires that leaders master the basics. Effective leaders have personal proficiency and can accomplish the roles of strategist, executor, talent manager, and human capital developer. These basics are the leadership code that is necessary, but not sufficient, for individual leaders and organizational leadership.

Start from the Outside In

Just as a product or firm brand matters only to the extent that consumers value it, a leadership brand needs to generate results that attract

TABLE A-1

Brand criteria for firms and leaders

Criterion	Lessons from product and firm brand	Application to leadership brand
Leadership code: Do the basics well. *Does the brand deliver what it promises?*	A brand must deliver on promises by ensuring that leaders master the core of leadership (Lexus).	All leaders must master a core set of leadership competencies (P&G).
Esteem: Start from the outside in. *Does the brand generate value and is it well regarded?*	A brand must create perceived value in the mind of customers or users of the product (Rolex).	Leadership success is measured by the value (results) that leaders create for employees inside and customers and investors outside the organization (Starbucks).
Knowledge: Communicate in customer terms *Does the brand elicit customer response?*	A brand must communicate to customers what it intends (FedEx).	Leadership brand inside a firm should connect to desired experience for target customers outside the firm (American Red Cross).
Evolution: Evolve along with the customers. *Does the brand keep up with growing customer expectations?*	A brand must stay aligned with current customers as the market changes (Pillsbury).	Leadership brand requires that leaders at every level adapt to changing business conditions (Payless ShoeSource).
Uniqueness and differentiation: Tell a story people want to hear. *Does the brand stand out in a unique way?*	A brand creates a unique and differentiated view of a product or firm (Rolls-Royce).	Leaders in the firm develop a reputation for delivering on promises in a manner consistent with firm identity (PepsiCo).
Pervasiveness: Spread the word. *Does the brand relate to users across segments?*	A brand resonates at different levels of market segmentation (Timex, P&G).	Leadership brand is pervasive through all levels of leadership in the organization (McKinsey & Company).
Sustainability: Have staying power and endurance. *Does the brand have staying power and endurance?*	A brand crosses products or services and is sustained over time (Pampers).	Leadership brand endures and ensures that it is not tied to one person or one strategic era (General Electric).
Efficacy: Make it work. *Does the brand deliver and communicate what we intend?*	A product brand delivers and communicates what it intends to deliver (Special K: weight loss).	The leadership brand communicates the desired leadership identity (Johnson & Johnson: trust, ethics, and integrity).
Relevance: Keep it relevant. *Does the brand align with strategy today and tomorrow?*	A brand matters to consumers (Kleenex).	Leadership brand matters to employees, customers, and investors (Apple).
Price/value: Sustain price and value. *Does the brand allow premium pricing?*	Consumers pay an average of one-third more for branded products (Starbucks).	Branded leaders deliver more value than other leaders (General Electric, P&G).

or please consumers, or it is useless. The key questions: "What do customers want this firm to be known for?" followed by "What do our leaders need to know, do, and deliver to make that customer identity happen?" With this approach, leadership matters not because leaders say so, or because employees will be happy, but because customers and investors will take money out of their wallets and hand it to the firm. Leadership brand requires that leadership results be assessed by the extent to which leaders deliver value to customers and investors outside the firm. And as customer expectations evolve, so must the brand.

Communicate in Customer Terms

A brand must communicate to customers what it intends. FedEx wants to be known as the "on time, every time" delivery service. This simple message must communicate to those who use the services what differentiates FedEx and makes it stand out. In the context of leadership brand, *building knowledge* means developing leaders' line of sight between customer expectations and leader performance. If customers could hire people to run the firm, would they choose the current leaders? If so, the leaders in place know and act on customer interests in ways that delight customers.

Evolve Along with Customers

Brands change with consumers. The Pillsbury Doughboy was a cute, chunky icon of the Pillsbury product line. With the advent of healthy choices and lifestyle, the Doughboy went on a diet and adapted to current consumer conditions. Kentucky Fried Chicken became KFC; March of Dimes went from solving polio to addressing childhood diseases in general; Marriott went from hotels to retirement centers; Nike moved from shoes to clothes. As brands evolve, so do leaders. Successful leaders continually tie their brand or identity to the changing expectations of customers and investors. As customers change, so must the leadership brand. Since it takes time (seven to ten years, depending on who's looking) to build a strong leader, it is important that all leaders master the leadership core.[1] When they have mastered the core, they are then able to adapt their core skills and abilities to the unique circumstances they face—applying what they know to what they must deliver.

Tell a Story People Want to Hear

Brand is unique and not generic—and that makes it rare in today's leadership world. We see this over and over in our training programs, where one of the exercises involves having participants bring in the leadership competency models that are used in their own 360-degree assessments and post them along the wall. We ask everyone to go around and name the company each list represents. Often, they cannot—the competencies are similar and generic (have a vision, communicate well, build teams, engage employees, and the like). A leadership brand pushes leaders to move from generic leadership to targeted leadership. And one simple question is enough to begin the move from generic attributes to focused results. For each competence, asking, "So that what?" leads you to a specific result that is tied to the strategy of the organization. (See chapter 3 for more on this.)

Spread the Word

Effective leadership brand must be reflected by leaders at all levels of an organization. A strong brand is universally understood to convey a specific message: Nike communicates athleticism to rich and poor—to both athletes in training and athletes in mind only. In the same way, a firm's leadership brand cannot be something that the top leaders in an organization do while others watch—or worse, do something else. Instead, it must engage and be reflected by leaders at every level of the organization. Organizations with an effective leadership brand have leaders throughout the organization that "be," "know," and "do" the leadership identity. If a leader two or three layers down the organization does not reflect the desired brand, that leader dilutes or pollutes an entire segment of the organization, affecting the response of employees, customers, and investors to the firm and undermining performance. Leaders who do not reflect the firm's leadership brand must be identified and upgraded or removed.

Have Staying Power and Endurance

Brand is sustainable, not tied to any individual model. Leadership brand is not tied to any one leader. It is embedded throughout the organization. When Bob Nardelli took the reins at Home Depot, he brought with him a disciplined, aggressive, and engaging style. This style was soon captured throughout the Home Depot network of stores. The company began to adopt the leadership brand he modeled. It was reinforced through the company's financial management, information technology, and human resource processes and systems. When money, data, and people all fit with the leadership brand, they communicate and reinforce that brand. We have worked in companies where the top leader wants to be "the" leader, the one who embodies the brand of the firm, leaving others to emulate rather than execute a defined, consumercentric leadership brand—and from this we conclude that corporate identity is *less* well focused rather than (as the leader fondly hopes) more so.

The ultimate test of success occurs only after the leader departs. Is the leadership brand effective enough and broadly enough executed to be recognized by the leader's successor? While a successor will bring new and innovative ideas, there is a substantive difference between building on your predecessor's work in establishing a leadership brand and creating a new leadership brand to suit yourself. It may be more tightly tied to business demands or more widely reflected in the organization.

Make It Work

A brand must have efficacy or it will not last. Unfulfilled promises are worse than no promises at all. More patron complaints are registered in a Four Seasons restaurant than in a Denny's diner, because the expectations of the patrons are higher in the high-end restaurant. Leaders who declare a leadership brand must live by it or they will die (or at least derail) by it. Leadership brand efficacy occurs when employees, customers, and investors believe that promises made at the top are promises that will be kept.

Keep It Relevant

The brand has to matter to the user of the brand. Brands work because consumers find them relevant. A consumer has to like the softness and moisturizing features of Kleenex, the comfort of Dockers, or the sound quality of Bose speakers. Likewise, the leadership brand has to matter to those who are exposed to leaders. Employees, customers, and investors need to believe that the leaders' reputation is solidly based and that their unique and collective contributions make a difference in the professional and personal lives of everyone they reach, directly or indirectly.

Sustain Price and Value

A simple test of a brand is the extent to which consumers pay a premium for the products or services to acquire them rather than those of a competitor. Starbucks charges more for coffee than a local gas station or grocery store can, Evian water costs more than the local store's branded water, and so forth. Consumers willingly pay the higher price because they get value either in perceived quality of the product or assigned reputation gleaned by using the product. Likewise, leaders must create perceived value by what they do and deliver or by the reputation they bring to their work, or both.

These tenets of a leadership brand may be used to diagnose the extent to which leadership brand exists within an organization. The survey in assessment A-1 may be used as a cursory diagnosis of the extent to which leadership brand exists.

These criteria lay out the expectations that branded leaders must meet. With them in mind, leadership rhetoric shifts from ambitious but fuzzy terms such as *transformation*, *vision*, *aspiration*, *character*, and *empowerment* and begins to focus on business terms such as *customer share* and *market value*. The ultimate return on a leadership investment should be a "return on intangibles" (a new ROI for leadership) that shows up in a firm's stock price.[2] When leadership brand meets these criteria and connects to customer share and market value, the rationale for leadership investment is much easier to make. For example, when Jack Welch retired and Jeff Immelt replaced him at the helm of GE, contenders for the top GE job left to head up other companies. For example, James McNerney Jr. went to 3M and then on to Boeing just a few years later. As most GE leaders moved, the stock of the company they joined went up and stayed up in anticipation of their delivering on future results.

ASSESSMENT A-1

Diagnosis for leadership brand

Diagnostic question on leadership brand *To what extent do leaders in my organization . . .*	Low						High
Do the basics well: Demonstrate a core set of desired leadership competencies?	1	2	3	4	5	6	7
Start from the outside in: Connect their actions inside the organization to the expectations of customers outside the organization?	1	2	3	4	5	6	7
Build knowledge: Communicate to employees what the company wants to be known for by key customers?	1	2	3	4	5	6	7
Develop along with the market: Adapt their knowledge and skills to changing business conditions and strategies?	1	2	3	4	5	6	7
Differentiate: Stand out in a unique and distinct way?	1	2	3	4	5	6	7
Spread the word: Demonstrate the appropriate leadership behaviors and results at all levels of the company?	1	2	3	4	5	6	7
Make it last: Endure over time by not focusing on any one individual?	1	2	3	4	5	6	7
Make it work: Have the right reputation from external stakeholders?	1	2	3	4	5	6	7
Keep it relevant: Align their actions and behaviors with the strategy for today and tomorrow?	1	2	3	4	5	6	7
Sustain price and value: Deliver more value to the organization than leaders elsewhere give theirs?	1	2	3	4	5	6	7
Total							

Key:

56 and over: Put your organization's name on a T-shirt; you have branded leadership.
42–55: You're well along the path; keep at it.
28–41: Your firm needs work but there is hope.
14–27: You have a lot of work to do.
13 and under: Sorry.

Appendix B

Firms with Branded Leadership

IT IS EASIER TO SPOT a good product or firm brand than a good leadership brand because the product is more visible. Sometimes leaders who embody their leadership brand work quietly behind the scenes. These are what Jim Collins calls "level 5 leaders," who deliver consistent results without calling attention to themselves. They become branded leaders when they transfer their talents to others and when they build a cadre of leaders inside the company who lead in similar ways.

There are a few ways to ferret out companies that have branded leaders and leadership. This appendix explores these methodologies and how we use them in this work. First, companies may develop reputations for their quality of management. One of the eight dimensions the Hay Group and *Fortune* identify as leading to most-admired status is perceived quality of management. Firms with higher perceived quality of management tend to demonstrate the kind of leadership brand we propose. They have more than competent or celebrity leaders; they build both current and next-generation leaders able to respond to today's and tomorrow's problems as defined by those outside their firms. The *Fortune* survey offers one glimpse into which firms make that reputation. Table B-1 tracks the top three firms on management quality for the last seven years.

Others have worked to identify firms with strong and credible leaders according to the reputation of the leaders, leadership, and leadership development efforts of these firms. In the Hewitt study, researchers identified twenty firms that became their exemplars of high-quality leadership. We are partnering with Hewitt and *Fortune* to identify firms with leadership brand. This research will not only highlight which firms demonstrate leadership brand but also specify ways to create sustainable leadership brand.

TABLE B-1

Top companies for management quality

Company	2000	2001	2002	2003	2004	2005	2006	Total appearances
GE	2						2	4
Berkshire Hathaway				2		3		2
Enron	1	2						2
Omnicom Group	3	1						2
Citigroup		3	3					2
Altria Group				1		2		2
Walgreens			2					1
UPS					1			1
Liz Claiborne					2			1
Kinder-Morgan Energy Partners						1		1
Procter & Gamble					3		3	2
United Health Group							1	1

Source: From "Most Admired Companies Survey," 2000–2006, *Fortune*, March 19, 2007, p. 88.

Jim Collins's research used economic indicators of transformation to identify companies that moved from good to great and sustained that position. One of the problems of almost any of these performance-based criteria for selecting good companies is that company performance changes. Of the forty-two original *In Search of Excellence* companies selected according to financial criteria, only thirteen still met the criteria a few years after the study. However, the firms that met the financial criteria even for a short period would be more likely to demonstrate a leadership brand. Clearly, more research on these issues is needed.

We decided to further identify firms with a leadership brand by surveying leadership thought leaders for their input on which firms most demonstrated the leadership brand criteria we proposed. The resulting list is remarkably similar to other lists: GE, PepsiCo, Johnson & Johnson, 3M, Motorola, Home Depot, Polaris.[1]

Finally, we felt that firms with a leadership brand would generally be net exporters of leadership talent. It is ideal for a firm to produce leaders it can promote from within, but in the process some firms may do so much to develop leadership talent that they overfill their bench and become net exporters to other firms. We call these firms *feeder firms* because they feed the demands for next-generation leaders in other firms. Obviously, one could argue that firms with a strong leadership brand would promote from within, which we agree with. But firms seeking external candidates are more likely to either go directly to a firm with a strong reputation for leadership or try to identify leaders who had sound leadership experiences earlier in their careers. Feeder firms would be those who produced leaders in other firms.

True leadership feeder firms are scarce. Leaders who rise to the top of an organization often come from within, and when they are sourced from another firm, either for the top job or a job leading to the top job, they seem to come primarily from just two places: General Electric and McKinsey. This is not new news. GE has a decades-old reputation for building leaders who go on to remarkable success at other firms. Former GE leaders have led such firms as Albertsons, Comdisco, Conseco, Home Depot, Honeywell, Intuit, 3M, and Boeing. While their success rate is not perfect, it is remarkably high. McKinsey as well has produced many CEOs and other senior leaders in other firms, including GE, PepsiCo, American Express, Sotheby's, Ashland, Northeast Utilities, IBM, Westinghouse Electric Corporation, Duracell International,

Levi Strauss, Merrill Lynch, and Raychem. Evidently, the experiences of consulting in multiple industries and solving their varied problems have helped many former McKinsey consultants become top senior executives.[2]

In examining the careers of the leaders of the *Fortune* 500 to see where they came from, we discovered that additional feeder firms exist at an industry level. This finding is interesting in that it suggests that part of leadership success is mastering not only the core elements of leadership but also the application of these core elements to the unique strategic challenges of an industry. So some industries seem to have their own feeder firms—firms that develop the next generation of leaders within that industry—as shown in table B-2.

So what have we learned about identifying the firms that excel at leadership brand? First, it is a small set. The same firms keep showing up on "good reputation" lists. This may be due to the reality of the leadership brand, or it may be because of social factors such as general reputations of high-performing firms. Second, it is a movable set. Reputations for quality of management often evolve with business conditions and performance. Third, it is generally not a generic insight for business as a whole (except perhaps for GE and McKinsey); it is a phenomenon found within specific industries.

TABLE B-2

Industry leadership feeder firms

Industry	Leader source	Examples
Automotive	Johnson Controls	Michael Johnston (Visteon), Charles McClure Jr. (ArvinMeritor)
	General Motors	John Finnegan (Chubb), Michael J. Burns (Dana), Lewis Campbell (Textron)
Consumer products	Kraft	Robert Eckert (Mattel), James Kilts (Gillette), Doug Conant (Campbell Soup), Rick Lenny (Hershey Company)
Financial services	Merrill Lynch	Jeffrey Peek (CIT Group), Herbert Allison (TIAA-CREF)
Medical	Pfizer	Stephen MacMillan (Stryker), Fred Hassan (Schering-Plough)
Oil	Texaco	Clarence P. Cazalot Jr. (Marathon), Glenn Tilton (United Airlines)
Computer	Hewlett-Packard	Michael Capellas (Compaq, MCI), Antonio Perez (Kodak)

Notes

Chapter 1

1. John H. Zenger and Joseph Folkman, *The Extraordinary Leader: Turning Good Managers into Great Leaders* (New York: McGraw-Hill, 2002).

2. Robert Eichinger (presentation at the Human Resource Planning Society annual meetings, Tucson, Arizona, 2006), citing David V. Day and Robert G. Lord, "Executive Leadership and Organizational Performance: Suggestions for a New Theory and Methodology," *Journal of Management* 14, no. 3 (1988): 453–464.

3. Bradford Smart, *Topgrading: How Leading Companies Win by Hiring, Coaching, and Keeping the Best People* (Paramus, NJ: Prentice Hall, 1999), 5.

4. All these topics are covered in leadership books published in the last five years. They show the array of metaphors for informing leadership thinking and action. See Wess Roberts, *Leadership Secrets of Attila the Hun* (New York: Warner Books, 1990); Eric Harvey, David Cottrell, and Al Lucia, *Leadership Secrets of Santa Claus* (Dallas: Walk the Talk Company, 2004); Jack Welch and Suzy Welch, *Winning* (New York: HarperBusiness, 2005); Mike Murdock, *Leadership Secrets of Jesus Christ* (Chicago: Honor Books, 1997); and John Wooden, *Wooden on Leadership* (New York: McGraw Hill, 2005).

5. Again, these exemplars are the topic of leadership books published in the last five years. They show the array of cases that are used to describe leadership.

6. Ram Charan, Stephen Drotter, and James Noel, *The Leadership Pipeline: How to Build the Leadership Powered Company* (San Francisco: Jossey-Bass, 2000).

7. Information on Canadian Tire comes from interviews with key executives and from their Web site (http://www.canadiantire.ca).

8. This material on Bon Secours is derived from interviews with its business leaders, a workshop with its board of directors, and an internal document titled "Continual Development System."

9. http://www.bonsecours.org/us/our_mission/index.htm.

10. Information on drugstore.com from author conversations with Robert Hargadon, vice president of human resources.

11. Leadership and Evolutionary Psychology symposium, Society of Industrial and Organizational Psychologists, April 2006.

12. We do not claim this to be a rigorous or thorough study. We targeted thought leaders who have shaped the study of leadership across organizations. This meant interviewing not leaders within one organization but those who studied leaders in many organizations. And we wanted to find out from those who have done extensive research what their findings are. Our list of individuals we interviewed and surveyed included Jim Bolt (working on leadership development efforts); Richard Boyatzis

(working on the competency models and resonant leadership); Jay Conger (working on leadership skills as aligned with strategy); Bob Fulmer (working on leadership skills); Bob Eichinger (working with Mike Lombardo to extend work from the Center for Creative Leadership and leadership abilities); Mark Effron (working on large studies of global leaders); Joe Folkman, (working on synthesis of the extraordinary leader); Marshall Goldsmith (working on global leadership skills and how to develop those skills); Gary Hamel (working on leadership as it relates to strategy); Jon Katzenbach (working on leaders from within the organization); Jim Kouzes (working on how leaders build credibility); Morgan McCall (representing the Center for Creative Leadership); Barry Posner (working on how leaders build credibility); and Jack Zenger (working on how leaders deliver results and become extraordinary).

13. There are much more thorough and comprehensive reviews of the leadership literature. See Bernard M. Bass, *Bass and Stogdill's Handbook of Leadership* (New York: Free Press, 1990); and Center for Creative Leadership, *The Center for Creative Leadership Handbook of Leadership Development* (San Francisco: Jossey-Bass, 1998).

14. Charles J. Fombrun and Cees B. M. van Riel, *Fame and Fortune: How Successful Companies Build Winning Reputations* (New York: FT Press, 2003).

15. Baruch Lev, *Intangibles: Management, Measurement, and Reporting* (New York: Brookings Institution Press, 2001); and Dave Ulrich and Norm Smallwood, *Why the Bottom Line Isn't! How to Build Value Through People and Organization* (Hoboken, NJ: Wiley, 2003).

16. Lev, *Intangibles*; and Robert S. Kaplan and David P. Norton, *Strategy Maps: Converting Intangible Assets into Tangible Outcomes* (Boston: Harvard Business School Press, 2004).

17. Nordstrom leaders, interview by Dave Ulrich, October 2006.

Chapter 2

1. Ray Oldenburg, *The Great Good Place: Cafés, Coffee Shops, Bookstores, Bars, Hair Salons, and Other Hangouts at the Heart of a Community* (New York: Marlowe, 1999).

2. Thomas J. Watson Jr., *A Business and Its Beliefs: The Ideas That Helped Build IBM* (New York: McGraw-Hill, 1963), 5.

3. Louis V. Gerstner Jr., *Who Says Elephants Can't Dance? Inside IBM's Historic Turnaround* (New York: HarperBusiness, 2002).

4. The case for value as the receiver more than the giver is made in Dave Ulrich and Wayne Brockbank, *The HR Value Proposition* (Boston: Harvard Business School Press, 2005).

5. Dave Ulrich and Norm Smallwood, *How Leaders Build Value: Using People, Organization, and Other Intangibles to Get Bottom-Line Results* (San Francisco: Wiley, 2006).

6. Darin Fonda, "Who Says GM Is Dead?" *Time*, May 22, 2006.

7. Anthony Rucci, Steve Kirn, and Richard Quinn, "The Employee-Customer-Profit Chain at Sears," *Harvard Business Review*, January 1998, 82–97.

8. *Fortune*, May 27, 2002, 162.

9. Moira Herbst, "The Costco Challenge: An Alternative to Wal-Martization?" Labor Research Association, *LRA Online*, July 5, 2005, http://www.laborresearch.org/print.php?id=391.

Chapter 3

1. Libby Sartain and Mark Schumann, *Brand from the Inside: Eight Essentials to Emotionally Connect Your Employees to Your Business* (San Francisco: Jossey-Bass, 2006); and Simon Barrow and Richard Mosley, *The Employer Brand: Bringing the Best of Management to People at Work* (San Francisco: Jossey-Bass, 2005).

2. Dave Ulrich, Jack Zenger, and Norm Smallwood, *Results-Based Leadership* (Boston: Harvard Business School Press, 1999).

3. Robert S. Kaplan and David P. Norton, *Alignment: Using the Balanced Scorecard to Create Corporate Synergies* (Boston: Harvard Business School Press, 2006); Robert S. Kaplan and David P. Norton, *Strategy Maps: Converting Intangible Assets into Tangible Outcomes* (Boston: Harvard Business School Press, 2004); and Robert S. Kaplan and David P. Norton, *The Strategy-Focused Organization: How Balanced Scorecard Companies Thrive in the New Business Environment* (Boston: Harvard Business School Press, 2000).

Chapter 4

1. Malcolm Gladwell, *Blink: The Power of Thinking Without Thinking* (New York: Little, Brown, 2005).

2. Lyle M. Spencer and Signe M. Spencer, *Competence at Work: Models for Superior Performance* (New York: Wiley, 1993).

3. Gene W. Dalton and Paul H. Thompson, *Novations: Strategies for Career Management* (Boston: Novations Group, 1986). Dalton and Thompson's work started in the 1960s at RCA and Lawrence Livermore labs and has continued over the years as a robust framework for developing professionals and leaders.

Chapter 5

1. A review of this work was presented by Richard Arvey, Maria Rotundo, Wendy Johnson, Zhen Zhang, and Matt McGue, "Genetic and Environmental Components of Leadership Role Occupancy" (paper presented at the 21st Annual Society for Industrial and Organizational Psychology, SIOP, conference, Dallas, Texas, April 2006). See also Thomas J. Bouchard Jr. et al., "Sources of Human Psychological Differences: The Minnesota Study of Twins Reared Apart," *Science*, October 12, 1990; Judith Rich Harris, *The Nurture Assumption: Why Children Turn Out the Way They Do* (New York: Free Press, 1998); Judith Rich Harris, "Where Is the Child's Environment? A Group Socialization Theory of Development," *Psychological Review* 102, no. 3 (1995): 458–489; and M. McGue et al., "Behavioral Genetics of Cognitive Ability: A Life-Span Perspective," in *Nature, Nurture, and Psychology*, ed. R. Plomin and G. E. McClearn (Washington, DC: American Psychological Association, 1993), 59–76.

2. Building on strengths is found in research by Jack Zenger and Joe Folkman, who show that if leaders are in the 90th percentile on at least one strength, they are seen as effective leaders (top third overall); if they are in the 90th percentile on two strengths, their overall leadership score reaches the 72nd percentile—nearly the top quartile. Marcus Buckingham argues that building on strengths helps leaders differentiate themselves.

3. Morgan W. McCall Jr., Michael M. Lombardo, and Ann M. Morrison, *The Lessons of Experience: How Successful Executives Develop on the Job* (New York: Free Press, 1988).

4. Cynthia McCauley, Ellen Van Vestor, and John Alexander, eds., *The Center for Creative Leadership Handbook for Leadership Development* (San Francisco: Jossey-Bass, 2003).

5. Warren R. Wilhelm, *Learning Architectures: Building Organizational and Individual Learning* (Albuquerque, NM: GCA Press, 2003).

6. Adapted from Hewitt Associates, "How the Top 20 Companies Grow Great Leaders 2005," http://www.hewittassociates.com/_MetaBasicCMAssetCache_/Assets/Articles/top_companies_2005.pdf.

7. Executive Development Associates, "Executive Development Trends 2004," cited by Robert Fulmer, Linkage OD Conference, Chicago, 2006.

8. Adapted from Hewitt, "How the Top 20 Companies Grow Great Leaders 2005"; and Duke Corporate Education, Corporate Leadership Project 2005, http://www.apqc.org/PDF/bestpractices/studies/2006/lds.pdf.

9. Michael Treacy, *Double-Digit Growth: How Great Companies Achieve It—No Matter What* (New York: Penguin Books, 2003); and Greg A. Stevens and James Burley, "3000 Raw Ideas = 1 Commercial Success!" *Research-Technology Management* 40, no. 3 (1997): 16–27.

10. This argument is made by Michael M. Lombardo and Robert W. Eichinger, *The Leadership Machine: Architecture to Develop Leaders for Any Future* (Minneapolis: Lominger Ltd. Inc., 2000).

11. John Battelle, *The Search: How Google and Its Rivals Rewrote the Rules of Business and Transformed Our Culture* (New York: Penguin Group, 2005); see also "The 70 Percent Solution: Google CEO Eric Schmidt Gives Us His Golden Rules for Managing Innovation," CNNMoney.com, *Business 2.0*, November 28, 2005, http://money.cnn.com/2005/11/28/news/newsmakers/schmidt_biz20_1205/.

12. McCall, Lombardo, and Morrison, *The Lessons of Experience*.

13. Executive Development Associates, "Executive Development Trends 2004."

14. Ibid.

15. Paul Russell (presentation at The Best of OD Linkage Conference, Chicago, May 2006).

16. Arthur Yeung, Dave Ulrich, Stephen W. Nason, and Mary A. Von Glinow, *Organizational Learning Capability: Generating and Generalizing Ideas with Impact* (New York: Oxford University Press, 1999).

17. Jeffrey Pfeffer and Robert I. Sutton, *Hard Facts, Dangerous Truths, and Total Nonsense: Profiting from Evidence-Based Management* (Boston: Harvard Business School Press, 2006).

18. Bob Eichinger (presentation at the 2006 Human Resource Planning Society Conference, Tucson, Arizona, April, 2006).

19. The concept of judging ourselves by our intent and others judging us by our behavior comes from conversations with Steve Kerr.

20. The concept of feed-forward comes from many conversations with Marshall Goldsmith.

21. Marshall Goldsmith and Laurence S. Lyons, eds., *Coaching for Leadership* (San Francisco: John Wiley & Sons, 2006); see also Dave Ulrich, "Coaching the Coaches," in *Coaching for Leadership*, 145–152.

22. See D. C. Hambrick, T. S. Cho, and M-J. Chen, "The Influence of Top Management Team Heterogeneity on Firms' Competitive Moves," *Administrative Science Quarterly*, December 1996; and D. C. Hambrick and G. Fukutomi, "The Seasons of a CEO's Tenure," *Academy of Management Review*, October 1991.

23. Paul McKinnon (presentation at The Best of OD Linkage Conference, Chicago, May 2006).

24. Thomas L. Friedman, *The World Is Flat: A Brief History of the Twenty-First Century* (New York: Farrar, Straus and Giroux, 2005); and Thomas L. Friedman, *The Lexus and the Olive Tree: Understanding Globalization* (New York: Farrar, Straus and Giroux, 1999).

25. Paul R. Bernthal, Sheila M. Rioux, and Richard Wellins, *Leadership Forecast: A Benchmarking Study* (Bridgeville, PA: Development Dimensions International, 2003); and Robert M. Fulmer and Jay Alden Conger, *Growing Your Company's Leaders: How*

Great Organizations Use Succession Management to Sustain Competitive Advantage (New York: AMACOM, 2004).

26. Robert M. Fulmer, "Choose Tomorrow's Leaders Today: Succession Planning Grooms Firms for Success," *Graziadio Business Report*, 2002; and Robert Fulmer, "Keys to Best Practice Succession Management," *Human Resources*, January 25, 2005.

Chapter 6

1. Bersin & Associates, *The Corporate Learning Factbook: Benchmarks and Analysis of U.S. Corporate Learning and Development*, March 2006.

2. New York State Department of Civil Service and Governor's Office of Employee Relations, "Report of the Competencies Working Group," 2002, http://www.cs.state.ny .us/successionplanning/workgroups/competencies/CompetenciesFinalReport.pdf.

3. Donald L. Kirkpatrick, *Evaluating Training Programs: The Four Levels* (San Francisco: Berrett-Koehler, 1996).

4. Jim Collins, *Good to Great: Why Some Companies Make the Leap . . . and Others Don't* (New York: HarperCollins, 2001); and Lyle M. Spencer and Signe M. Spencer, *Competence at Work: Models for Superior Performance* (New York: Wiley, 1993).

5. Dave Ulrich and Norm Smallwood, *How Leaders Build Value: Using People, Organization, and Other Intangibles to Get Bottom-Line Results* (New York: Wiley, 2006).

6. Our earlier work, *How Leaders Build Value*, really builds on this logic.

7. Dave Ulrich and Norm Smallwood, "Capitalizing on Capabilities," *Harvard Business Review*, June 2004.

Chapter 7

1. George Will, *Men at Work: The Craft of Baseball* (Boston: G. K. Hall, 1991).

2. www.McKinsey.com

3. All Music Group and MTV, "Milli Vanilli," http://www.mtv.com/music/ artist/milli_vanilli/bio.jhtml#/music/artist/milli_vanilli/bio.jhtml.

4. Three Chords and the Truth, "U2 Biography," http://www.threechordsandthe truth.net/u2bios/.

5. General Electric, *Annual Report*, 2000.

6. General Electric, *Annual Report*, 2003.

7. Thomas J. Watson, Jr., *A Business and Its Beliefs: The Ideas That Shaped IBM*, 2nd edition (New York: McGraw Hill, 2003).

Chapter 8

1. Sun Microsystems Leadership Development and Compensation Committee Charter.

2. Hewlett-Packard Company Board of Directors HR and Compensation Committee Charter.

3. Google Corporate Governance Guidelines.

4. Doris Kearns Goodwin, *Team of Rivals: The Political Genius of Abraham Lincoln* (New York: Simon & Schuster, 2005).

5. Lawrence Mishel, Jared Bernstein, and Sylvia Allegretto, *The State of Working America, 2006/2007* (Ithaca, NY: ILR Press, 2006).

6. Dave Ulrich and Wayne Brockbank, *The HR Value Proposition* (Boston: Harvard Business School Press, 2005); and Edward E. Lawler III, John W. Boudreau, and Susan Albers Mohrman, *Achieving Strategic Excellence: An Assessment of Human Resource Organizations* (Palo Alto, CA: Stanford University Press, 2006).

7. See many examples of the customer and investor participating in HR practices in Dave Ulrich, "Tie the Corporate Knot: Gaining Complete Customer Commitment," *Sloan Management Review*, Summer 1989; and Ulrich and Brockbank, *The HR Value Proposition*.

8. The ways in which HR professionals help build brand are adapted from a paper by Dave Ulrich and Dick Beatty, "From Partners to Players: Extending the HR Playing Field," *Human Resource Management* 40, no. 4 (2001): 293–308.

9. Wayne Brockbank and Dave Ulrich, *HR Competencies of the Future* (McLean, VA: Society for Human Resource Management, 2003).

10. Warren R. Wilhelm, *Learning Architectures: Building Organizational and Individual Learning* (Albuquerque, NM: GCA Press, 2003).

Chapter 9

1. Tom Peters, *The Brand You 50: Or Fifty Ways to Transform Yourself from an "Employee" into a Brand That Shouts Distinction, Commitment, and Passion!* (New York: Knopf, 1999).

2. Jeffrey R. Immelt and Thomas Stewart, "Growth as a Process: The HBR Interview," *Harvard Business Review*, June 2006, 60–70.

3. "Marshall Goldsmith: Biography," http://www.marshallgoldsmithlibrary.com/html/marshall/biography.html.

4. Gary Hamel, personal contact with authors, April 11, 2006.

5. Linda Tischler, "Herman Miller's Leap of Faith," *Fast Company*, June 2006, 52.

6. Malcolm Gladwell, *Blink: The Power of Thinking Without Thinking* (New York: Little, Brown, 2005).

7. Part of this list is adapted from Taylor Hartman, *Color Your Future: Using the Character Code to Enhance Your Life* (New York: Scribner, 1999); the list also includes input from Professor Wayne Brockbank.

8. Ann Crittenden, *If You've Raised Kids, You Can Manage Anything* (New York: Penguin, 2005).

9. These words were actually written by Marianne Williamson, in *A Return to Love: Reflections on the Principles of a Course in Miracles* (New York: Harper Collins, 1992), 190–191. However, Mandela's admirers believe he *should* have said them because they are exactly what he stands for. The concepts are Mandela's brand, and the myth that he said these words is believable and perpetuated because they are so well aligned with that brand.

10. Michael M. Lombardo and Robert W. Eichinger, *FYI: For Your Improvement* (Bloomington, MN: Lominger Ltd. Inc., 2004).

Appendix A

1. Robert Eichinger and James Peters, "There are seven CEOs working for your organization today—do you know who they are and do you know what to do?" Working paper, Lominger Ltd, Minneapolis, MN.

2. Dave Ulrich and Norm Smallwood, *Why the Bottom Line Isn't! How to Build Value Through People and Organization* (Hoboken, NJ: Wiley, 2003).

Appendix B

1. We interviewed a number of thought leaders on leadership and asked them, "Who are the firms with a distinct leadership style or brand?" Results include: *Warren Wilhelm*: "GE, Dell, Pepsi, McKinsey, Goldman Sachs, Bank of America, Southwest

Airlines. Non- or not-for-profit sector: Drucker Foundation, UNICEF/other UN subsidiaries, maybe the World Bank, IMF."*Marshall Goldsmith*: "J&J, IBM, GE, Dell, General Mills, McKinsey." *John Katzenbach*: "The U.S. Marine Corps is the very best I know at understanding the 'basics' of leadership—and the best at developing leaders at all levels. Their mantra is simple and compelling, and I first heard it articulated by Brig. General John Ryan (ret.) as follows: 'We want all of our leaders—at every level—to focus on only two things: First, mission accomplishment; you will accomplish your mission no matter what [interestingly, Gen. Ryan won the Medal of Honor by single-handedly blowing up a bridge after all members of his platoon had been killed or wounded]. Second, and of equal importance, you will take care of each and every one of your Marines—let me repeat that, you will take care of each and every Marine in your unit.' I have often thought that if all aspiring young leaders focused on these two things they would be a long way down their journey to becoming admirable leaders at whatever level they gravitate to. Other institutions, of course, are pretty well known, e.g.: General Electric (particularly adept at senior leadership), Southwest Airlines (particularly adept at frontline leadership), and perhaps McKinsey (for professional leadership development)."

2. Wikipedia reports that as many as eighty *Fortune* 500 companies are or have been run by former McKinsey consultants. See http://en.wikipedia.org/wiki/McKinsey.

Index

About the Authors

DAVE ULRICH is Professor of Business Administration at the University of Michigan and a partner at The RBL Group, a consulting firm focused on helping organizations and leaders deliver value. He has developed ideas with impact around leadership, organization, and HR.

He has published over one hundred articles and book chapters and twelve books, including *The HR Value Proposition* (with Wayne Brockbank), *Why the Bottom Line Isn't: How to Build Value Through People and Organizations* (with Norm Smallwood), *The HR Scorecard: Linking People, Strategy, and Performance* (with Brian Becker and Mark Huselid), *Results-Based Leadership: How Leaders Build the Business and Improve the Bottom Line* (with Jack Zenger and Norm Smallwood), *Human Resource Champions: The Next Agenda for Adding Value and Delivering Results*, and *The Boundaryless Organization: Breaking the Chains of Organization Structure* (with Ron Ashkenas, Steve Kerr, and Todd Jick).

Dave was the editor of *Human Resource Management Journal* (1990–1999) and served on the editorial board of four other journals. He is on the board of directors for Herman Miller, is a Fellow in the National Academy of Human Resources, and is Cofounder of the Michigan Human Resource Partnership. In 2006, he was ranked the number-one most influential person in HR by *HR Magazine*, and was named by *Fast Company* as one of the ten most innovative and creative thinkers of 2005. He has consulted and done research with over half of the *Fortune* 200.

Dave can be reached at dou@umich.edu.

NORM SMALLWOOD is a recognized authority in developing businesses and their leaders to deliver results and increase value. His current work relates to increasing business value by building organization, strategic HR, and leadership capabilities that measurably impact market value.

He is Cofounder (with Dave Ulrich) of The RBL Group, a firm of well-known and broadly experienced management educators and consultants.

In 2005 and 2006, The RBL Group was ranked as the number-one leadership development firm in the world by Leadership Excellence.

He is coauthor of five other books, including *Real-Time Strategy: Improvising Team-Based Planning for a Fast-Changing World* (with Lee Tom Perry and Randall G. Stott), *Results-Based Leadership: How Leaders Build the Business and Improve the Bottom Line* (with Dave Ulrich and Jack Zenger), *Why the Bottom Line Isn't: How to Build Value Through People and Organizations* (with Dave Ulrich).

He has contributed chapters to multiple books, and has published more than fifty articles in leading journals and newspapers, including two *Harvard Business Review* articles: "Capitalize Your Capabilities" (June 2004) and "Building a Leadership Brand" (forthcoming in July 2007).

He was selected as one of the top 100 Voices in Leadership by *Executive Excellence* magazine in February 2005.

Norm can be reached at nsmallwood@rbl.net